*The Abortion Question*

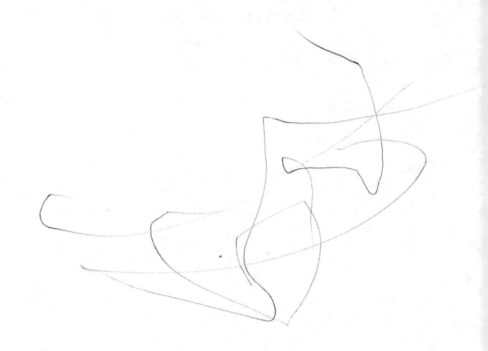

# THE
# ABORTION
# QUESTION

## HYMAN RODMAN
## BETTY SARVIS
## JOY WALKER BONAR

COLUMBIA UNIVERSITY PRESS
*NEW YORK*

**Library of Congress Cataloging-in-Publication Data**

Rodman, Hyman.
  The abortion question.

  Bibliography: p.
  Includes index.
  1. Abortion—United States.  2. Abortion—United
States—Moral and ethical aspects.  3. Abortion—Law
and legislation—United States.  I. Sarvis, Betty,
1943–     .  II. Bonar, Joy.  III. Title.
HQ767.5.U5R63  1987        363.4'6'0973        87-5219
ISBN 0-231-05332-0
ISBN 0-231-05333-9 (pbk).

*Book designed by Laiying Chong*

Columbia University Press
New York   Oxford

Printed in the United States of America

c 10 9 8 7 6 5 4 3 2
p 10 9 8 7 6 5 4 3 2 1

# Contents

# *Preface*

When the U.S. Supreme Court effectively legalized abortion in the United States on January 22, 1973, Patrick Cardinal O'Boyle saw it as "a catastrophe for America," while abortion law reformers hailed it as a victory for reproductive freedom in America. Both before and after the Court's decision, the battle lines have been drawn between those who favor legal abortion and those who oppose it. Since the Court's decision the battle has become more intense, and the contending forces, self-named pro-life and pro-choice, have engaged in constant warfare. As one side gains some advantage, the other side gathers its forces and strives harder. The political and rhetorical battles continue to rage at the local, state, and federal levels.

Why do the battles continue, seemingly without end? It is because each side has powerful arguments and devoted adherents. One side sees itself fighting for the life of millions of humans who are being slaughtered in the womb. The other side sees itself fighting for a woman's freedom to control her body, her childbearing decisions, and her life. These are transcendent issues. Defeat is not taken in stride with the intention of waging a fight on the next issue that comes along. *Abortion is the issue,* and the pro-life and pro-choice forces are engaged in a protracted struggle for the hearts and minds and votes of American policymakers and the American public.

One intention of this book is to convey the moral position of each of the contending sides and to show how morality colors the vision of each side. Because of the intensity of the abortion question and the strength of convictions, each side is often swept along by its own rhetoric. Most partisans do not grant any rationality to the arguments of their opponents, or for that matter to the opponents themselves. Searching for a civilized side to the debate, Sidney and Daniel Callahan (1984) suggest many points of agreement—for example, the need for improved social and educational programs that would sharply reduce the demand for abortion. Despite such potential for agreement, bottom-line disagreement remains, with one side opposing the legality of abortion because abortion is the greater evil and the other favoring it because it is the lesser evil.

A second intention of the book is to present a useful and relevant history of the abortion controversy in the United States, especially from the mid-1960s to the present. We focus on constitutional and legal issues, and on the actions of the U.S. Supreme Court, because that is where the major decisions have been made. Those favoring legal abortion are looking to the Court to uphold the constitutional basis of a woman's right to choose an abortion. The opponents of abortion are looking to the Court to uphold statutes that effectively hobble access to abortion; and the Court (perhaps a reconstituted Court) has become the chief target for their hope that abortion will once again be prohibited.

A third intention of the book is to provide important information about the context for the current abortion debate. This includes information on the medical, psychological, and social aspects of abortion. Does abortion have a detrimental effect on women's physical or mental health, or on the relationship between men and women? In addressing such questions, we are less concerned with portraying the arguments of each side and more concerned with presenting the research evidence. Of course, the research evidence does not speak for itself, and ideology often influences interpretation. Even where the research evidence is rather clear—for example, that induced legal abortion is not a risk factor for women's emotional and mental health—there are counterarguments, opposing interpretations, and contrary anecdotal evidence.

Finally, in chapter 9, we predict that the abortion debate will eventually be resolved: perhaps early in the twenty-first century, perhaps by the turn of the century, the controversy will have run its course. That does not mean that there is any reduction in the strength of the current battle. If anything, the battle grows more intense as each side sees the possibility of major changes. Will Congress or state legislatures pass new statutes to hamper access to abortion? Will the U.S. Supreme Court accept further restrictions, giving states greater leeway to control abortion? Will President Reagan, or a future president, be able to appoint enough anti-abortion justices to the Court so that it will overturn its decisions legalizing abortion? Since these are all possible, and since the stakes are high, the contending abortion partisans are highly motivated to intensify the battle and to find new rhetoric and new tactics to further their cause.

The three of us are in favor of maintaining the legality of abortion. We consider ourselves pro-choice. Nevertheless we have attempted to present a fair and objective picture of the abortion situation in the United States. Not many books have attempted to do this; most books are frankly pro-choice or pro-life. No doubt those opposed to abortion will be unhappy with some of our statements and interpretations, and will blame them on an underlying pro-choice bias. Those favoring legal abortion will also be unhappy with some of our statements and interpretations; perhaps they will blame them on an unseemly attempt to bend over backwards to be fair to the pro-life movement. We have argued among ourselves about how to present and to interpret some issues. Several passages in the book are compromises that emerged out of serious disagreement and debate.

Is legal abortion a symbol of liberty or oppression? Perhaps time will tell. In the meantime, this book tries to paint a realistic picture of abortion in the United States. Some of the colors are bright, some are dark, and some clash harshly; some of the images are bathed in mottled light.

The only thing clear about the abortion controversy is that it generates a great deal more heat than light. In this book we have aimed for the light. Our overriding goal is to inform readers about abortion in the United States. By taking a concise, factual, objective approach—insofar as we possibly could—we hope to provide an understanding of the historical, moral, legal, medical, emotional, and cultural aspects of abortion in the United States. If we are successful, most readers will finish the book with enhanced understanding. Moreover, some readers who are ambivalent about abortion will find that a better understanding helps them to make more informed decisions about the difficult questions surrounding abortion.

# Acknowledgments

Many people have helped in the preparation of this book. In particular, we appreciate the reviews of earlier drafts of the manuscript by Hani K. Atrash, Robert A. Bonar, Daniel Callahan, Lynn Sanford Koester, Patricia Meador, Mary Lou Moore, and Rebecca B. Saunders. Each read portions of the manuscript and gave us valuable feedback and advice.

We thank Mable B. Anderson, Mary T. Curran, and Derek Rodman for research assistance and Janet Poole and Elizabeth R. Hunt for typing the manuscript.

The libraries of Duke University, University of North Carolina at Chapel Hill, and University of North Carolina at Greensboro provided unfailingly excellent service and we thank the staff members of these libraries. We are also appreciative of the general encouragement provided by the administration of the University of North Carolina at Greensboro.

The statements made and views expressed in the book are our own and should not be attributed to any of the individuals or institutions acknowledged above.

Abortion is a matter that is morally problematic, pastorally delicate, legislatively thorny, constitutionally insecure, ecumenically divisive, medically normless, humanly anguishing, racially provocative, journalistically abused, personally biased, and widely performed.

Richard A. McCormick, S.J.

When people with differing philosophies sit down and listen to one another ... they learn that those who lean towards the right-to-life and those who lean towards the right-to-choice are both striving to create a situation with the minimum amount of artificially produced fetal wastage. With a subject as complex and intractable as [abortion], common goals about the welfare of individual women and respect for the awesome processes of human reproduction can still lead to different policies, but we should learn to respect one another's point of view.

Malcolm Potts, M.B., B.Chir., Ph.D.

*The Abortion Question*

CHAPTER 1

# THE RISE OF
# THE ABORTION
# CONTROVERSY

THE BIRTH OF A CHILD is supposed to be a joyous event. Often, however, the facts do not conform to that ideal. Currently, about 1.5 million American women are terminating a pregnancy by induced abortion each year (Henshaw 1986). Over half of these women are pregnant for the first time; about one-fifth of them are married; approximately 30 percent are nonwhite. Of women choosing abortion, roughly one-third are teenagers, one-third are 20 to 24, and one-third are 25 or older. More than one pregnancy out of four is being terminated by induced abortion (Henshaw et al. 1985). Despite these statistics (some might say because of these statistics) the abortion question continues to stir strong emotions.

Although induced abortion was not legally available throughout the United States during the years between the mid-nineteenth century and 1973, evidence gathered by Kinsey and his associates (1954) indicated that nearly one of every four American women had an induced abortion at some time in her life and the rate was thought to be even higher among poor women.

The abortion question has generated a tremendous amount of controversy in the United States since the late 1960s. When induced abortion was generally illegal during the 1960s and early 1970s, pro-abortion groups grew in strength as they dramatized the plight of women desperately seeking illegal abortions, often with harmful or fatal results. Since the 1973 U.S. Supreme Court decisions that legalized abortion, anti-abortion groups have grown in strength by dramatizing the millions of legally induced abortions as millions of deaths of "unborn children." The controversy has centered around legal and moral questions, physical and mental health issues, evidence of discrimination against poor women, and charges of black genocide. It has drawn the attention of many religious groups, especially the Roman Catholic Church. It has swept into local and national elections and into Congressional and judicial debates. Some families have been torn apart by the controversy, as husband and wife or parent and child adopt opposing positions. The questions are difficult, controversial, emotionally laden, and often impossible to deal with objectively because people's values are so strongly involved. But although the current questions are difficult and the current controversy bitter, abortion and the basic questions about abortion have been with us for a very long time.

## Historical Overview

Induced abortion has been practiced for thousands of years. Aristotle recommended that couples practice induced abortion as a means of maintaining population at an optimal size (Dedek 1975). Early Greek and Roman restraints on abortion were intended to protect the pregnant woman from mutilation or to guarantee that husbands would not be deprived of children by wives who were unwilling to become mothers. Early Christian objection to abortion was related to speculation about the existence of a soul, particularly a soul which was the creation of God. In the fourth century, Augustine concluded that "no soul was present in fetal life until the moment of quickening, when the mother-to-be detected the first stirrings of life within her body" (Smith 1970:27).

In the thirteenth century, Thomas Aquinas concluded, as had Aristotle, that the soul is "infused" into the body of the male embryo at about forty days after conception and at about the eightieth day in the female embryo. Not until the seventeenth century did Roman Catholic thought crystallize against induced abortion by assigning fetal life at any stage equal importance with that of the mother.

According to Farr (1980), the principal medical textbook in use in the Western world during the tenth through seventeenth centuries mentioned therapeutic abortion as a surgical procedure. In Roman Catholic countries, however, the church hierarchy discouraged abortion for either medical indications or as a means of fertility control. During the Renaissance, advances in surgery, combined with the rise of Protestant opposition to Roman Catholic doctrine, encouraged the use of induced abortion not only when the mother's life or health were threatened by the pregnancy, but also as a method of fertility control. During the sixteenth century, induced abortion became so prevalent in France, for instance, that population maintenance appeared significantly threatened.

The written record left by doctors, herbalists, midwives, and lawyers of preindustrial England indicates that herbal abortifacients were in frequent use and were not legally restricted before the nineteenth century (McLaren 1981:224–237). Abortion literature of the seventeenth and eighteenth centuries, most of it written by men who opposed abortion and sought to control women's childbearing, indicates that both single and married women used common herbal remedies in hopes of inducing miscarriage.

In the United States, laws restricting induced abortion became part of statute law during the nineteenth century and were based on English common law. Even those opposed to abortion agree that, in English common law, abortion was not a crime before quickening and was a "misprision" or misdemeanor after quickening. Quickening, the woman's first feelings of fetal movement, usually takes place between the sixteenth and eighteenth week of pregnancy, although its occurrence varies for different women and in the same woman for different pregnancies. In the United States, however, the common law distinction of quickening disappeared when the early abortion statutes were passed.

In 1930 Pope Pius reaffirmed the position of the Roman Catholic Church that fetal life was equally sacred with the life of the mother. He reviled medical and therapeutic indications for abortion, saying that they "excused the direct murder of the innocent" (quoted in Smith 1970:29).

Despite the opposition of religions such as Roman Catholicism and Islam, abortion has become common throughout the world. In an effort to alleviate the problems caused by poverty, burgeoning population, and illegal abortion, many countries, including Scandinavian, Eastern European, and several Asian countries, adopted liberal abortion legislation long before the United States.

In the middle years of the twentieth century, American physicians increasingly voiced their concern about the mutilation and death of women who sought illegal abortions. Many reputable physicians struggled with the problem of obeying anti-abortion statutes as they sought to provide safe care to women who would otherwise seek a dangerous illegal abortion.

### Thalidomide and German Measles

Two events of the early 1960s received international publicity and brought abortion and related social problems to the attention of a mass audience. Prior to the thalidomide tragedy most physicians advised their patients that the "placental barrier" protected the developing fetus from almost anything the mother might ingest. The thalidomide experience changed that. In the early 1960s thousands of pregnant women used this mild tranquilizer, which was effective against insomnia and nausea. The drug was available without a prescription in Europe. Later, it was found that at least 8,000 deformed babies were born to mothers who took thalidomide. Babies whose mothers took thalidomide during the first fifty days of pregnancy developed without ears, without arms, without legs, or with very deformed arms and legs (Schardein 1976; Saxen and Rapola 1969).

The abortion-related aspects of thalidomide received the most publicity in the United States in 1962. Mrs. Sherri Finkbine learned, when she was two months pregnant, that she might bear a deformed child because she had taken a thalidomide-containing tranquilizer obtained in Europe. Although Arizona law permitted abortion only to save the pregnant woman's life, her doctor recommended an abortion. Hospital approval was given and arrangements were made for the operation. In an effort to warn others of the dangers of the drug, Mrs. Finkbine phoned a local newspaper and talked with the medical reporter, who agreed not to use her name in the article. Mrs. Finkbine recalls that, rather than an article warning of the drug, "the front-page, black-bordered story screamed in bold print: 'Baby-deforming drug may cost woman her child here.' That did it. The story went out on the wire, and before the day was two hours along . . . it stirred international interest" (Finkbine 1967:18).

The publicity led to the cancellation of Mrs. Finkbine's abortion through fear that the doctor, hospital, or Mrs. Finkbine could be criminally prosecuted. The hospital unsuccessfully petitioned the state supreme court of Arizona in the hope of obtaining judicial clarity of what it considered vague laws. At this point the names of the Finkbines became a matter of public record, and they subsequently received thousands of letters filled with advice and hate. After numerous inquiries and much anxiety, the couple went to Sweden and waited a week for a decision from a Swedish medical board. The abortion was approved and done (Finkbine 1967:15–24).

The same question of performing abortions in cases of possible fetal deformity arose in 1964 when a German measles (rubella) epidemic hit the United States. About 20,000 severely handicapped children were born in the United States as a result of that epidemic and similar epidemics have occurred about every twenty-five years (Berger 1980). The 1964 epidemic once again focused the attention of the public on the abortion issue. It again raised questions that the Finkbine case had brought to public attention—medical, social, and legal questions: (1) Why were hospital practices not strictly in compliance with the law? (2) What should be done about socioeconomic inequalities in access to abortions (the Finkbines could afford to go out of the country to obtain an abortion but others could not)? (3) What was the purpose and effectiveness of abortion laws? (4) Should a woman have the right to abort a fetus which is likely to be severely handicapped?

## Recent Developments

From the 1960s to the present, many groups of Americans demanded that their rights be recognized. Ethnic and racial minority groups, homosexuals, indigent mothers, the elderly, and many others fought for their civil rights, in and out of the courts. Meanwhile, the role of women in American society changed dramatically. Women moved into the world of employment in ever-increasing numbers. By 1985, more than 54 percent of adult women were in the labor force. Among married women with children under six, and with husband in the household, the percentage in the labor force climbed from 19 percent in 1960 to 53 percent in 1985 (U.S. Bureau of the Census 1985).

In just two decades dramatic changes occurred in marriage and family structures. By the early 1980s people married, on the average, two years later than they did in 1960, the birth rate dropped below the replacement level, and many women were postponing the birth of their first child. For the first time, as many women as men were entering college. Increasingly, women sought employment in jobs which were formerly open only to men. New living patterns emerged as single person households, single parent families, and cohabiting unmarried couples became increasingly common. Divorce rates rose dramatically.

Effective contraception, particularly birth control pills, and the 1965 U.S. Supreme Court decision *(Griswold v. Connecticut)* which declared most restrictions on the sale of contraceptives to be unconstitutional were the forerunners of a sexual revolution. As many women became self-supporting, and as highly effective, available contraception made it possible for women to be sexually active with less likelihood of becoming pregnant, women demanded the right to make decisions about their own lives and their own bodies.

More permissive attitudes toward sexual behavior, particularly women's sexual behavior, became generally accepted. Premarital sex, extramarital sex, cohabitation, divorce, remarriage, and abortion were openly practiced and discussed.

Not everyone accepted these changes, however. Political and social conservatives, typified by the Moral Majority (now part of the Rev. Jerry Falwell's Liberty Federation), viewed permissive sexual attitudes, changing gender roles and family patterns, and abortion as grave threats to society. Their influence increased considerably in the 1980s, with the election of Ronald Reagan in 1980 and again in 1984.

Those opposed to abortion and to the provision of information about fertility control sought to prohibit such activities through restrictive laws and through constitutional amendments. In many cities anti-abortion groups picketed agencies which provided fertility control information and services. Women seeking help from these agencies were often harassed by the picketers. In numerous instances agencies providing abortion services were blown up, set afire, or vandalized.

By 1980 the great majority of American women in their fertile years were using contraception to control the number and spacing of their children and the birth rate had dropped dramatically. When unplanned pregnancies did occur many women were choosing to have abortions.

Sexually active women under 18 were least likely to be protected against unwanted pregnancy and pregnant women in that age group were most likely to delay abortion to the more dangerous time beyond the first trimester (Rodman, Lewis, and Griffith 1984; Henshaw et al. 1985). Nevertheless, during the late 1970s and early 1980s, anti-abortion groups argued strongly for laws restricting the provision of fertility control services to women under 18 and to poor women who were least able to afford contraception, abortion, or children.

At the same time, many other Americans became concerned about overpopulation. Some argued that only with strong efforts at fertility control, through contraception, abortion, and sterilization, could we halt a dangerous population explosion.

The notion that adequate health care is not a privilege, but a right, became a heated issue. In many European countries free health care, including abortion and contraception, is available to all citizens (Rodman and Trost 1986). This is not true in the United States. The National Organization for Women, the Black Congressional Caucus, and groups concerned with public health placed a high priority on safe, legal, inexpensive abortion.

Not just life, but the quality of life, became an issue. Is merely being born more important than being born healthy, wanted, and loved? Should a pregnancy be terminated if it is known that the expected child is likely to be severely handicapped? Should a woman be forced to bear a child conceived by rape? What if a woman feels unable to meet the physical or emotional needs of the expected child? In the years after abortion became legally available, the number of children put up for adoption decreased dramatically, while the number of aborted pregnancies increased until it exceeded 1.5 million a year. Clearly, most women with an unplanned pregnancy preferred to abort the pregnancy rather than give birth to a child to be given up for adoption.

The issues of changing sex roles, overpopulation, equitable health care, women's rights, the rights of the unborn, and the quality of life all fueled the burning fires of the abortion controversy, turning abortion into a symbolic issue for many competing groups. After all, what can surpass in emotional intensity a single controversy that embraces sex, religion, and politics?

# CHAPTER 2

# THE SOCIAL AND CULTURAL DYNAMICS OF FERTILITY CONTROL

IN THE TWO HUNDRED YEARS from 1650 to 1850 the number of people living on earth approximately doubled, from about 500 million to a little over 1 billion. In the one hundred years from 1850 to 1950 the world's population more than doubled again, from about 1 billion to 2.7 billion. Since 1950 the world's population has been increasing at an even faster rate.

Rapid population growth has occurred because birth rates have not decreased while death rates have. Improved medical and public health measures have resulted in greatly decreased death rates among children under five, and people who survive childhood are more often living to old age. Antibiotics have reduced deaths due to infectious diseases; pesticides have reduced deaths due to insect-born diseases such as malaria and yellow fever and other diseases caused by parasites; and public health measures such as immunization and water purification have virtually vanquished typhoid fever, diphtheria, smallpox, and other plagues of the past.

There is disagreement about the necessity for controlling population growth. In the eighteenth century Malthus questioned the ability of world resources to support unlimited population growth. Since then many economists and demographers have warned that there is a limit to the number of people the earth can support. In contrast, others, including Pope John Paul II, have argued that the problem is one of distribution of resources, not of population growth.

## Cultural Differences

There are vast national and cultural differences with regard to abortion. Most contemporary societies permit and some encourage induced abortion as a method of fertility control, but others prohibit abortion. Among those nations that legally prohibit abortion, some are tolerant of illegal or quasi-legal abortions, while others are antagonistic. In conjunction with differences about the legality of abortion, nations also differ in their public attitudes on abortion, their public support of abortion as a method of family planning or reproductive control, and their rates of induced abortion. There are also sharp differences about abortion *within* societies; these differences, especially in the United States, will be discussed in chapter 8.

Infanticide provides another example of societal differences. Some societies, without access to modern medical technology, have used infanticide as a means of population control. There is evidence of infanticide, at least in the past, in China, India, and Europe. "Infanticide has been practiced on every continent and by people of every level of cultural complexity, from hunters and gatherers to high civilizations, including our own ancestors" (Williamson 1978:61). In a sample of fifty-seven societies, Minturn and Stashak (1982) report that infanticide was practiced in thirty. In virtually all cases infants were killed at birth, before a birth ceremony occurred. Typically, the infants killed were illegitimate, part of a multiple birth, or weak and deformed. Many of them would not have survived for very long. In hunting and gathering societies requiring constant movement to obtain food, infants might be killed if an older sibling still required nursing (Hawkinson 1976). Infanticide is condemned in most modern societies, but its practice illustrates the sharp social and cultural differences in the area of family planning and population control.

In the United States, numerous cases of infanticide and infant abandonment are reported every year. Often these involve an infant born out of wedlock and left in a trash can or a public restroom by a distraught woman. Depending on circumstances, the woman may be defined as criminal or as emotionally ill. Did she stifle the child's first breaths, or refrain from encouraging the child's breathing, or abandon the young child in freezing weather or without food, or leave the child on a doorstep where someone would find it? Each of these actions is subject to differing interpretations by the authorities, depending on the woman's intent and her emotional and physical condition. If she is criminally charged, her ability to hire skilled lawyers who can vigorously defend her becomes critical. In similar fashion, many physicians have chosen not to sustain the life of a child born with serious physical handicaps, such as Down's syndrome. Decisions about the effort to be made to keep such a child alive have sometimes been made by the physician, sometimes by the parents, and sometimes by both. Such decisions are subject to differing interpretations about criminality, and ethical and legal guidelines for physicians and parents are murky and controversial. In the United States, attempts by the Reagan administration to intervene in these decisions were struck down by the U.S. Supreme Court in 1986.

Anti-abortion rhetoric includes a "slippery slope" argument which says that once we accept abortion we are on the way toward accepting infanticide, euthanasia, and other assaults on individual lives. The slope, however, runs in both directions. Perhaps pro-choice rhetoric should argue that the acceptance of abortion makes it possible to eliminate other, more questionable methods, such as infanticide. Although not put in terms of infanticide, or of slippery slopes, the pro-choice rhetoric does include such an argument: once we accept legal abortion, we can eliminate dangerous illegal abortions; and should we return to the "dark ages" of criminalization, we will reap a whirlwind of illegal abortions and dead women.

When does personhood begin? A cultural ethic colors our answer. In most contemporary societies, the answer ranges from conception to birth: implantation, quickening, and viability are in the middle of the range. In many societies, however, personhood begins with a birth ceremony. Killing a child after birth but before the birth ceremony can therefore be used as a means of social and population control. Devereux (1976) reports that infanticide typically occurs immediately after birth and before nursing. Among the Hopi, infanticide occurred during birth, with the woman squeezing the baby between her thighs.

Focusing on cultural differences raises the question of morality. Clearly, if we equate morality with majority views, we can be led astray. In Salem, Massachusetts, in the early seventeenth century, the moral majority succeeded in hanging twenty "witches" and tormented another woman until she died of exposure. In the view of the "moral leaders" of the community, morality and justice prevailed. In retrospect, most of us would not agree with the verdict. Even in that time and place, many disagreed. Precisely because of such religious persecution, the U.S. constitution sought to protect individuals from the majority and to provide for freedom of religion and freedom of speech.

When are we dealing with culturally relative moral issues and when with issues of universal morality? Moving food to one's mouth is a culturally relative matter. Some societies use chopsticks, some use forks, and others use fingers. Although the people of a society may be attached to one way as the right way, from an objective moral viewpoint we can probably agree that there is nothing superior or inferior about chopsticks, forks, or fingers.

We can probably also agree that murder is a matter of fundamental morality and should be universally condemned. There are strong differences of opinion, however, about what should be defined as murder. Many cultures condone the killing of people in some circumstances, especially when the victims are members of a cultural outgroup.

It is difficult to achieve moral consensus about abortion. Some condemn abortion at any stage of embryonic development, regardless of circumstances. Others accept abortion through the second or even the third trimester of pregnancy. Yet others accept infanticide, as long as it takes place before the birth ceremony. Most contemporary moralists have little difficulty in condemning infanticide (Burtchaell 1982); such moral condemnation may be appropriate in modern society but inappropriate in societies that do not have the technology to safely perform induced abortion (Hawkinson 1976). Some have emphasized the importance of taking into account the situation of a particular person when making a decision about the morality of abortion (Bolton 1979; Gilligan, 1982; Luker 1975). It may also be important to take into account the situation of a particular society when making judgments about the morality of its practices (see Callahan 1972; Gilligan 1982; Michel 1982). If a large proportion of a population is facing starvation, abortion and infanticide may seem less immoral than starving older children and adults. In some societies, having more than a given number of children is considered more immoral than abortion. To many people, forcing a woman to deny other potentialities because she is potentially a mother is more immoral than early abortion. They argue that women will remain oppressed "unless they are given full control over that element of their life which most stands in the way of full self-determination—bondage to the biological function of childbearing" (Callahan 1977:442).

## *Policies to Control Fertility*

Thousands of people in Africa are dying of famine brought about by drought, destructive agricultural practices including deforestation, and uncontrolled fertility. India experienced similar famines during the 1960s; since then, government policies have encouraged fertility control and change in agricultural practice, with the result that pervasive famine is not presently a problem in that country.

Faced with inadequate supplies of food and other resources, many countries have tried to reduce birth rates as they have tried to reduce deaths due to malnutrition and disease. India, Pakistan, Bangladesh, China, Japan, the United Kingdom, Austria, Hungary, Sweden, the Dominican Republic, El Salvador, and the Philippines are among the countries that have adopted national policies designed to facilitate fertility control and limit population growth.

Methods of fertility control include sexual abstinence, delayed marriage, contraception, abortion, and sterilization. Government policies may be designed to encourage, support, provide, or even require the adoption of one or more of these measures. One widely used voluntary approach is to take advantage of existing retail outlets to market contraceptive products at subsidized prices that are affordable (Population Reports 1985). Although government programs to encourage voluntary methods of control may seem ethically preferable to Americans, some nations have used various degrees of coercion to achieve what they perceive to be the overriding goal of population control. Some governments offer financial incentives to citizens who limit family size or who undergo voluntary sterilization. Some impose financial or social penalties on those who have more than a certain number of children (Tietze 1983).

Not all countries seek to limit population growth. Most eastern European countries adopted liberalized abortion laws prior to 1960. In response to very low birth rates, however, several have recently adopted more restrictive abortion laws.

In France, where the birth rate dropped below the replacement level several years ago, government policies are now designed to encourage families to have at least three children. Several reasons have been cited for encouraging higher fertility in France (Tomlinson 1984). When the birth rate drops significantly, the proportion of elderly to young people increases and this may eventually place a burden on younger working people. Another concern in France has been that population decline reduces the country's influence in world affairs. In addition, a significant proportion of the French labor force consists of recent immigrants, and some argue that the "Frenchness" of the country is threatened by the low fertility of native French citizens.

Fertility control policies have also been promoted for reasons other than underpopulation or overpopulation. Some labor leaders have argued that restricting the supply of workers by reducing the birth rate among the working class would increase the workers' value and power in the marketplace.

## Fertility Policy in the United States

The vast majority of adults in the United States use contraception or sterilization to control their fertility. When unwanted pregnancy occurs, many resort to abortion to prevent unwanted childbirth. Yet the United States has never had a comprehensive policy to encourage fertility control (Gould 1979). When federal funds were made available in the 1960s for "family planning" they were available only to low-income women. In contrast, many countries make fertility control services available to all of their residents, regardless of ability to pay.

About one-quarter of the U.S. population is Catholic. Officials of the Catholic Church attempt to influence population policy in the United States. They have often been successful in getting restrictive state laws on the books and have been instrumental in delaying or preventing the passage of federal legislation designed to facilitate fertility control. The Church hierarchy maintains that the primary purpose of marriage is procreation and that all methods of fertility control except the rhythm method are illicit. Most Catholic couples, however, use "illicit" means and Catholic women have abortions in about the same proportion as other women (Westoff 1973).

Access to contraception, abortion, and voluntary sterilization has often been restricted by state law. Federal legislation has only occasionally addressed issues of fertility policy. The U.S. Supreme Court has therefore been asked to decide on the constitutionality of state laws restricting access to methods of fertility control. For instance, the Court ruled in 1965 that the decision to use contraception should be a private one, and could not be restricted by state laws against the sale of contraceptives *(Griswold v. Connecticut)*. In 1973, in *Roe v. Wade,* the Court ruled that a woman's right to privacy includes the right to choose abortion before the fetus reaches the point of viability.

Although federal family policy has been a popular catchword it has not been feasible. Specific federal policies to promote the health, education, and welfare of children have been adopted. But comprehensive family policy formulated by federal legislation has been difficult to pursue. There are several reasons for this: our diversity of ethnic background, religious belief, and family life-styles; our tradition of Western expansion and the relative abundance of natural resources, which permitted us to support a growing population; our tradition of individualism and freedom from government intervention; and our emphasis upon states' rights. These factors have discouraged the formulation of a national family policy or fertility control policy (Gould 1979; Steiner 1981; Westoff 1973). Moreover, fertility control measures could be made available for use on a voluntary basis without imposing constraints on individual rights or even on states' rights. Another explanation for American reluctance to provide government help in achieving fertility control probably lies in our ambivalence about sexuality, about children, and about the role of women in our society.

## The Ambivalence of Americans Toward Fertility Control

Until quite recently, federal policies to encourage fertility control were nonexistent. As late as the 1950s President Eisenhower said, "This government will not ... as long as I am here, have a positive political doctrine in its program that has to do with the problems of birth control. That's not our business."

Social and political attitudes changed during the 1960s. In 1965, President Johnson stated he would "seek new ways to use our knowledge to help deal with the explosion in world population and the growing scarcity in world resources." In 1969 President Nixon proposed to Congress that "we should establish as a national goal the provision of adequate family planning services within the next five years to all those who want them but cannot afford them." Congress responded by authorizing funds for family planning services to the poor and for population research (Westoff 1973).

A poll conducted in 1971 found the "American public ... overwhelmingly in favor of the government providing birth control, ... split on the question of abortion, and favoring high schools offering information on ways of avoiding pregnancy" (Westoff 1973). About two-thirds of the respondents thought that population growth was a problem in the United States. American legislators, however, have been extremely reluctant to enact laws that would provide fertility control services to all who want them.

American attitudes about sexual behavior, sex education, fertility control, and population policies can best be described as ambivalent. The gap between our stated beliefs and our actions reflect ambivalence about children as well. Politicians like to say that children are our most precious resource, yet many refuse to support programs that provide an adequate standard of living for children who have the misfortune to be born into disadvantaged families. We have few programs, at the state or federal level, to encourage good care for children whose mothers must work to support their families. Disadvantaged families are often held responsible and blameworthy for their condition of poverty (Rodman 1965, 1968), and public policy often seems designed to punish poor families rather than to assure them a fair share of national resources.

Ambivalence about sexuality, about children, and about poverty creates some strange situations. For many years it was possible for affluent women to obtain effective contraceptives and to obtain safe abortions from a physician when an unwanted pregnancy occurred. In contrast, poor women faced obstacles in their attempt to prevent unwanted births, even though additional children would only drive the family deeper into poverty. Federal and state funds were not made available until the 1960s to help poor women control their fertility, and some of that funding was withdrawn during the Reagan administration.

At the same time that poor women faced difficulties in gaining voluntary access to fertility control measures, they were sometimes the target of involuntary fertility control measures. State laws permitting the sterilization of mentally retarded individuals were most actively enforced during the 1930s, especially against the poor and the black. As a result of such discriminatory treatment, sterilization is viewed suspiciously by some people. Among middle-class white men and women, however, voluntary sterilization has become the most frequently used method of fertility control once they have all the children they desire.

TEENAGE PREGNANCY

Ambivalence is particularly prevalent in American attitudes toward teenage sexual activity. Research indicates that a majority of teenagers over 16 are sexually active. Pregnant women under 18 are a "high risk" group in terms of their ability to support a child, in terms of the effect of pregnancy on their own education and future employment, and in terms of producing low-birth-weight infants disproportionately susceptible to developmental problems.

Despite the risks involved in teenage pregnancy, there are strong pressures in the United States to restrict adolescents' access to information about sexuality and to contraceptive and abortion services (Rodman, Lewis, and Griffith 1984). Although many teenagers are sexually active, many of their elders insist that teenagers "should be" sexually abstinent. It is exceedingly difficult for any society to be totally successful in preventing postpubertal teenagers from participating in sexual activity. The biological changes of puberty focus a young person's attention on his or her sexual maturing at the very time when the maturational thrust to become independent of parents and to develop self-identity makes the young person turn to peers for personal relationships and intimacy.

Some societies are permissive about early sexual activity. Others, including the English-speaking countries, have often invoked strict social sanctions against teenage and premarital sexual activity. Unmarried young women have been forced to give away children born out of wedlock, and often the young woman was forced to leave school and reside in a "home for unwed mothers" until her child was delivered. Sweden, in contrast, has never had a "cult of virginity" and no stigma is attached to unmarried sexual relationships or unmarried parenthood. Early marriage and early parenthood, however, are discouraged.

Some societies sanction sexual pleasure that does not result in pregnancy (e.g., masturbation) among young people who, financially and developmentally, are not in a position to support children. Western societies, influenced by Roman Catholic doctrine, have tended, until recently, to exert sanctions against such behavior. Today, in the United States, many marriage counselors and sex therapists believe that teaching self-stimulation is the most effective way to help preorgasmic women become sexually responsive to their sexual partners. Yet, present generations of Americans have often been told by parents, ministers, and even physicians, that "self-pleasuring" is unhealthy and sinful.

Our ambivalence about sexuality, poverty, and fertility control is also evident in our attitudes toward repeat abortion and in our vacillating support of fertility control in developing countries. Many people, including some family planning counselors who generally support contraception and abortion on demand, express disapproval of women who seek more than one abortion. Yet statistics show that women seeking a repeat abortion are more likely to have been using contraception at the time of conception than are women seeking a first abortion. Women who seek an abortion are women who are sexually active and fertile. Tietze (1983) noted that one or more unplanned pregnancies are highly probable events among sexually active, fertile women. Many woman are reluctant to use oral contraceptive pills or IUDs continually for the twenty-five or more years during which they expect to be sexually active and fertile. All other available methods of contraception are less than 95 percent effective, and unexpected pregnancies for women who use them are fairly frequent. It is therefore not surprising that many people choose to be sterilized.

## Models of Fertility Control

The dynamic relationships between abortion, fertility, and population control vary with "demographic, sociocultural, economic, and political variables" (Omran 1976:18–45). Omran proposed three models of interaction among these variables: (1) the "Classic Western" model where socioeconomic change brought about a gradual decline in mortality, and later, in fertility; (2) the "Accelerated" model of Japan and eastern Europe, where socioeconomic changes caused demographic changes such as longer life expectancy and lower rates of infant and maternal mortality; and (3) the "Delayed (Third World)" model where countries experienced epidemiological transitions only recently, usually since World War II.

In the Classic Western model, Omran suggests that legalization of abortion had less effect on fertility than did the concomitant increase in contraception (1976:29–30). In societies fitting this model, abortion is used mostly by unmarried women; legalization of abortion, therefore, reduced the number of out-of-wedlock births and decreased discrimination against indigent women who previously had less access to "medical" abortions than more affluent women.

In the Accelerated model, legalization of abortion sharply reduced the birth rate and reduced the number of illegal abortions. "Medical progress partly influenced mortality decline, while abortion unequivocally accelerated fertility decline" (Omran 1976:19). In countries such as Japan abortion is commonly used to limit family size and most abortions are obtained by older married women. Abortion was common prior to legalization and contraceptive methods tended to be the traditional ones of coitus interruptus, abstinence, rhythm, or douching.

Some demographers and epidemiologists (Omran 1976; Tietze 1983) estimate that, on average, it takes two or more abortions to avoid one birth in a noncontracepting population, compared to about 1.2 abortions to avoid a birth in a contracepting population. Tietze (1983:98) noted that the "interval between two successive conceptions has three components: (a) the pregnancy itself, (b) a postgestational anovulatory period during which conception cannot occur, and (c) an ovulatory period during which the monthly probability of conception is more than zero but less than one." Induced abortion reduces (a) from nine months to about three months. Period (b) may be shorter after abortion, if the woman would otherwise breastfeed her infant. Period (c) is probably not affected by induced abortion. Effective contraception may extend period (c).

In economically underdeveloped countries resembling Omran's Delayed (Third World) model, use of contraception has been limited by norms favoring large families, high valuation of children, and low status of women. "Mortality declined in response to major breakthroughs in medical technology, usually imported. . . . Fertility . . . has been sustained at high levels. . . . The role of social change . . . is very limited" (Omran 1976:19). The effect of abortion liberalization in these countries is difficult to predict. Omran suggests that confidentiality and effective health delivery systems may be crucial determinants of fertility control in this model. It may be difficult for indigent women in these countries to obtain contraceptives or surgical procedures, including abortion. Even when available, women may have to use them secretly to avoid censure.

## The Medical Model in Fertility Control

Pregnancy is a normal physiological event for a woman although the state of pregnancy differs from her normal nonpregnant state.

In societies where the care of women in childbirth has been assigned to physicians, especially where most physicians are men, pregnancy tends to be defined as pathological. In "treating" pregnant women, the physician often demands control over social and sexual activities, diet, medication, time of delivery, and mode of delivery. Women who do not follow the physician's instructions and prescriptions risk verbal abuse and the threat of denial of medical care should a medical emergency develop during pregnancy or delivery.

Most women agree that it is helpful to have an attendant knowledgeable about childbirth present at the time of delivery. There is little evidence to support the idea that the attendant must be a physician. Prenatal screening can usually identify potential problems and emergency situations that might call for hospital delivery and a physician's attention. Countries such as Great Britain and the Netherlands deliver most babies without physicians and outside of hospitals, yet they have better records of maternal and infant mortality than does the United States. In the United States, however, the availability of a physician's help in a medical emergency during delivery is usually made contingent on choosing to have the baby in a hospital, in the presence of a physician, whether or not a medical problem exists.

Imposition of a medical model on pregnancy and fertility control may be unfortunate. Antiseptic conditions are desirable for normal deliveries and for surgical procedures, including sterilization and abortion procedures. However, physicians are not the only people capable of maintaining antiseptic conditions. In many countries non-physicians provide safe, sanitary delivery care, sterilization, and abortion procedures, and distribute contraceptives and information about their use. The use of non-physicians has made safe childbirth and effective fertility control available to many women who could not otherwise be reached.

Safilios-Rothschild (1974:128) found that women in several Mediterranean societies associated oral contraceptives and IUDs with physicians and illness. Many women mistrusted hospitals, physicians, and medical procedures. Providing fertility control services and prenatal care as part of a preventive health delivery system was therefore not an effective approach. Safilios-Rothschild suggested that corrective (abortifacient) techniques rather than preventive (contraceptive) techniques were more acceptable to many of the women since "the motivation to suppress the known pregnancy" was much greater than the motivation to use suspect birth control "medication."

Similar considerations may operate in the fertility control decisions of many American women. Luker (1975) found that many women who sought abortions in California had weighed the costs and benefits of contraception against the costs, benefits, and probability of getting pregnant and had chosen not to contracept. The effect of contraception on her relationship with her sexual partner or her family was considered, as was the effect of contraception on her health. Two-thirds of the women in Luker's study had been advised by a physician that they might have trouble conceiving. Such advice may have affected the women's assessment of the probability of pregnancy and may have motivated some of them to test their fertility.

## The Relationship Between Abortion, Contraception, and Sterilization

Interaction among the various methods of fertility control is complex and difficult to interpret. Abortion and contraception are sometimes seen as competing ways to control fertility and sometimes as complementary. Some argue that liberalized abortion laws open the floodgates to induced abortion and encourage less dependence upon contraception; widespread abortion then becomes the greatest obstacle to the spread of contraception. Seen as complementary methods, abortion "does not compete with contraception but serves as a backstop when the latter fails or when contraceptive devices or information are not available. As contraception becomes customary, the incidence of abortion recedes even without its being banned" (Davis 1967:733).

Tietze (1981:97) noted that the relationship between the abortion rate and the pregnancy rate depends on a variety of factors including "changes in the age distribution of women within the reproductive age range.... The proportion of women who are sexually active ... the proportion married ... and changes in the sexual behaviors of the unmarried." The abortion rate also depends on "the proportion of sexually active women who *intend* to give birth and on the contraceptive behavior of sexually active women." Also of importance are changes in contraception and abortion methods, as well as changes in the frequency of "illegal abortions not included in the official statistics."

## CHANGES IN THE ABORTION RATE

It is difficult to determine whether the legalization of abortion increased the percentage of pregnancies ending in induced abortion (although it seems logical that there would be an increase). Because large numbers of women had been victims of unsafe, illegal abortion and because physicians disliked having to choose between their commitment to uphold the law and their commitment to the welfare of their women patients, many physicians sought the legalization of induced abortion. A significant decrease in the incidence of serious complications due to "spontaneous" abortions occurred after legalization, suggesting that many "spontaneous" abortions prior to legalization were, in fact, illegally induced abortions (Neubardt and Schulman 1977).

We can only estimate the number of illegal abortions obtained prior to legalization. It is known that many American women obtained abortions from their private physicians, and that many women who could not afford private medical care obtained illegal abortions from more dangerous sources. Kinsey and his colleagues (1958) estimated that one of every four American women had at least one induced abortion during her fertile years. Surveys using randomized response techniques and retrospective estimates (Abernathay 1976; Tietze 1983) support estimates of roughly one million induced abortions per year in the United States prior to legalization.

The frequency of illegal abortions not included in official statistics appears to be quite low at present (CDC 1985). Since 1973 the number of legal abortions reported in the United States has increased from about 740,000 to more than 1.5 million per year. We cannot conclude, however, that an increase in the absolute number of abortions represents an increase in the abortion rate (the number of abortions per 1,000 women aged 15–44) or in the abortion ratio (the number of abortions per 1,000 known pregnancies or per 1,000 live births; the CDC uses abortions per 1,000 live births). With the maturation of the "baby boom" generation (those born between 1945 and 1960) an unprecedented number of women reached the age of fertility at precisely the time when anti-abortion laws were being repealed or reformed. Even if the abortion rate remained constant, an increased number of women aged 15 to 44 would be associated with an increased number of abortions.

## CHANGES IN THE PREGNANCY RATE AND IN THE BIRTH RATE

Beginning in the late 1960s the birth rate (the number of live births per 1,000 women aged 15–44) fell markedly. Presently, women aged 15 to 44 are having, on the average, fewer than two children each. The average American woman is experiencing fewer pregnancies than earlier cohorts. There has been a decrease in the pregnancy rate (the number of known pregnancies per 1,000 women aged 15–44) as well as in the birth rate. Changes in the birth rate may be due to a number of factors: women are marrying somewhat later than in the preceding generations; more women are using effective oral contraceptives and IUDs; barrier methods such as condoms, foams, gels, and diaphragms have improved in effectiveness and in esthetic acceptability, although such methods remain less effective than oral contraceptives and IUDs; voluntary sterilization has become common and is a highly effective and usually irreversible method; when unwanted pregnancy does occur, more than 1.5 million women per year are choosing abortion.

## THE REVOLUTION IN GENDER ROLES AND SEXUAL BEHAVIOR

Evidence indicates that a major change in gender roles (the behaviors which society expects from men and from women) and in attitudes toward sexual behavior, a true "sexual revolution," has occurred in the last two decades. Traditional expectations were that women would have numerous children, spend most of their lives caring for home and children, and have little involvement in business or political affairs outside the home. Traditional methods of fertility control included abstinence, coitus interruptus, delay of marriage to the later, less fertile, years, and socialization of women to the norm that they should not enjoy sexual expression, except for procreation within marriage.

Sexually active women deprived of contraception face the prospect of a pregnancy every year or two from sexual maturity to menopause. Coitus interruptus (withdrawal of the penis before ejaculation) may leave a woman feeling frustrated rather than relaxed and satisfied by sexual intercourse, especially if no other stimulation is used to bring her to orgasm. Women threatened with frequent pregnancy, or frustrated by coitus interruptus, may be motivated to inhibit their sexual activity. Traditionally, socially tolerated prostitution provided an outlet for male sexual activity, using a small group of women who were relatively infertile due to venereal disease, and who had access to contraception which was denied "respectable" women. The increasing availability of esthetically acceptable, effective contraception, along with women's increasing economic and social independence, has permitted many women to achieve increased sexual pleasure and freedom of sexual expression even as the birth rate has declined.

Divorce is now commonplace in the United States. Many women are raising children outside of traditional two-parent marriage relationships. Unmarried mothers, either divorced from or never married to the fathers of their children, now comprise a substantial proportion of women in many Western societies. In some Scandinavian countries, no stigma is attached to unmarried pregnancy. In a mobile society unmarried mothers are soon indistinguishable from divorced mothers. In several states, birth certificates list the father's name and the mother's maiden name, making it difficult to identify a child as "illegitimate." In these circumstances, living with a single parent, unmarried or divorced, may not be the traumatic experience it was thought to be in times past. This is especially true if the woman and her children have an adequate income.

A majority of women are now employed outside the home. In

1985, 54 percent of married women, 61 percent of separated women, and 75 percent of divorced women were in the labor force (U.S. Bureau of the Census, 1985). On the average, women are not paid as much as men, even for the same job; nevertheless, women have achieved a considerable degree of economic independence. Many women perceive that they have choices: they can have careers, they can have children, or they can have both careers and children, concurrently or sequentially. A corollary is that men, too, may have more choices. Often they can count on their wives to help support the family financially and they can spend more time with their children and in their homes.

These aspects of the "sexual revolution" have affected the factors cited by Tietze (1981:97) as influencing the pregnancy rate and the abortion rate. Women are marrying at a later age; a smaller proportion of women have married; a higher proportion of unmarried women are sexually active and more people consider it socially acceptable for unmarried women to be sexually active. It seems clear that American women, married and unmarried, have become effective contraceptors. Women are having, on the average, fewer pregnancies. Most of all, evidence suggests that the sexual revolution has permitted many women and men to enjoy sex for pleasure without procreation. When contraception is not used, or when it fails, many women are using abortion to avoid unwanted childbirth.

### ADOPTION VERSUS ABORTION

People who oppose abortion often advocate adoption as an alternative. Several studies have reported that most unmarried pregnant women prefer to abort during the first trimester of pregnancy rather than carry the pregnancy to term and give up a child for adoption. The statistics on adoption and abortion support those findings. The number of infants made available for adoption has decreased significantly in the last decade, at the same time that the number of abortions has increased to more than 1.5 million per year in the United States. Some single women, of course, are choosing to bear and keep their children, rather than turning to adoption or abortion.

## Effectiveness and Risks

We have examined relationships among fertility control methods, considering the effect of abortion availability on the use of contraception and on the birth rate. The sweeping changes in the number of women in the fertile years, in attitudes about sexuality and about the role of women, and in the availability of safe, effective methods of contraception and abortion have all been considered as part of the dynamics of fertility control. Other dimensions of fertility control are the relative effectiveness of various methods and their relative risks to the woman's health and to her future ability to carry a wanted pregnancy to term (Tietze 1981).

### THE RISK OF METHOD FAILURE

Sterilization is the most effective method but is usually irreversible. Oral contraceptive pills and IUDs are nearly 100 percent effective, if used properly. They are reversible methods. Occasionally, they may not be tolerated by the woman's body. Properly used, barrier methods (foams, gels, other spermaticides, condoms, and diaphragms) seem to be about 95 percent effective. They are perhaps less likely to be used appropriately and consistently.

Periodic abstinence (rhythm) is 100 percent effective when there is no intercourse during the fertile period. It is, however, difficult to ascertain just when the fertile period occurs, and the method depends on both partners being willing to abstain for one-third or more of each month.

Birth rates are lower in populations where sterilization and contraception are widely used and where most women are not dependent only on abstinence, rhythm, coitus interruptus, and douching. Cause and effect relationships are confounded, however, by demographic, sociocultural, economic, and political variables, such as those described by Omran's models (1976).

### THE RISK TO SUBSEQUENT PREGNANCIES

The effect of abortion on a woman's ability to carry a later pregnancy to delivery of a healthy child is discussed in chapter 4. In short, if a D&E procedure is performed by competent personnel, one abortion procedure appears to have little effect on later pregnancies. The evidence is less clear in the case of two or more abortions. A confounding factor is that the statistics on repeat abortions often include abortions by older methods which are no longer used because they are less safe.


RISKS TO THE PREGNANT WOMAN

In developed countries, among women under age 30 (excepting smokers using oral contraceptive pills), risks for each method—abortion, oral contraceptives, IUDs, and barrier methods—are about equal, and are significantly lower than the "birth-related risk to the life of women without fertility control. Beyond age 30 . . . the risk to life increases rapidly for pill users, especially those who smoke. . . . For all other methods, the risk . . . remains far below the level of mortality associated with complications of pregnancy and childbirth without fertility regulation. At all ages the lowest level of mortality by far . . . is achieved by the use of barrier contraceptives with early abortion in case of failure" (Tietze 1981:98).

In short, voluntary sterilization, contraception, and abortion have become relatively safe choices for women who wish to control their fertility. Although some change has occurred in recent years, the major responsibility for fertility control rests with women. Despite some continuing ambivalence and controversy, and despite the absence of a 100 percent safe and effective contraceptive, most American women are effectively controlling their fertility.

# CHAPTER 3

# THE MORAL DEBATE

THE UNITED STATES IS a pluralistic society where people of many moral and religious persuasions exist side by side. Constitutional protection of religious freedom and of the right to privacy was designed to protect this diversity of belief, particularly to protect individuals from pressure to conform to majority views. As stated in 1973 by the U.S. Supreme Court, in *Roe v. Wade,* the right to privacy "is broad enough to encompass a woman's decision whether or not to terminate her pregnancy." This ruling had the effect of returning the abortion decision to the individual conscience. The tolerance of most Americans for a diversity of beliefs and practices is illustrated on the abortion question by the distinction made between private morality and public policy, a theme we explore more fully in chapter 8.

After 1973 several states passed laws intended to restrict or discourage access to abortion, particularly for minors. The U.S. Supreme Court, however, rejected most of these statutes. At present no American law says a woman must have an abortion; neither is a woman legally constrained from choosing to have an abortion during the early months of pregnancy.

To many people this seems a just solution of the issue. But many others consider abortion to be the killing of a living person and argue that abortion should be prohibited. They contend that accepting abortion places us on a slippery moral slope that can lead to the acceptance of killing of other defenseless groups. The alliance of this moral position with politics, indeed the responsibility many pro-life advocates feel to translate this moral position into law, continues the controversy.

The abortion controversy pertains not only to what is just but to what is possible. Women throughout history have subjected themselves to abortion when they perceived it to be preferable to other alternatives. Many physicians throughout the world urged that abortion be legalized because it was clear that desperate women would have an abortion even though it was illegal and dangerous.

For many social observers, the central issue in the abortion controversy is the moral debate between those arguing for the fetus' right to live and those arguing for the woman's right to choose to terminate the pregnancy. Does a fetus have an absolute right to life, regardless of the pregnant woman's situation? Does the woman have an absolute right, even a responsibility, to control her own fertility, including the right to an abortion? Controversy about these questions is highly emotional and partisan. The central legal issue may have been resolved by the U.S. Supreme Court decisions of 1973, but the moral issues—involving questions of privacy, of controlling one's own body, of defining life and death—have proven more difficult to resolve. Theologians and philosophers have argued the morality of abortion and their varying conclusions testify to the difficulty of the questions. Arguments may be framed in rational and objective terms, but the conclusions are typically linked to subjective beliefs and values.

Surveys of anti-abortion and pro-choice advocates indicate that their moral differences on abortion are closely tied to differences about political and religious issues and about the roles of women. Anti-abortion partisans tend to favor political conservatism, sexual conventionality, and religious orthodoxy. Granberg (1981:157–163) found that 70 percent of a sample of members of the National Right to Life Committee, an anti-abortion activist group, were Catholic (compared to 28 percent of the U.S. population). Religion was extremely important to 59 percent of the sample, and 95 percent of sample members attended church at least once a month. Nine in ten opposed the Equal Rights Amendment. Sex education in the public schools, with or without community or parental involvement, was opposed by 36 percent of the members. In sharp contrast, among Granberg's sample of members of the National Abortion

Rights Action League, a pro-choice activist group, 4 percent were Catholic, 20 percent attended church at least once a month, 93 percent approved of the Equal Rights Amendment, and only 1 percent were opposed to sex education in the public schools. Similar differences between anti-abortion and pro-choice advocates have been reported by Ray (1983) and Luker (1984).

## Central Issues in the Controversy

This brief discussion points to some of the central issues of the abortion controversy: (1) When does human life begin? (2) Under what circumstances, if any, may life be terminated? (3) What is the proper role of women? and (4) What role should the law play?

### WHEN DOES LIFE BEGIN?

The empirical evidence of scientific observation tells us that reproduction is a continuous process. A live sperm must merge with a live egg and the fertilized egg must divide and redivide into the millions of cells which make up the human body; after implantation in the uterus these cells must differentiate into organs and tissues which must integrate and become capable of functioning outside the woman's body. Cell biologists have learned that a woman is born with all of the eggs (ova) she will ever produce. Of the several hundred ova in her ovaries, typically only a few are ever fertilized. Many fertilized ova do not survive to the stage of implantation. Similarly, although the human male produces millions of sperm for each ejaculation, only a very small fraction of his sperm ever fertilize an ovum and develop into a new human being. Even if conception occurs, about one-third of the fertilized ova are aborted spontaneously, apparently because they are defective (Snell 1983).

The study of embryology has identified much of the biological process of conception, implantation, and fetal growth (Snell 1983). During her fertile years (roughly ages 12–50) a woman's ovaries usually release an egg once a month, about two weeks after the start of her last menstrual flow, in a process known as ovulation. The egg passes from the ovary to the uterine tube and makes its way to the uterus. If the egg is not fertilized it passes out of her body.

At each ejaculation, mature men normally discharge 250 million to 300 million sperm cells, each of which carries genetic information. When ejaculation occurs with sexual intercourse, millions of sperm pass through the uterus and into the uterine tubes. If egg and sperm meet, one sperm may penetrate the egg, resulting in fertilization or conception. Any sperm which do not penetrate an egg die within a few days. When the sperm penetrates the egg, changes occur that prevent any other sperm from penetrating. Each egg and each sperm cell normally carry one-half of the chromosomes necessary to complete the transfer of genetic information. The two half-complements of genetic information, from the sperm and the egg, form a full complement of information in a new and unique combination.

The fertilized egg, a single cell known as a zygote, continues its passage through the uterine tube. The zygote then begins mitosis, or cell division, so that two, then four, then eight, etc., cells are formed, each with a full complement of genetic information, half received from the sperm and half received from the egg. The small cluster of cells polarizes into the blastocyst and the trophoblast. The blastocyst becomes the embryo and the trophoblast develops into the yolk sac, the umbilical cord, part of the placenta, and other tissues which serve to protect the developing embryo, to remove wastes, and to transmit nourishment to the embryo from the woman's body (Snell 1983; Berger 1980).

Following fertilization, hormones are released which cause the uterine wall to proliferate, providing a nourishing environment for the embryo. Between the fifth and ninth day after conception the small cluster of polarized cells normally attaches to the uterine wall. Unless prevented by drugs or intrauterine devices, about 75 percent of all fertilized ova survive to the stage of uterine implantation. Implantation usually triggers hormonal changes which prevent monthly menstruation for the duration of the pregnancy. Without such hormonal changes the embryo would be swept out of the body in the next menstrual flow. Implanation is usually well established within fourteen days after fertilization—which is about one month after the beginning of the last menstrual period (LMP) (Snell 1983).

Between the fourth and eighth week after fertilization the embryo develops rapidly. Major organs are formed, limb buds appear, and the embryo attains a length of about one inch.

By the end of the first trimester of pregnancy (three months LMP) the developing organism, now known as a fetus, is about two inches in length from the top of its head to the lower end of its spine. The fetus has a somewhat human appearance, bone and cartilage are recognizable, simple reflex movement may occur, and the fetal heartbeat may be detected by electrocardiogram (Moore 1982; Snell 1983).

Spontaneous abortion of the living fetus before the twentieth week is called miscarriage. About one-third of all pregnancies terminate in miscarriage. Natural expulsion of the fetus occurring after the twentieth week, but before normal prenatal development, is called premature birth. Between 20 weeks and the usual gestation period of about 40 weeks the brain, heart, and lungs undergo rapid development. For that reason, infants with a gestational age of less than 24 weeks have, until recently, rarely been viable (able to live after birth). With most pregnancies, development proceeds from zygote to embryo to fetus, and about 40 weeks after fertilization, to delivery of an infant capable of living outside the womb without life-support technology, though it will require years of nurturance and care.

The view of the Roman Catholic Church, as stated in the 1968 encyclical *Humanae vitae*, is summarized by McCormick: "Every contraceptive act is intrinsically evil. . . . Intercourse is a single act with two aspects or inner meanings, the unitive and the procreative . . . by divine design inseparable, so that one who deliberately renders coitus sterile attacks its meaning as an expression of mutual self-giving" (1981:218–219).

From this it follows, in Catholic theology, that any sexual expression that does not have the potential for procreation is also intrinsically evil. This is one basis for the Roman Catholic prohibition not only against contraception and abortion, but also against masturbation and voluntary sterilization by vasectomy or tubal ligation.

Current Roman Catholic doctrine also holds that life begins at the moment of conception, a view shared by some other religious groups. It is clear that most Americans do not support a prohibition against contraception and sterilization, and similarly, most Americans do not support the official Roman Catholic position on abortion or on the moment of personhood.


## PERSONHOOD

Much debate centers around the somewhat murky concept of meaningful human life or personhood. Scholarly arguments and Senate hearings have not resolved the issue. From the biological viewpoint, the fertilized egg may divide into more than one individual any time during the early days or weeks after fertilization. Such division results in monozygotic (identical) twins, since one set of genetic information is shared by both embryos. Because individualization is not determined until after the first stages of cell division are completed, some people do not consider that a new individual exists until those early days (about one month LMP) have passed. By that line of reasoning, personhood may be defined as occurring when there is no longer the possibility that the developing embryo may divide into two or more individuals.

Others define personhood in terms of some particular level of brain function. Brain development proceeds rapidly between three and six months LMP. By the end of the second trimester (six lunar months or 24 weeks LMP) the fetus can move its eyes, though they are not yet open, and can move its hands, and has slight sucking and kicking reflexes. These reflex movements, evidence of central nervous system activity, are perceived by the pregnant woman or others who feel for them through her abdomen. These are the movements of "quickening," the ancient criterion of personhood.

For many people the crucial criterion of personhood is viability, the ability of an organism to maintain life outside the womb with the help of parents or other caretakers. Legally, the U.S. Supreme Court stated in its 1973 ruling on abortion (*Roe v. Wade*): "The unborn have never been recognized in the law as persons in the whole sense" and that the rights extended to the unborn, in tort law, are contingent upon live birth. However, the Court did state that "with respect to the State's important and legitimate interest in potential life, the 'compelling' point is at viability."

In summary, the biological evidence is that only a small fraction of eggs and sperm ever realize their potential for fertilization. Of those which do join to become zygotes, at least a quarter pass out of women's bodies by the time of the next menstrual flow, probably because the zygotes are in some way defective. If the zygote survives to implantation, individuation is not determined until about one month LMP. During the process of development from a one-celled zygote to the millions of cells differentiated into the organs and systems of a viable newborn infant, various points of development have been cited as the moment of personhood. The chosen point may be conception, implantation, quickening, viability, or some degree of brain function deemed uniquely human.

## THE MEANING OF "LIFE" AND "DEATH"

Personhood is not the only concept that has been debated. The meaning of "life" and "death" is also subject to interpretation. Testifying before a Senate subcommittee, Leon Rosenberg (1981), a Yale University embryologist, stated that science cannot define life or death. Rather, that definition is a matter of personal belief, i.e., of one's religious belief or world view.

Medical technology has made it possible to maintain certain essential body processes such as blood circulation and oxygenation, breathing, and waste disposal, even when the heart, lungs, or kidneys are not functional or when the brain is no longer integrating the activity of other organs. Thus, it has become difficult to define the moment of death if brain activity has ceased but support technology continues other biological functions. So, too, has the definition of life become ever more difficult. Incubators, artificial wombs, implantation in surrogate mothers, and other technological life-support systems are presently possible.

## Under What Circumstances, If Any, May Life Be Terminated?

Beginning with the premise that God infuses the soul at the moment of conception, Roman Catholic doctrine maintains that

every unborn child must be regarded from the moment of conception as a human person, with all the rights thereof, and that to
destroy the fetus is to commit murder. However, Roman Catholic
doctrine distinguishes between direct and indirect abortion.

Direct abortion, "the deliberate attempt to kill the fetus or in-
capacitate it in such a way that it is likely to die" (Smith 1970:30),
is always forbidden because maternal and fetal life are considered
equal. Indirect abortion may be permitted under the doctrine of
double effect, which supposes that an action may have an intended
good effect and an unintended (yet inevitable) evil effect. If a woman
would die from a cancerous uterus, for instance, her pregnant uterus
might rightfully be removed, even though that results in the death
of the fetus. In this example the intent is preservation of the mother's
life. The death of the fetus is not intended nor directly induced,
though that is the indirect result of removing the cancerous uterus.

Many who believe that human life begins at the moment of
conception are truly horrified by abortion, which they regard as the
deliberate destruction of human life. Yet many people realize that
social or medical conditions may force a woman to choose, not
between good and evil, but between the greater and lesser of two
evils.

The Roman Catholic theologian Richard A. McCormick (1981)
directly addresses the need for compassion for women caught in
difficult social situations and he distinguishes between the dictates
of applied, pastoral care and moral arguments. Since pastoral care
deals with individuals as they are, in terms of their strengths and
perceptions, McCormick does not foreclose abortion at the pastoral
level, although at the moral level he considers abortion unaccept-
able. Aware of the complexity of abortion and sensitive to varying
positions, he recognizes the "tension between the good and the
feasible" and recommends societal changes that would lessen the
abortion problem. He also refrains from taking a legal position that
would align him with either prohibition or permissiveness and opts
for returning the abortion decision to each of the fifty states.

The Protestant theologian Harmon Smith states that the abortion
decision must be made in a context of competing values. "I believe
it arguably the part of mercy to foreclose the birth of nascent life
which is or promises to be severely deformed, defective, or disad-

vantaged." He accepts that people will differ in their decisions about abortion, depending on their situation. And he rejects the idea that abortion is murder: "It is a premeditated but not thereby malicious action; it can, and ought always to be, a genuinely regretable alternative to unwanted pregnancy" (Smith 1970:52–54).

These two theologians (McCormick 1981; Smith 1970) exemplify two views of morality. One ethic assumes that right and wrong are absolutes (decreed by a higher authority such as God, church leaders, or the state) and that individuals have a duty to behave according to the prescribed moral code. A second ethic, reflected in the writings of Gilligan (1982), Luker (1984), and Smith (1970), is that decisions must often be made within a context of conflicting interests. For example, what is good for one (the unborn child) may be bad for others (the pregnant woman, her family, her sexual partner, or the society in which she lives). Moral decisions, in this view, are made within the context of a network of relationships; whatever decision the woman makes may have negative consequences for someone. Moral behavior does not involve subscribing to an absolute code of right and wrong behavior laid down by a higher authority; rather, moral behavior is taking responsibility for making choices. It may be moral to choose to use contraceptives. If the contraceptive fails, it may be moral to choose to abort the pregnancy, given the network of relationships and competing claims within which the woman lives.

With an absolute ethic, abortion may be defined as always wrong. With a contextual ethic, abortion may be wrong in one situation but may be the best choice available in other situations.

A variety of other moral positions on abortion have been developed and debated. The arguments can become tortuous and can taken on the character of an academic game, as McCormick (1981) has pointed out. The usual critical and contentious issues emerge in these debates: the humanity of the fetus; the development of the fetus' human potential; the woman's right to control her fertility; the woman's right to control her body; the woman's circumstances; the relative moral weight to assign to the fetus' rights and the pregnant woman's rights. The moral arguments are more convoluted and subjective than the legal arguments. Paralleling the legal arguments, however, the conclusions range from a moral position that places paramount emphasis upon a woman's right, or even obligation, to choose an abortion to a moral position that places paramount emphasis on the fetus' humanity and therefore would prohibit abortion.

## What Is the Proper Role of Women?

As we have seen, many people do not believe that abortion during the early weeks or early months of pregnancy involves killing a living person. Presently in the United States over 90 percent of abortions are obtained during the first trimester of pregnancy. When one listens to women who are considering induced abortion, it becomes apparent that many women do not feel that they are destroying a human life. Rather, they realize that continuing the pregnancy beyond the early months would eventually result in the birth of a child for whom they feel unable to provide—financially, emotionally, or physically. Clearly, many pregnant women distinguish between the potential life represented by the fetus in the first or even second trimester of pregnancy and the living human being which may develop if the pregnancy is carried to term. This view is in harmony with the legal distinction that exists in the United States.

For many men and women abortion remains an abstract issue to be decided in terms of moral or religious codes. Research studies have found, however, that many women who were generally opposed to abortion changed their minds when they personally faced an unwanted pregnancy (Freeman 1977). The teenager who has not finished high school, the professional woman who wants children but not until she has completed her training and established her career, the outstanding athlete who is at the peak of her ability, the young couple with a beloved child, just barely making ends meet on their two salaries, the woman in her late thirties or forties who welcomed her earlier children but does not want another child at her age, the woman whose child is at high risk for severe developmental problems such as Down's syndrome—many such women are choosing induced abortion when an unplanned pregnancy occurs. Moreover, there are women impregnated by acts of rape and

incest. To many people it seems immoral that these women should
be forced to continue their pregnancies.

While some religious and political leaders argue about the morality of abortion, many women see it as a practical issue. They
perceive that sexual relationships are a normal part of human behavior and that unwanted pregnancy, even with contraception, is
always a possibility. Pregnancy sometimes occurs at a time when a
woman is unable or unwilling to support an additional child. Thus,
she chooses abortion.

Some argue that abortion decisions are the private concern of
the woman. Others claim that the potential father or that society
has a right and even an obligation to intervene. Attitudes about sex
roles, sexuality, and the employment of women, as well as religious
beliefs, all interact to affect an individual's attitudes about the morality of abortion.

According to McCormick, "when relating abortion to women's
liberation, Pope Paul insists that true liberation is found in the
vocational fulfillment of motherhood" (1981:133). Despite the
views of the official Roman Catholic hierarchy, the sexual revolution
in Western society has profoundly changed the ways in which men
and women relate to each other. Women and men often have sex
for pleasure and not for procreation. The use of contraception,
particularly birth control pills, has become widespread. Voluntary
sterilization has become the most frequently used method of fertility
control for American married couples with children. Women are
postponing childbearing and are having fewer children. In the
United States the traditional family of breadwinning father and
homemaking mother is no longer the modal pattern. Even among
women with children under age 6, the employment rate is greater
than 50 percent.

Some social commentators are concerned that these new patterns
reflect an uncaring attitude toward people, especially "the most defenseless members of society—orphans, the poor, the aged, the
mentally and physically sick, the unborn" (McCormick 1981:11).
Noonan says, abortion "is the reverse of a mother's care of her
offspring. Its exercise is a betrayal of the most paradigmatic of trusts,
that which entrusts to a mother the life of her helpless child"
(1979:190). Others would argue that a caring attitude toward peo-

ple does not mean that women should have many children, or that
women must remain in traditional roles, or that the fetus should
be placed in the same category as the poor and the sick. Furthermore, many would argue that caring moral people refrain from
having more children than the world's resources can support.
Clearly, attitudes toward abortion are closely tied to attitudes about
the proper role of women.

## What Role Should the Law Play?

A moral position is one thing. A law is something else again.
The moral values of a particular religious group, for example, can
be backed by the teachings of the clergy and by requiring adherence
in order to maintain membership in good standing. To the extent
that the moral teachings are successful they will be supported by
the force of individual belief, commitment, and guilt. But the sanctions of the state do not back them up and individuals are free to
disregard the values and to leave the group.

A legal prohibition with criminal sanctions is quite different.
Regardless of an individual's moral beliefs, the state can punish the
individual, and the individual is generally unable to leave the state
to avoid sanction. States therefore always face a difficult question:
which moral positions should be embodied in the law? Some groups
in American society are opposed to birth control and divorce. Some
are opposed to alcoholic beverages and marijuana. Should the moral
position of a segment of society be made the law of the land? And
which segment's moral position will prevail?

Where there is moral consensus there is no problem. Homicide,
robbery, and rape are morally reprehensible to virtually all members
of society, except under unusual circumstances, and laws against
these actions are approved. Universal values are involved and consensus about legal statutes to make these acts criminal are widely
accepted. But the prohibition of birth control, divorce, alcohol, or
marijuana does not rest upon universal values and does not have
moral consensus. When banned, as with marijuana currently, there
is a great deal of deviance and subterfuge.

Abortion occupies a unique position. If we put it in a category with contraception and divorce, as pro-choice partisans would, then the issue is simple. The law would permit abortion. Those groups that regard it as morally reprehensible (primarily the Roman Catholic Church, but several other conservative religious groups as well) can preach their message and attempt to persuade women not to exercise their legal right to abortion. Those who hold a different moral position can exercise their choice to have, or not to have, an abortion.

If we put abortion in a category with homicide and robbery, as pro-life partisans would, then the issue is also simple. These are acts that are universally recognized as reprehensible and therefore moral suasion should be backed up by legal prohibitions and sanctions. No one, regardless of her moral beliefs, would be permitted to have an abortion.

The abortion debate is exacerbated by the question of the role the law should play. That moral positions differ greatly is one thing; these value differences can be accommodated as long as no attempt is made to enact one set of values into law. For example, there is no social movement in the United States to require everyone to attend church, or to be baptized, or to refrain from eating pork. Substantial numbers of people are morally committed to these practices, but they do not regard them as universal values requiring legal backing and universal compliance.

Pro-choice partisans see abortion values in the same light. They acknowledge that various groups can use moral suasian to gain compliance with their position, but insist that legal sanctions are inappropriate. The anti-abortion position is that abortion is the taking of human life, is akin to murder, and that legal sanctions are therefore required.

It appears that the controversy is intractable. But this is so only if we focus on the polar positions and the opposing partisans. Most people fall between the poles and are uncertain or ambivalent about abortion. Many who are personally opposed to abortion confront the gnawing question of what to ask of the law. This applies particularly to Catholic legislators. Several officials within the Roman Catholic hierarchy have openly questioned whether Catholics could, in good conscience, vote for anyone who accepts abortion. During the 1984 presidential election campaign in the United States, Geraldine Ferraro and Mario Cuomo, both Catholic, were upbraided by Catholic Church officials for not following through on their personal opposition to abortion with public opposition. But Ferraro and Cuomo carefully separated their personal moral views from their political and legal positions. As Cuomo said to a group of theology students at the University of Notre Dame, "We know that the price of seeking to force our beliefs on others is that they might someday force theirs on us."

Although the public confrontations during the 1984 presidential campaign raised the morality versus legality issue to new and controversial heights, such confrontations are part of a long history of controversy about separation of church and state. Earlier, Joseph Califano, Jr., as Secretary of the Department of Health, Education, and Welfare, faced the same kinds of questions and wondered how to deal with carrying out an abortion law that he was personally opposed to. He sought advice from his pastor, Father James English, and from Richard A. McCormick, a Jesuit scholar at Georgetown University, before his Senate confirmation hearings. They assured him that he could administer laws on abortion as a public official even though he was, as a matter of personal and religious conviction, opposed to those laws.

Califano's compromise was to clearly indicate his personal opposition to abortion and to the use of federal funds to support abortion, while also clearly indicating his commitment to uphold the law (Califano 1981). Although religion and morality can deal in absolutes, politics deals in compromise. Abortion partisans who do not hold public office, however, are not inclined to compromise. This is readily seen in the reactions of the partisans to several compromise positions that have been offered on abortion.

In the 1960s and early 1970s one set of legal recommendations took the position that abortion should be permissible only under certain circumstances. The American Law Institute's Model Penal Code proposed that these circumstances should be cases of rape, incest, fetal deformity, and threats to the physical or mental health of the woman. Neither the pro-choice nor anti-abortion forces accepted the idea that legalizing abortion under certain circumstances was a satisfactory solution. Opponents of abortion were not prepared to accept any justification for abortion except, perhaps, a threat to the woman's life. Robert Drinan explained the anti-abortion objection to this kind of law:

> [The] major premise assumes that the state should grant to the parents the right to terminate a pregnancy when these parents consider a temporal good to themselves of more value than the very existence of the life of the fetus. The Model Penal Code puts into operation for the first time in American law the concept that the state may grant to individuals the right to terminate a life which is inconvenient for these particular individuals.
>
> The law under this so-called model abortion legislation allows mothers to prefer their own mental health to the very existence of a forthcoming child, and tells married people that they may not terminate the life of a healthy fetus (unless it results from rape or incest) but may snuff out the entire future of a child whose physical or intellectual qualities might not be perfect. Such a provision in the law is primarily social or non-medical and, at least to me, appears to have ominous overtones. (Drinan 1970:16)

On the other hand, pro-choice advocates believe that abortion should be legally available without requiring special justification or circumstances. They object to restrictions which place the abortion decision in the hands of legal or medical authorities rather than under the control of the pregnant woman.

Many who are pro-choice or anti-abortion would agree that abortion involves complex questions for which each of us has a degree of responsibility. Poverty, the ways in which we meet the problems of severely handicapped children, and attitudes about religion, sexuality, and women's roles all contribute to the abortion controversy. These issues will not be resolved easily.

# CHAPTER 4

# MEDICAL ASPECTS
# OF ABORTION

W HEN LEGAL ABORTIONS are not available, many desperate women seek illegal abortions. Defying the law to seek an illegal abortion is stressful, but the prospect of continuing the pregnancy is often judged to be even more stressful by many women. As a result, it has been estimated that "from 30 to 55 million abortions . . . take place annually throughout the world" and that "about half of them are illegal." It has also been estimated that "about 84,000 women die each year from complications of illegally induced abortion" (Population Reports, 1980:F105). Illegal abortions are often dangerous because they are more likely to be performed clandestinely by unskilled persons under septic conditions, and are more likely to be delayed to later stages of pregnancy, which require more dangerous methods. In many countries where abortion is not legally available, more than half of all gynecology patients are the victims of botched abortions. When abortion is legally available, the number of such patients drops dramatically, as does the number of women who claim to be experiencing spontaneous abortion (Ahmad 1984:11–24).

When a society makes abortion legally available at the woman's request, it becomes possible to maximize the safety and reduce the emotional and physical trauma of abortion. Research efforts can then focus on the development of safer and more acceptable methods of fertility control. Abortion services can be part of broader public health programs that include contraception, prenatal and neonatal care, Pap smears, venereal disease control, education about parenting and nutrition, immunization, and other preventive health measures. The evidence is clear that when a country includes legal abortion in its public health program, the incidence of maternal morbidity and mortality and of perinatal mortality is significantly reduced (Andolsek 1985).

In 1965, when abortion was illegal in the United States, 235 abortion-related deaths were reported. In 1976, three years after *Roe vs. Wade* legalized abortion, there were 27 abortion-related deaths, and only two were due to illegal abortion (Cates 1982). Now that abortion is legal in the United States there are relatively few illegal abortions and very few deaths from illegal abortion— between 1975 and 1979 there were 17 deaths due to illegal abortion (Binkin, Gold, and Cates 1982). In 1981, there was only 1 death due to illegal abortion (CDC 1985).

Prior to the U.S. Supreme Court's 1973 abortion decisions, many women sought legal abortions to preserve their life or health. This frequently presented difficult medical, legal, and ethical questions for physicians and hospital abortion committees: Was a woman's suicide threat genuine and did it justify abortion under a state statute which permitted abortion only to preserve the woman's life? What about various heart or kidney diseases? Medical judgments varied considerably on such questions (see Table A.2 in the appendix). A woman might have been granted an abortion by one hospital while another hospital in the same state judged the abortion to be un-justified under state law. It was widely recognized that access to abortion ultimately depended on the physician's or the hospital's attitude toward the social desirability of abortion. Some physicians stated flatly that there were no medical justifications for abortion while other physicians did anything they could to find legal justi-fication for an abortion.

For many decades the medical profession interpreted the validity of different indications for abortion. With the passage of repeal laws in some states and subsequently with the 1973 U.S. Supreme Court abortion decisions, the need for a "justifiable reason" for a "thera-peutic" abortion became legally irrelevant, and the interpretive func-tion of the medical profession changed abruptly. Medical judgments about legal justification for an abortion were no longer necessary.

This does not mean, however, that medical advice about abortion became unnecessary. Since abortion became legal, the physician's role has been to advise the woman on the medical aspects of abortion and to provide the technical expertise that assures the safest outcome of the procedure. The physician's role is no longer that of moral judge, dispensing or withholding abortions according to personal moral convictions. David (1981:5–18) noted that efforts to professionalize the status of physicians developed after the American Medical Association was founded in 1847. "An anti-abortion campaign, portraying doctors fighting the health risks associated with botched abortions and opposing the brazen advertisements of greedy abortionists, seemed a 'perfect' way to further these objectives" (1981:7). Abortion was soon criminalized in all states and "mainstream medicine increased its disdain for contraception, abhorred abortion, and avoided all issues relevant to human sexuality when it could but, when pressured, recommended abstinence and prayer" (G. Davis, quoted in David 1981:7).

David also noted that the liberalization of abortion laws in many parts of the world can be attributed to "a) general recognition of the threat of illegal abortion to public health, b) support for women's rights to terminate an unwanted pregnancy under safe conditions at an early state of gestation, and c) provision of equal access to abortion for rich and poor women alike. . . . In only a few lands was abortion legalized expressly to limit population growth and enhance socioeconomic development" (1981:12).

## The Folklore of Abortion

Historical and anthropological evidence indicates that women of virtually every society have used, or have been subjected to, herbal abortifacients, drugs, and mechanical trauma to prevent the birth of unwanted children. Limited resources and sexual taboos have sometimes forced women to seek abortion. Cultural and social patterns that give men effective control over women's fertility have sometimes dictated abortion and at other times forced women to continue unwanted pregnancies.

A wide variety of largely ineffective and sometimes dangerous techniques have been used to attempt abortion. Ergot, knitting needles, coat hangers, quinine, lye, starvation, papyrus, magic, and strenuous physical activity have all been tried. A Kgatla woman took a drug after coitus to expel the semen. A woman of the Loyalty Islands drank boiled seawater to abort. The Romans inserted papyrus into the cervix. Women in the United States asked a druggist for "something to bring down my period" and received a catheter, quinine, and penicillin. Abortion is currently illegal in Thailand, but practitioners who deliver babies and abort pregnancies are widely and easily contacted. About 80 percent of abortions in Thailand involve a massage technique. The practitioner presses and kneads the woman's abdomen from ten minutes to nearly an hour, until vaginal bleeding begins. The technique is common throughout Malaysia and Indonesia (Singnomklao 1985), but its relative safety is unknown.

An infinite variety of drugs have been taken to cause abortion. If taken in doses large enough to induce abortion some of these drugs can injure or kill the woman; others are simply useless. Women who fear an unwanted pregnancy may have a delayed period due to psychosomatic reasons. Many women have irregular periods for unknown reasons. If menstrual flow begins following ingestion of one of these drugs the folklore that the drug is effective is perpetuated (Bates and Zawadski 1964).

Drug-induced abortion can offer significant advantages over the surgical abortion procedures presently in use in many parts of the world. Contraceptive pills (estrogen-progesterone pills) and contragestive pills (prostaglandins and antiprogestins) can make it possible for women to truly control their own fertility in the privacy of their homes. These approaches will probably be available to women around the world in the near future (Baulieu 1985) and will be discussed later in this chapter.

## The Development of Medically Safe Procedures

Although Lister published his revolutionary concept of antiseptic surgery in 1867, it was not until after the turn of the century that his techniques were well enough understood and widely enough practiced to be considered a major medical advance. After the wide-spread adoption of Lister's techniques, safe procedures for specific operations, including dilatation and curettage, were developed. Continuing refinements in the use of general and local anesthesia and the availability of antibiotics after World War II also made surgery significantly safer. Induced abortion performed by skilled personnel under sanitary conditions has become the most frequent, and one of the safest, surgical procedures.

Since the late 1960s legal abortion has been available to women in many countries (Omran 1982; Tietze 1981). Today, nearly two-thirds of the world's women live in countries where abortion is legally available on request or for social reasons (Ahmad 1984:12). Concern about public health has promoted research on fertility control, the development of safer techniques of contraception and abortion, and epidemiological studies of the risks and aftereffects of various techniques. Contemporary abortion techniques can best be considered by gestational age and by type (instrumental evac-uation of uterine contents, uterine surgery, or medical induction by drugs or mechanical irritants which stimulate uterine contractions).

Our discussion of current abortion techniques is obviously not a "how-to" guide for physicians. Rather, it provides an overview of technical procedures and underlying considerations so that in-telligent readers can have a better understanding of what is involved and can make more informed judgments and decisions.

## *First Trimester Interruption of Pregnancy*

The first trimester refers to the first twelve weeks of gestational age, that is, the first twelve weeks after the first day of the last menstrual period (LMP). Most women ovulate about fourteen days LMP and conception can take place when coitus occurs within a few days before or after ovulation. Some women are aware of ovu-lation because they experience sharp pain or tenderness in the pelvis, particularly over the ovary. In addition, a clear mucous discharge from the vagina and a change in body temperature may indicate ovulation. These signs have frequently been used to facilitate conception, or the reverse, to avoid conception. However, women vary greatly in the pattern of their menstrual cycle and the fertile period may be difficult to identify.

Normally, the fertilized ovum takes six to twelve days to pass through the Fallopian tube and implant on the wall of the uterus. Embryologists estimate that as many as two-thirds of all fertilized ova fail to implant and are carried out in the woman's next menstrual flow. Often this happens without the woman ever suspecting that fertilization took place (Cook 1985). Biological "overproduction and programmed wastage" is common to many biological processes, allowing organisms to reproduce despite the high frequency of destruction by natural events; Potts noted that "the world of the embryo is a world of biological error and wastage" (1985:266). And Cook commented, "until implantation, one cannot know whether the conceptus will be a hydatidiform mole, a chorionic tumor, or an individual" (1985:223).

Potts suggests that a pregnant woman knows more about her situation than anyone else and that she can be trusted "to behave responsibly towards the fetal life in her womb" (1985:267). Given the frequent and natural occurrence of delayed menstrual flow, many women are sensitive to, and react differently to, different phases of their pregnancy. Potts noted that women throughout the world, faced with an unintended pregnancy, recognize three phases of that pregnancy. "First they say 'My period is late' and I think nearly all will accept anything that will bring it on. Secondly they say 'I am pregnant' and I think most will accept an early abortion if appropriate. Thirdly, a woman says 'I'm having a baby,' and then I think she is very ambivalent and probably is not going to end the pregnancy unless she perceives an extreme threat" (1985:267).

Even when a pregnancy is highly desired, many women are reluctant to announce their news before the end of 12 weeks LMP, because miscarriage is so common. Neither the woman nor a clinician can be sure that the woman is pregnant when she misses a period. Many women have cycles that are much longer than twenty-eight days. Consequently, many women do not feel they are aborting a pregnancy when they take something to "bring down their period."

## DEFINITIONS OF FERTILITY CONTROL TERMS

Increasingly, clinicians are distinguishing between five different types of fertility control measures although contradictions and inconsistencies sometimes occur in the literature. According to Potts (1985), *contraception* prevents the fusion of the gametes, i.e., prevents fertilization. *Postcoital* procedures affect events between fertilization and implantation. *Contragestional* agents may be used between implantation (six to twelve days after fertilization) and the time when fetal organs are formed (up to 6 weeks after fertilization, i.e., 8 weeks LMP). *Abortion* is then reserved for termination of a pregnancy at least 8 weeks LMP and late abortion refers to termination after 14 weeks LMP.

Baulieu (1985) suggested that the term "contragestion" should mean procedures used before pregnancy can be confirmed. Oral contraceptive pills and IUDs were found to be effective in preventing childbirth and to be safer than childbearing; thus they were widely used even though the way they worked was not completely understood. Recent research suggests that they are probably postcoital or contragestional agents rather than contraceptives as defined above; i.e., they may prevent or disrupt implantation rather than prevent fertilization.

Timing may be crucial. Depending on when they are taken during the ovarian cycle, some agents may prevent fertilization, or they may prevent implantation, or they may cause the uterine lining to shed (CIBA 1985; Hafez 1984).

The term "gestational age" is a source of some confusion in the literature on abortion. For most authors, 10 weeks of gestational age means 10 weeks since the last menstrual period (LMP); for others a gestational age of 10 weeks means 10 weeks since conception (i.e., 12 weeks LMP). Stubblefield notes this confusion by clarifying his own usage: "We assume here that gestational age is dated in terms of the number of weeks since the start of the last normal menstruation, even though conception cannot occur until ovulation, which, on the average, occurs 14 days later" (1985:161).

*Sterilization* procedures, generally distinguished from contraceptive procedures, act by preventing sperm from leaving the man's body in his ejaculate or by preventing sperm from traveling through the Fallopian tubes to reach the ovum. Like contraception, sterilization prevents fertilization.

## MENSTRUAL REGULATION

Edelman and Berger (1981:209) define menstrual regulation as "any procedure used to terminate a suspected pregnancy no later than 14 days after the expected onset of a menstrual period" (i.e., 6 weeks LMP). Menstrual regulation has also been called "endometrial aspiration, menstrual extraction, menstrual induction, and miniabortion" (Hodgson 1981:228). Menstrual regulation may be accomplished by surgical procedures or by the use of drugs.

Menstrual extraction techniques are sometimes used for diagnostic or therapeutic purposes rather than for interruption of pregnancy. Also, pregnancy tests are not always reliable during the early weeks LMP; pathological tissue growth such as hydatidiform moles and some tumors may also give positive pregnancy tests. Within 4 weeks LMP, "uterine size and shape . . . and changes in the consistency of the cervix are not always discernible" (Edelman and Berger 1981:210). Because menstrual extraction is sometimes performed therapeutically and before pregnancy can be diagnosed, some women find it easier to accept as a method of "bringing on their period." They reason that a pregnancy may not have been terminated, since delayed menstruation often occurs in women who are not pregnant.

The surgical procedure for menstrual induction involves vacuum aspiration of the uterine lining. When performed between 2 and 6 weeks LMP, no dilation of the cervix is necessary before the physician can insert a slender, flexible cannula (tube), which is then attached to a vacuum source. From a clinical standpoint, vacuum aspiration is simple, safe, and inexpensive. It carries little risk and causes minimal discomfort to the woman. Local cervical anesthesia may be used, often in conjunction with analgesics. Hospitalization is not necessary. A follow-up pregnancy test should be obtained within a few weeks (Edelman and Berger 1981; Hodgson 1981).

High dosages of diethylstilbesterol (DES) are effective in preventing implantation when they are taken within 48 to 72 hours after coitus. Because high doses of synthetic estrogens have unde-sirable side effects, DES, popularly known as "morning-after pills," has been used primarily for exceptional circumstances such as rape.

## PROSTAGLANDINS, ESTROGEN, AND PROGESTERONE

Prostaglandins, estrogen, and progesterone occur naturally in the body. These substances are involved in fertility, in the regulation of menstruation and ovulation, and in the onset of labor. Their effects depend on their interactions with each other and with other substances in the body. The relative proportions of each vary nat-urally to control the events of the ovulatory cycle. Natural changes in the proportions appear to be important for precipitating normal full-term labor. In recent decades these substances or their analogues (chemically similar substances) have been used to treat infertility problems and, conversely, to prevent unwanted pregnancy.

Because prostaglandins cause smooth muscle to contract, they have been used for some years to induce labor, both for full-term delivery and for second trimester induced abortion. Some of the prostaglandins are highly unstable compounds that metabolize quickly, so they must be administered directly into the uterus. Their instability, and their unpleasant though relatively minor side effects (headache, nausea, vomiting, diarrhea) have discouraged their use for first trimester abortion although their safety, compared to other second trimester techniques, has made them a frequent choice for abortion after eighteen weeks (Hodgson 1981; Bygdeman 1981; Kerenyi 1981). Besides causing uterine contractions, prostaglandins also soften the cervix, making dilation less traumatic.

Interestingly, research suggests that naturally occurring prosta-glandins are also responsible for much menstrual discomfort, such as headache, diarrhea, nausea, and uterine cramping. Treatment of dysmenorrhea (menstrual discomfort) seeks to inhibit the effects of prostaglandin with nonsteroidal, anti-inflammatory drugs such as aspirin and ibuprofen (Toppozada 1984).

Vaginal suppositories containing prostaglandin analogues in a high-melt base have recently been developed and have been used to induce abortion. These suppositories reduce the instability of the prostaglandin; they are noninvasive and easy to insert; they can be administered by the woman herself. Several researchers have reported the successful use of these suppositories at 6 to 12 weeks LMP (Arias 1984; Baird and Cameron 1985; Embrey 1984; Foster et al. 1985; Lauerson and Graves 1984). Side effects may include moderate amounts of vaginal bleeding and one or more episodes of vomiting or diarrhea in some cases. In general, investigators report that the suppositories are safe and highly effective, but that fewer side effects would be desirable. Many women, however, did not suffer from side effects and women who had experienced both the prostaglandin analogue approach and surgical evacuation found the suppositories an acceptable alternative.

It has been suggested that menstrual extraction might be practiced monthly as a means of shortening the inconvenience, irregularity, and discomfort of menstruation, as well as avoiding an unwanted pregnancy. Millions of women presently take oral contraceptive (usually estrogen-progesterone) pills for three-quarters of each month. Despite the side effects which may occur, women have accepted these pills because they are highly effective in preventing pregnancy, can be ingested easily, and are much less costly and much less dangerous than childbearing (Tietze 1983). Research suggests that estrogen-progesterone pills may achieve their effect through modification of the body's reactivity to prostaglandins (Toppozada 1984:27–57). Direct use of prostaglandins would require taking a pill for only a few days after coitus at mid-cycle, and would be at least as natural as estrogen-progesterone pills.

ANTIPROGESTINS

European scientists have sought to develop a fertility control agent which would act by inducing menstruation. According to Baulieu (1985; cf. Healy and Fraser 1985), a new steroid compound, RU 486, meets the requirements for an almost ideal fertility control agent. It need be taken for only a few days of the month and it gives rise to few long-term side effects as it acts quite specifically on well-defined processes. It can be safely taken whether or not the woman is pregnant and it is effective at any time during the first several weeks LMP. This antiprogestin facilitates menstrual induction by interfering with the action of progesterone. When used by 200 women, RU 486 successfully induced menstruation for more than 70 percent. When combined with small amounts of prostaglandin, 100 percent success was achieved without the unpleasant side effects of the larger doses required for prostaglandins alone.

Clinical research is seeking an optimal method for administering RU 486. Baulieu (1985:209) predicts that "we will have a successful recipe for a safe, self-administered compound in a couple of years." Of course, there is an extended time lag between a drug's availability for clinical investigation and its approval for general use. David (Ciba 1985:188–189) suggests that prostaglandins and antiprogestins may soon become available for self-administration in early pregnancy, entirely without medical supervision. "Women will then be able to decide whether they want to remain pregnant or if they want to bring on their period. . . . The question will have to be raised . . . of the extent to which contraception and abortion are the problems of physicians or of women independent of the medical profession."

These compounds would be especially beneficial in developing countries that are unable to meet the medical needs of women. If such drugs become available in some countries without a prescription, they would quickly make their way to other countries as well. It would be difficult to control their distribution, and countries that did not make them legally available would face problems of bootlegging and black markets. Efforts might be made, in conservative countries, to keep women in ignorance of the new and beneficial methods legally denied to them, just as the conservative religious establishment in the United States successfully limited access to information about contraception for many years.

## DILATATION AND SHARP CURETTAGE (D & C)

This was formerly, and in some areas of the world is still, the preferred method of abortion between 6 and 12 weeks LMP. After dilation of the cervix, the lining of the uterus is scraped by sharp curettage. The method is relatively safe and takes only a few minutes. General anesthesia is usually required.

## DILATATION AND EVACUATION (D & E)

In the United States and many other countries, over the last decade, D&E has become the method of choice for abortion between 6 and 12 weeks LMP, the period when most abortions are obtained. Following mechanical or chemical dilation of the cervix a cannula is inserted for vacuum extraction of the uterine contents. When gestational stage is accurately identified the method is safe, takes only a few minutes, and requires only local cervical anesthesia. Analgesics and an antibiotic may be administered just prior to the procedure; the woman is asked to remain at the clinic for an hour after the procedure is completed. It is cheaper to give each Rh-negative woman $RH_o$ (D) immune globin than to test for antibodies (Hodgson 1981:263). The aspirated tissue is routinely saved for examination, to verify the diagnosis of pregnancy, to determine the stage of gestation and the intra- or extra-uterine location of the pregnancy, and to verify that evacuation is complete (Hodgson 1981).

### LAMINARIA

Neubardt and Schulman (1977:133) noted that "Japanese physicians have perfected safe, dependable techniques for both early and late abortion based on mechanical irritation of the pregnant uterus." Laminaria sticks about two inches long are made of sterilized, compressed seaweed, with a thread attached for easy removal from the cervix. Properly placed in the cervix they painlessly dilate the cervix as they expand by absorbing cervical secretions, and they also mechanically stimulate the uterus to contract, resulting in abortion within a few days. Japanese medical journals have reported no serious complications from the use of laminaria in thirty years of legal abortion (Neubardt and Schulman 1977). Anesthesia is not required for insertion of laminaria.

In Japan laminaria sticks are used for legal abortion at 10 to 14 weeks LMP. Japanese women, long accustomed to legal abortion, are not likely to delay seeking abortion of an unwanted pregnancy. Thus, they rarely request abortion after 14 weeks LMP. An exception may be when amniocentesis indicates maldevelopment of the fetus, since such diagnosis may not be possible during the first trimester. Until recently, laminaria have been used in the United States primarily for second trimester abortions (Hodgson 1981).

## Second Trimester Abortion (13 to 27 weeks LMP)

In the United States many second trimester abortions are the result of delay caused by the woman's ambivalence or by objections from her male partner, friends, or family members. In some cases the woman may be ignorant about the symptoms of pregnancy or the availability of abortion services. Occasionally, women deny their pregnancy until they are beyond the first trimester. Some adolescents delay seeking help because of embarrassment or fear that their parents will be informed (Rodman, Lewis, and Griffith 1984).

Though second trimester abortions presently account for somewhat less than 10 percent of all abortions in the United States, that percentage represents more than 100,000 abortions per year, indicating a need for safe procedures and earlier detection and care (Grimes and Schulz 1985). Methods presently in use in the United States include instrumental evacuation of the uterus and induction of labor. Evacuation may be either by aspiration or curettage or by hysterotomy or hysterectomy. Techniques to induce labor may be subdivided according to "the type of abortifacient used (e.g., hypertonic saline or prostaglandin $F_2$) or according to the route for administering the abortifacient (e.g., interamniotic or extraovular)" (Grimes and Schulz 1985:84).

Abortions based on hysterectomy, hysterotomy, or urea instillation, in addition to carrying the risk normally associated with labor and delivery (estimates range from 12 to 18 deaths per 100,000 deliveries), carry additional risk due to massive saline infusions, to water intoxication, or to hemorrhage and infection.

In 1978 D&E became the leading method for early second trimester abortions. Although D&E abortions after 13 weeks LMP are more dangerous than abortions performed by D&E or D&C before 13 weeks LMP, D&E is safer than the other second trimester methods commonly used in the United States. Though less safe than D&E, intra-amniotic instillation of urea and prostaglandin $F_2$ is much safer than hysterotomy or hysterectomy (Grimes and Schulz 1985).

In 1973 the U.S. Supreme Court ruled that the states could not intervene in the abortion decision during the first three months of pregnancy, but during the second trimester, when abortion is more hazardous for the woman, the state's interest in the health of the woman permits the enactment of regulations to protect maternal health. Many states, therefore, enacted legislation requiring hospitalization for second trimester abortions. Since D&E at 13 to 16 weeks LMP is no more dangerous when performed in outpatient facilities than when performed in hospitals, and since outpatient abortions are cheaper, more convenient, and more easily available than hospital abortions, Cates and Grimes suggested that "policy makers should reconsider laws requiring all second trimester abortions to be performed in hospitals" (1981b:401). They suggested that 16 weeks LMP is presently a more appropriate threshold. In 1983 the U.S. Supreme Court did rule that the states could not require all second trimester abortions to be performed in a hospital *(City of Akron v. Akron Center for Reproductive Health).*

Because relatively few (100,000 per year) second trimester abortions are performed in the United States, it has been difficult to obtain epidemiologically adequate samples. However, a recent review of the effect of vacuum aspiration on future childbearing (Hogue, Cates, and Tietze 1983:125) found some evidence that second trimester methods, including D&E, which require dilation of more than 12 millimeters "may lead to problems of cervical incompetence," and they suggested that further study of second trimester methods is needed.

Second trimester methods such as intra-amniotic instillation, prostaglandins, and laminaria act by inducing labor. As with any pregnancy, the labor process can be painful and the pain can be exacerbated by stress due to ambivalence about the abortion, or by punitive attendants. Women having second trimester abortions need emotional support, training in relaxation techniques, and pain-relieving medication, just as do other women in labor.

Early second trimester fetuses aborted after induced labor are rarely viable when delivered. However, delivery of a fetus that shows reflex movement even briefly may be a very traumatic experience for medical personnel and for the aborting woman. In some cases the attending physician has been charged with murder or manslaughter because measures were not taken to try to keep the fetus alive (Nolen 1978). Such incidents usually occur because the woman has mis-informed her physician about her stage of pregnancy, either delib-erately or because her calculations were in error. If the physician is misinformed, or if the length of pregnancy is misjudged for other reasons, the fetus may have developed to the point of reflex movement or even to the point of viability.

Within the second trimester, prostaglandin-induced abortions are apparently more likely to expel fetuses which exhibit reflex activity. For this reason and because prostaglandin may cause side effects in some women, combination methods (such as the combined use of laminaria prior to infusion with urea and prostaglandin) are being investigated by clinical researchers (Grimes and Cates 1981; Hern 1984).

## Third Trimester Abortion

The phrase "third trimester abortion" is rarely seen in the medical literature. During the third trimester of pregnancy physicians often induce labor when that seems to be in the best interest of the woman and/or the expected child. Barring medical complications, such in-duced labor usually results in the birth of a viable child.

A low incidence of third trimester abortions—less than 1 percent of all induced abortions—has been reported by the Centers for Disease Control. A careful review of reported third trimester abor-tions in the state of Georgia (Spitz et al. 1983) indicates that the actual percentage may be substantially lower than the reported per-centage. Of the eighty-six women whose third-trimester abortions had been reported to the Georgia Department of Human Resources in 1979 and 1980, only three were clearly identified as induced third trimester abortions. In fifty-eight cases, labor was induced to expel a dead fetus, a procedure that is not considered to be induced abortion. In fifteen cases, the induced abortion actually took place in the first or second trimester; misclassification was due to errors in transcription, coding, or keypunching. Two cases had other outcomes and in eight cases there were insufficient data available to classify the pregnancy outcome. That left only three cases that were classified as third trimester induced abortions; in two of these cases the terminated pregnancy involved an anencephalic fetus.

In an attempt to locate other third trimester abortions, Spitz et al. reviewed an additional 170 cases in which the woman reported the LMP as greater than or equal to 25 weeks. The authors verified the pregnancy outcome of 142. No true third trimester abortions were confirmed in this group. Pathology reports, sonography, and physicians' estimates identified the fetuses as less than 25 weeks in 126 cases, and 16 involved fetal deaths *in utero*.

Spitz et al. concluded that the true rate of induced third trimester abortions in Georgia in 1979 and 1980 was 4.3 per 100,000 total abortions. They suggest that the same kind of overreporting of third trimester abortions may occur in other states as well, and that the actual number of these abortions may be much less than is generally believed.

### Summary of Abortion Methods Currently in Use

We have summarized currently used abortion procedures in table 4.1. Administration of DES within a few hours of insemination may prevent pregnancy. Because of its unpleasant side effects, however, use of DES has been restricted to extreme situations such as rape.

Implantation of a fertilized ovum, at about 10 to 14 days after conception, may be prevented by the use of an IUD.

Between 5 and 7 weeks LMP, vacuum extraction, without dilation of the cervix, is simple and safe. Prostaglandins and prostaglandin analogues may also be used at this stage. By 8 weeks the embryo is about one inch in length.

Table 4.1.
**Abortion Procedures in the United States, 1985**

| Weeks Since Last Menstrual Period (LMP) | Developmental Stage | Preferred Procedure |
|---|---|---|
| LMP | 0 | |
| Ovulation | 2 | Conception at 2 weeks ± a few days | DES—"morning-after pill" |
| Expected menstrual flow | 4 | Implantation usually well-established | (Implantation may be prevented by IUD) |
| | 5 to 7 | | Menstrual regulation by vacuum extraction without dilation |
| | 7 to 12 | | Dilation and evacuation (D&E) |
| End of first trimester | 13 to 16 | | D&E |
| | 14 to 24 | After 20+ weeks fetus may show reflex activity or be capable of sustaining life | Induction of labor by laminaria, PG, urea instillation, or combination methods |
| | | | (Induced abortion after 24 weeks may be legally forbidden except for medical emergencies) |
| End of second trimester | 38 to 42 | Normal full-term delivery | (Induction of labor to deliver a live infant is quite common, but this is not abortion) |

From 7 to 16 weeks LMP, dilation of the cervix, followed by vacuum extraction of the uterine contents, is presently the recommended procedure and requires only a local anesthetic. The procedure may be combined with the use of prostaglandins or laminaria. At 14 weeks LMP the fetus is about three inches long.

Presently, over 90 percent of all abortions are obtained during the first trimester of pregnancy. The risk to the woman increases with each week of delay. Procedures used after 16 weeks LMP, including laminaria, prostaglandins, or urea instillation, induce labor. They may abort a fetus which shows some reflex activity.

Induction of labor during the third trimester is a common medical procedure, undertaken with the intent of delivering a healthy infant with minimum risk to the mother. Often labor is induced when there is an indication of fetal or maternal distress. States have the option of prohibiting third trimester abortions, under *Roe v. Wade,* as long as an exception is made for abortions intended to protect the life or health of the woman. There is little evidence of induced third trimester abortions.

## Abortion Related Risks and Complications

Many factors combine to make the estimation of the risks and complications of induced abortion very difficult. When induced abortion is illegal, or is legal only under specified circumstances, many abortions are obtained clandestinely and are not likely to be reported to official agencies. In many parts of the world physicians' professional organizations have supported the legalization of abortion because physicians often observed the tragedy of women who died or suffered permanent damage to their health as a result of illegal abortion. As Neubardt and Schulman said:

> The medical effects of legal abortion have been dramatic. There has been a significant decline not only in maternal morbidity and mortality, but in perinatal mortality as well. We have been impressed with the change in the character of "spontaneous" abortion since induced abortion has become legal. We no longer see the hemorrhaging, septic, hypotensive women having "miscarriages" who need an immediate transfusion and surgical curettage. It appears that the truly spontaneous abortion is gradual and rather benign.

The others are almost certainly crudely induced. The experienced gynecologist . . . need only make rounds on the gynecology ward of any municipal
hospital to recognize the difference that legal abortion has made. (1977:viii–
ix)

Even when abortion is legal, it is very difficult to obtain accurate
estimates of the risks involved. The techniques available, the medical
conditions under which abortions are obtained (walk-in clinic with
excellent facilities, hospital, isolated or primitive clinic) and the skill
of those performing the procedures all affect the outcome. Moreover, cultural and demographic variables may also have an important
influence on the outcome.

Ethical considerations preclude good experimental designs for
studying the outcome of various abortion methods. Patients usually
cannot be assigned to treatment groups randomly. It is, therefore,
important to choose comparison groups carefully. For instance,
clinic clients apparently differ in important ways, both medically
and demographically, from hospital clients. Age, life-style, smoking
habits, gestational stage, and preexisting conditions may be confounding variables.

Estimating and comparing risks of different techniques can also
be complicated because the terminology in the literature is not
consistent. "Vacuum aspiration" may refer to menstrual extraction
by suction, without dilation of the cervix, before 7 weeks LMP.
The term "vacuum aspiration" has also been used for a procedure
performed as late as 16 weeks LMP, with dilation of the cervix and
vacuum aspiration of the uterine contents. The risks, complications,
and future pregnancy outcomes of two "vacuum aspiration" procedures may thus be quite different. Similarly, "curettage" may refer
to either suction or sharp curettage (Hodgson 1981).

Inappropriate generalizations from one technique to another have
also interfered with the accurate estimation of risk. In the United
States, insertion of laminaria to cause slow dilation of the cervix
and uterine contractions was long considered a relatively dangerous
technique with high risk of infection because similar techniques,
used for centuries by pregnant women and abortionists, were associated with illegal abortion in the minds of American physicians.
In Japan, however, physicians using sterilized laminaria and preventive antibiotics have found the procedure a safe and nontrau-

matic method for legal abortion. In recent years, as this information has overcome the earlier erroneous generalizations, an increasing number of American physicians have adopted the technique (Stubblefield, Altman, and Goldstein 1984).

Another confounding factor in assessing risks involves the comparison of hospital and outpatient facilities. Today in the United States most induced abortions are obtained in outpatient facilities—physicians' offices or walk-in clinics. The crude death-to-case rates are 1.5 deaths per 100,000 hospital procedures and 0.6 deaths per 100,000 nonhospital procedures (Grimes, Cates, and Selik 1981). It thus appears that clinic abortions are safer than hospital abortions. These figures, however, must be adjusted for preexisting conditions, concurrent sterilization procedures, and the stage of pregnancy. With such adjustments, Grimes et al. found the "death-to-case rates for first-trimester abortions performed in both kinds of facilities were about 0.7" per 100,000 (1981:30).

The Centers for Disease Control (CDC) of the U.S. Public Health Service have collected and reported abortion statistics since 1969. The objectives of their epidemiologic surveillance of abortion have been "(1) to document the number and characteristics of women obtaining abortions, and (2) to eliminate preventable mortality and morbidity related to abortion" (CDC 1985). The CDC receives statistics (by state of occurrence) from central health agencies, from hospitals and other facilities, and from the National Center for Health Statistics. Not all states report all data every year. In such circumstances estimates are based on projections from past years and on reports from other agencies.

Risks and complications of induced abortion can be assessed in terms of mortality or morbidity rates for women obtaining an induced abortion. The CDC (1985) considers deaths to be abortion-related when they occur within 42 days (6 weeks) of an induced abortion procedure. The CDC usually does not include in its statistics cases where an ectopic pregnancy was an unexpected complication. (An ectopic pregnancy is one in which the fetus develops outside of the uterus, usually in the Fallopian tube).

It is also important to assess the effect of prior induced abortion on the later ability to have a child. Over 60 percent of American women who had an induced abortion in the last decade had no children. Most of these women plan to have children at a later date. The long-term effect of abortion on future pregnancies is therefore of great importance. Inability to conceive, cervical incompetence, miscarriage, vaginal bleeding during pregnancy, low birth weight, prematurity, and other developmental disadvantages to infants of subsequent pregnancies are some possible outcomes which have been considered or for which empirical data are available.

ABORTION-RELATED MORTALITY

Legal abortion, performed during the first trimester of pregnancy, has become one of the most common, and safest, of all surgical procedures. About 1.5 million American women are now having an induced abortion each year (CDC 1985; Henshaw et al. 1986). More than 90 percent of these abortions are obtained during the first trimester of pregnancy, over two-thirds of them at walk-in clinics or physicians' offices. Under these conditions the death-per-case rate was 0.5 deaths per 100,000 abortion procedures in 1981 (CDC 1985:39). The rate for first trimester abortions performed in hospitals is similar, when adjusted for preexisting conditions and concurrent sterilization. By comparison, pregnancy carried to term has a maternal death rate of 12 to 18 deaths per 100,000 deliveries. Some other common surgical procedures, such as tonsillectomy and laparoscopic tubal sterilization, have a death rate of more than 10 per 100,000 procedures.

During the years 1974 to 1977, 36 women in the United States died as a result of legal first trimester induced abortion (Grimes, Cates, and Selik 1981). From 1978 through 1981, 43 women died of legally induced abortion (CDC 1985). Reaction to anesthesia and embolic events were the most frequent causes of death, followed by hemorrhage and infection.

After 12 weeks LMP, the woman's risk of dying as a result of abortion increases 50 percent for each week of delay (Cates and Grimes 1981). Thus, delays created by laws which require approval from a hospital abortion committee or which require parental consent for minors, may increase the risk of death significantly (Rodman, Lewis and Griffith 1984). Similarly, the enactment of legislation that denies Medicaid payment for abortion may cause delay while women seek the necessary funds, and may increase the risk of death by abortion among indigent women (Cates and Grimes 1981).

Selik, Cates, and Tyler (1981) described a new approach to abortion mortality studies that is now being used by the CDC. They "calculated the proportion of deaths to which various measurable risk factors contributed." These factors are called behavioral risk factors because they "consisted of any human behavior . . . that increased the patient's risk of death." These include (1) community factors such as lack of services for legal abortion or medical care, or deterrents to use of services, such as laws requiring parental consent; (2) patient factors such as delay in obtaining abortion or delay in seeking medical care for complications; (3) physician factors including "delay in diagnosis or treatment, or use of relatively ineffective or hazardous treatments"; and (4) health care facility factors, including deficient resources such as drugs or equipment, inadequately skilled personnel, and policies that contribute to delayed or inadequate treatment.

Behavioral risk factors may or may not be preventable. The focus is on the factors needing attention, not on the responsible individuals. The CDC found that most abortion deaths involved multiple behavior factors. For the 106 abortion deaths reported in the United States between 1975 and 1977 (55 legal, 10 illegal, 41 spontaneous abortions) "physician factors contributed to 68 percent of the deaths, patient factors to 62 percent, facility factors to 11 percent, and community factors to 5 percent" (Selik, Cates, and Tyler 1981:632). Patient delay in obtaining an abortion contributed to nearly half of the deaths from legal abortion. Incomplete emptying of the uterus and uterine perforation each contributed to one-sixth of the deaths. These two problems are often associated with inaccurate assessment of gestational age.

Delay in obtaining an abortion until after 12 weeks LMP, and delay in seeking help when infection develops, stand out as the chief causes of abortion deaths. Fewer than 10 percent of legal abortions are presently being obtained after 12 weeks LMP; these second trimester abortions are associated with a much higher risk of death.

Cates and Grimes (1981) noted that, for D&E procedures, "black and other" women had death-to-case rates three times that of white

Table 4.2.
Abortion-Related Deaths in the United States, 1977–1981

| Abortion Procedure | Number of Deaths | Number of Abortions | Deaths per 100,000 Abortions |
|---|---|---|---|
| Instrumental evacuation | 46 | 5,787,000 | 0.8 |
| Intrauterine instillation | 11 | 223,000 | 4.9 |
| Hysterotomy/ hysterectomy | 3 | 5,090 | 58.9 |

SOURCE: CDC 1985:41.

women, a discrepancy which they suggest reflects the influence of economic status on access to good, timely medical care.

A summary of abortion deaths in the U.S. (1977–1981) is shown in table 4.2.

ABORTION-RELATED MORBIDITY

Abortion-related morbidity—nonfatal complications of abortion—may be difficult to define. Women normally have monthly bleeding and many women have cramps or pain with every menstrual cycle. Body temperature normally fluctuates a few degrees with the menstrual cycle. Furthermore, bleeding is expected with any surgical procedure. What constitutes "normal" bleeding or pain or temperature fluctuation is thus a matter of subjective judgment. Even if a complication is defined objectively, for example, in terms of a certain number of sutures taken in the cervix, "two physicians may have different thresholds for deciding when to suture and when to apply other treatment" (NAS, 1975:47).

Nonfatal complications of abortion can be categorized as minor or major, and as early or long-term. Early complications may be due to the woman's preexisting medical state or to the skill of the operator, or they may be related to gestational stage. Early complications may include hemorrhage, infection, cervical injury, and uterine perforation. The use of laminaria can reduce the risk of cervical injury and uterine perforation. Second trimester abortion presents additional risk due to incomplete abortion, i.e., the partial retention of uterine contents, resulting in infection, though that may also be a problem in first trimester vacuum evacuation, especially at 4 to 8 weeks LMP (Lauersen and Graves 1984:91). Earlier abortions are safer; delay always increases the risks.

According to Cates and Grimes "about 12 percent of women undergoing legal abortions sustain complications of any type, while fewer than one percent develop a major complication" (1981:158). If women with preexisting conditions are excluded from the calculations, the rates are lower. In a study of 2,458 abortions in Vermont, complications were reported in 2.91 percent of the cases (Freedman et al. 1986).

The method of abortion affects the risk of complication. D&E at less than 13 weeks gestational age has been safest. From 12 to 16 weeks, D&E is safer than saline or PG instillation. Hysterotomy and hysterectomy are so dangerous that they should not be considered appropriate as routine abortion methods (Cates and Grimes 1981b).

FUTURE PREGNANCY OUTCOMES

A major concern about induced abortion is whether it has an adverse effect upon the outcome of later pregnancies. Does it increase the likelihood of sterility, ectopic pregnancy, spontaneous abortion, premature delivery, low infant birth weight, or birth defects? The published findings on such questions have been conflicting, and this has led to a continuing controversy about pregnancy outcome. Several states passed legislation requiring physicians to inform their patients about the supposed negative effects of abortion; such requirements were quashed by the U.S. Supreme Court in *City of Akron v. Akron Center for Reproductive Health* (1983).

Some early studies did find evidence of poor outcomes at subsequent pregnancies, while later studies did not. Abortion techniques used in earlier years, involving greater dilation of the cervix, may have been associated with increased risk of spontaneous abortion or prematurity at a later pregnancy. Schoenbaum et al. (1980) also suggest that the conflicting findings may reflect the salutary effects of legalizing abortion—increasing skill of physicians, abortions obtained at earlier stages of pregnancy, and the use of D&E rather than sharp curettage. In addition, earlier studies may have confounded the issue by using inappropriate comparison groups, since first pregnancies carried to term are more likely to have complications than second pregnancies carried to term. Women with one prior abortion are most appropriately compared to women with no prior pregnancies rather than to women who have had a prior pregnancy carried to term.

It is known that first pregnancies have a higher risk of spontaneous abortion, prematurity, and birth defects than second pregnancies. Schoenbaum et al. (1980), taking this information into account, compared four groups of pregnant women:

a. Women whose only previous pregnancy was terminated by induced abortion;
b. Women whose one previous pregnancy was carried to term;
c. Women who had not had a previous pregnancy;
d. Women whose only prior pregnancy had terminated by spontaneous abortion.

With regard to prematurity and birth defects, group a and group c resembled each other more than either resembled group b. That is, presently pregnant women whose only other pregnancy was terminated by induced abortion resemble women with a first pregnancy more than they resemble women with a second pregnancy. Women who had experienced a previous spontaneous abortion were at the highest risk for a poor outcome to their present pregnancy. Schoenbaum et al. (1980) and Daling and Emanuel (1977) did not find that women with one previous abortion are more likely to experience poor outcomes at a subsequent pregnancy.

In 1983, Hogue, Cates, and Tietze reviewed the findings from more than 150 studies conducted throughout the world to assess the impact of abortion on future childbearing. They focused on studies dealing with vacuum aspiration procedures carried out during the first trimester, the type of abortion that is most common in the United States and involves approximately 500,000 women each year. Only ten of the studies reported on such abortions and met the additional criteria of controlling for some confounding variables and of comparing "second pregnancies among women who terminated their first pregnancy with first or second pregnancies among women who had no previous experience of induced abortion" (p. 120). The ten studies were consistent and suggest that "the risk of low birth weight, preterm delivery or midtrimester spontaneous abortion in a pregnancy following one that is terminated . . . is not significantly higher than the risk of adverse outcomes of a first pregnancy carried to term" (p. 125). The most favorable results, as expected, were found for women who were delivering their second pregnancy.

REPEAT ABORTION

As the number of women experiencing legal abortion grows, an increasing number of women become subject to repeat abortion. Tietze (1974, 1978, 1983) pointed out that contraceptive failure and human imperfection inevitably result in repeat abortions. He demonstrated that even among those women using the most effective contraceptive—oral contraceptive pills—nearly one out of four will have an unwanted pregnancy within ten years after their first induced abortion. Howe, Kaplan, and English (1979) found that women having repeat abortions were more often using contraception at the time of conception than were women having first abortions. Many noncontracepting repeaters were not contracepting because of medical contra-indications or lack of supplies. Repeaters were sexually more active than nonrepeaters and thus were at greater risk of conception.

Howe, Kaplan, and English (1979) questioned the idea that repeaters are less motivated or less responsible about contraception. Their data "clearly reject the premise that abortion is a primary or even back-up birth control method" in the population they studied. Despite findings such as these, many professional and lay people continue to blame women who seek repeat abortions.

Hogue, Cates, and Tietze, in their comprehensive review, found thirteen studies that report on pregnancy outcome following more than one induced abortion. "No definite conclusions can be reached about the impact of multiple induced abortions, since the results of 13 different epidemiologic studies are almost evenly divided between those that show no effect and those reporting related reproductive problems" (1983:119).

# CHAPTER 5

# PSYCHOSOCIAL AND EMOTIONAL ASPECTS OF ABORTION

IN 1973 THE U.S. SUPREME COURT legalized abortion, leaving the abortion decision to the woman and her physician. However, the influence exerted by a century-long legal prohibition against abortion did not disappear overnight. Even though attitudes toward abortion have become more favorable since the 1960s, anti-abortion sentiments still exert considerable pressure. They are seen in some groups' moral codes, in the punitive attitudes of some health professionals, and in the way a woman's social role is sometimes viewed by herself and others.

Before the 1973 Supreme Court decisions on abortion many American physicians assumed that abortion was emotionally traumatic for the patient (Kummer 1963) or that only an emotionally unstable patient chose abortion. These assumptions were based on flawed evidence about negative psychological aftereffects of induced abortion. They developed in a situation in which abortion was generally illegal, difficult to obtain, and dangerous, and at a time when many believed that woman's main purpose was to bear and rear children (Freud 1963; Hubbard 1977).

## Illegal Abortion

The clinical literature during the 1960s was confused and contradictory on the psychological aftereffects of illegal abortion. The lack of conclusive data and the partisanship were singled out in a review article by Simon and Senturia. They examined twenty-seven books and articles, representing the research and clinical literature from 1935 to 1964, and their conclusion was widely repeated:

> It is sobering to observe the ease with which reports can be embedded in the literature, quoted, and requoted many times without consideration for the data in the original paper. Deeply held personal convictions frequently seem to outweigh the importance of data, especially when conclusions are drawn. In the papers reviewed, the findings and conclusions range from the suggestion that psychiatric illness almost always is the outcome of therapeutic abortion to its virtual absence as a post-abortion complication (Simon and Senturia 1966:387).

The most serious problem in the studies reviewed by Simon and Senturia is the poor methodology. A few case histories, limited clinical experience, and an uncritical review of the literature were often used as the basis for wild generalizations. As Simon and Senturia say, "although Taussig makes only the most cursory references to psychiatric sequelae of therapeutic abortion, he is quoted by nearly every author since 1936 as warning against serious psychiatric sequelae to abortion" (1966:378).

Gladston, a psychiatrist, aptly points to his limited clinical experience with the effects of abortion and indicates that "the psychiatrist generally does not have contact with masses of people, but rather with single individuals. Hence, the psychiatrist can report cases but he finds it rather difficult to draw generalizations or broad deductions" (1958:117). A few pages later he overcomes this difficulty and states, "I think any abortion is likely to have serious traumatic sequelae" (p. 121).

A major methodological flaw prior to 1973 was that evidence regarding the emotional effects of aborting a pregnancy was confounded with the emotional effects of breaking the law. A second methodological problem is related to attitudes about the appropriate role of women. Prior to the sexual revolution of the 1960s and early 1970s, many psychiatrists and other physicians assumed that a woman who did not want her pregnancy, or who was willing to terminate her pregnancy, was by definition emotionally deviant and pathological.

Before abortion was legalized, many abortions were performed furtively, often under septic conditions, by people who preyed on other people's misery. In that environment, conducive to serious physical and emotional risk, the medical profession took a prominent role in pushing for more liberal abortion laws. Physicians had to deal with the results of "botched" abortions—infection, hemorrhage, death, sterility. Many physicians insisted that no one should have the right to tell them how to provide medical care for their patients or to tell them they could not provide care which the physician deemed necessary or which the patient would obtain from highly risky sources if she could not obtain it legally.

Nevertheless, under reform laws that permitted abortion on physical or mental health grounds, some physicians concluded there were no legal indications for an abortion on physical health grounds. They felt that any woman could be carried to term, no matter what her physical condition. Not even heart disease, renal disease, pulmonary disease, or malignancy were accepted by all physicians or all hospital abortion committees as legally acceptable reasons for induced abortion (Packer and Gampbell 1959).

Because many physicians experienced conflict between their obligation to obey laws that restricted abortion and their commitment to patients who sought an abortion, it became customary to pass the problem on to psychiatrists, who were expected to make a decision based on the woman's mental health.

## THE PSYCHIATRIST AS DISPENSATOR

When access to abortion is restricted, but legally available on mental health grounds, psychiatrists may play a very special role in deciding who gets an abortion. This role was played by psychiatrists in some states prior to 1973 (Sarvis and Rodman 1974). In states with "reform" laws, a diagnosis that pregnancy threatened the woman's mental health could sanction an abortion. Under such circumstances the psychiatrist "is a legally authorized bootlegger. In this role, the law empowers the psychiatrist to grant permission for otherwise prohibited acts. . . . He is authorized to prescribe abortion as though it were treatment, provided he can find the pregnant woman to be mentally ill (so as to justify his prescription)" (Szasz 1962:347). A similar point was made by Levene and Rigney, who noted that "legislators, in liberalizing existing antiabortion laws by including mental health provisions, . . . placed the psychiatrist in the

role of dispensator—quite different from his usual role of consultant. . . . In essence, he is able to grant dispensation from the law's
restrictive consequences" (1970:52, 54).

In such context the woman had a vested interest in manipulating
the psychiatrist by appearing sufficiently ill to justify an abortion.
According to Pfeiffer, the law encouraged women "to feign psychiatric symptoms, to mouth suicidal ideas, and to present themselves generally as emotionally disordered when in fact they are not"
(1970:405). With a lack of clear evidence for making a decision,
the psychiatrist was often forced to fall back upon his own moral
and ideological convictions. Enough strands of evidence were available to enable the psychiatrist, whether anti-abortion or pro-abortion, to rationalize his position, or he could forthrightly state that
the evidence for a decision was lacking and then proceed to act
principally in terms of his own values.

## HARASSMENT BY HEALTH CARE PROVIDERS

Ambivalent or negative attitudes of physicians and other hospital
personnel sometimes influenced a woman's reaction to an abortion.
Marder gave several examples of harassment of abortion patients
and pointed out that on some occasions "nurses, interns, and residents, as well as medical students, demonstrated anger and re-
sentment toward a patient by voicing an old theme: 'You've had
your fun and now you want us to take care of it for you' "
(1970:1236). In addition, certain hospital policies were highly punitive. In some hospitals, for example, certain women received abortions only if they agreed to be sterilized at the same time.

## THE EMOTIONAL TRAUMA OF ILLEGAL ABORTION

The illegality and shame which our society attached to abortion,
and the danger associated with illegal and delayed abortion, made
many women fearful, angry, anxious, and depressed. Deliberately
choosing to participate in an illegal act was traumatic for many
women. Nevertheless, even a dangerous illegal abortion was often
perceived to be a better alternative than carrying the pregnancy to
term. Given societal sanctions against pregnancy out of wedlock,
the other alternatives to abortion—raising a child out of wedlock

or giving the baby up for adoption—were perceived to be even more traumatic. Since legalization of abortion, the number of babies made available for adoption has dropped dramatically. Although others may advocate adoption as preferable to abortion, women with an unwanted pregnancy clearly prefer abortion. An increasing number of women are also choosing to be single mothers.

Another choice, marrying her sexual partner, has been very common. Over the last thirty years, more than a third of women who married were pregnant at the time of the wedding, despite social pressure against premarital sexual intercourse. It is likely that many couples were planning to marry anyhow. For those who were not, forced marriage is no longer the only socially acceptable choice.

Of course, premarital intercourse resulting in pregnancy has never been the only reason that women choose abortion. Many women had illegal abortions because they had more children than they and their husbands could support, physically or emotionally. Today, many women are choosing abortion when there is a high risk of fetal deformity or when they do not want to change a desired lifestyle by bearing and rearing children. In the United States, most married women are using effective contraception or sterilization, so that only one abortion out of four is obtained by a married woman.

## Legally Induced Abortion

The 1973 U.S. Supreme Court decisions *(Roe v. Wade, Doe v. Bolton)* decreed that a state could not intervene in the abortion decision during the first three months of pregnancy, and could intervene during the second trimester only to protect maternal health. Between 1973 and 1978, 4 million American women chose to have an induced abortion. Since 1978 more than 1.5 million induced abortions have been performed each year, over 90 percent of them during the first trimester.

After about fifteen years of nationwide legalized abortion, a considerable body of evidence has accumulated on the psychological and emotional aspects of induced abortion. This evidence will be reviewed as we deal with the factors leading to an unwanted pregnancy, the emotional reactions of the woman having an abortion procedure, and the involvement of the male partner—his relationship with the aborting woman, his role in the decision-making process, and his feelings about the pregnancy and the abortion. We will also consider the emotional and psychological response of those who provide abortion services, and finally, we will examine evidence concerning the children born to women who wanted to have an induced abortion but were denied that option.

Emotions run high in an abortion clinic. One of us (Bonar) spent several months of observation in a clinic. Women express anger, grief, and fear; after the procedure, they often express relief. The procedure itself takes only a few minutes and is usually performed under local anesthesia. Many women, however, have heard "old wives' tales" about abortion, so that even today women seeking safe, legal abortion are often very apprehensive.

Women seeking abortion are often angry at themselves for getting pregnant, at their sexual partners for getting them pregnant, at a biological situation that makes women pay a heavy price for sexual pleasure without effective contraception, at parents or partners or a society that coerces them into making an abortion decision about which they are ambivalent.

## FACTORS LEADING TO UNWANTED PREGNANCY

Luker found an astonishing degree of ignorance among people who thought they would not conceive if—if it was a certain time of the month, if she douched, if he withdrew or did not penetrate, if it was the first time, if she prayed, if she was lactating, if he or she were very young.

According to Luker (1975) an unplanned pregnancy is often the result of conscious "risk-taking." If one considers that many people have sexual intercourse several times a month for many years, yet have only a few children, then it may be tempting to take a chance. Before the early part of this century, relatively few American couples used contraceptives. Families of nine or ten children were common, the result of a pregnancy every year or two from the time a woman married to her mid-forties. Nowadays, few Americans have such large families, and today's women are likely to underestimate the probability of getting pregnant.

Luker interviewed women seeking abortion at clinics in California. Many of the women reported that they had weighed the costs and benefits of getting pregnant against the costs and benefits of abstaining from sex or of using contraception. Often they had chosen to take a chance on getting pregnant.

***Iatrogenic factors.*** With appalling frequency, a physician had told the woman, or her partner, that she or he would not be able to conceive. Thus, the couple did not perceive a need to protect against pregnancy. Sometimes a couple were motivated to test their fertility. In some cases a physician had urged the woman to give up an effective method of contraception because it might affect her later ability to bear children, even though there is little evidence to support that advice.

***Guilt and embarrassment.*** Luker (1975), Henshaw and Wallish (1984), Rosoff and Kenney (1984), and others found that many women, particularly very young women, are reluctant to admit that they may be sexually active. Thus their first coital experiences take place without any contraception.

Feelings of guilt and embarrassment prevent many young people from taking responsibility for their sexuality (Rodman, Lewis, and Griffith 1984). In the United States, compared to other developed countries, sexual guilt contributes to less effective use of contraceptives and higher rates of fertility and abortion for teenagers (Jones et al. 1985). Mosher (1973) found that sexually experienced women who scored high on "sex guilt" reported less effective use of contraception and had more conservative attitudes about premarital sex. Sex guilt was defined as a personality disposition manifested by "resistance to sexual temptation, inhibited sexual behavior, and the disruption of cognitive processes in sex-related situations" (Gerrard 1977:708). When Gerrard compared 45 abortion clients with a matched group of sexually active, nonpregnant women at the same university, the abortion clients scored significantly higher on Mosher's measures of sex guilt.

Freeman (1977) interviewed 329 applicants at a Philadelphia abortion clinic. Few of the women had expected ever to have an abortion. Rather, abortion was a "necessary response to unexpected conditions and the abortion decision frequently was inconsistent with their self-perceptions" (Freeman 1977:505). Four months after the abortion, only 10 percent of the women reported that they regretted their decision to abort.

EMOTIONAL REACTION TO LEGALLY INDUCED ABORTION

In Freeman's (1977) study, a pre-abortion questionnaire showed high levels of anxiety and depression related to the pregnancy. The frequency of anxiety and depression was low four months after abortion. Many of the women (39 percent) reported they had wanted the pregnancy but had then faced the realities of economics or marital status. Another 31 percent stated they had not wanted the pregnancy, but had not used contraception; 16 percent had not anticipated the possibility of pregnancy; 13 percent reported that their contraceptive method had failed.

Women who had originally wanted the pregnancy less often experienced relief and more often experienced depression at the time of abortion. However, most had resolved their negative feelings by the four-month follow-up.

Before collecting the data Freeman hypothesized that women who had abortions perceived themselves as agents, that is, as people who acted vigorously on their own lives. Freeman concluded, however, that "the need for abortion resulted from *not* perceiving oneself as agent." Most of the women had not been "pro-abortion" prior to their pregnancy. They had, however, avoided conscious consideration of the possible result of their sexual activity. Freeman concluded that abortion is "a symptom of contradictory social expectations for women. Social mores value self-management and individual choice in sexual behavior, while paradoxically, women's sexual activity is expected to be compliant and naive. Social pressures support individual management of fertility, but simultaneously support contraceptive sophistication only among women who have produced several children" (Freeman 1977:511–512). These conclusions are consistent with Luker's (1975) findings that many women were willing to risk pregnancy and avoid using contraception to preserve their relationships. Other researchers have reported similar findings (Berger et al. 1984; Henshaw 1984).

A Canadian study of 50 adolescent girls two years after abortion reported that "most did not regret their abortion and considered it a positive experience. Most said they would not have another abortion, although adoption was unanimously rejected as a choice for the pregnant teenager. Relations with their parents were generally good, and the families were supportive.... The proportion using contraception before the abortion was 2%, and two years after the abortion, 84%" (Cvejic et al. 1977:44). These authors reported that the decision-making process was the most difficult aspect of the experience for these girls; most of their anxiety related to telling their parents (parental consent was required for girls under 18).

In a prospective study of post-abortion psychosis in Britain, Brewer (1977) collected information from 21 consultant psychiatrists serving catchment areas with a total population of 1.3 million. He (1977) found only one reported case of post-abortion psychosis over a fifteen-month period. That one woman had a history of two previous attacks of psychosis associated with childbirth. The incidence of post-abortion psychosis was 0.3 per 1,000 legal abortions, compared to 1.7 per 1,000 full-term deliveries. These figures are similar to those reported by Tietze and Lewit (1972). Brewer concluded that physiological changes are more profound following childbirth, as compared to abortion, thus accounting for the higher rate of psychosis following delivery.

In Shusterman's study emotional reactions to the reality of pregnancy included anxiety and disbelief. Although the women were nervous about abortion, most felt relieved, and even somewhat happy afterward. They did not feel guilty or resentful about the abortion and "almost all said that if they had the decision to make over again they would definitely decide to abort" (Shusterman 1979:686).

Shusterman found three variables predictive of post-abortion emotional adjustment:

(1) Pre-abortion satisfaction with the decision. More satisfied women had received more support from partner, parents, and friends, but the decision had been the women's and was not forced on them by someone else.

(2) Relationship with the male partner. Women involved in more intimate, permanent relationships received more positive support from their partners and could share their feelings.

(3) The woman's initial response to her pregnancy. If the woman was especially angry or anxious at the first suspicion of pregnancy, she was more likely to experience post-abortion disturbance. Such women were less likely to have intimate, permanent, and positive relationships with their male partners.

When Belsey et al. (1977:71) assessed the emotional attitudes of 360 British women immediately before and three months after a first trimester legal abortion, the dominant factor was found to be the "degree of adjustment existing before the pregnancy. Those most likely to be disturbed after the abortion had a history of psychosocial instability, poor or no family ties, few friends, and commonly had failed to take contraceptive precautions."

In a Danish study, computerized records were used to track admissions to psychiatric hospitals of all Danish women under 50 who carried to term or had an induced abortion in 1975. Only first admissions recorded within three months after delivery or abortion were considered. There was

> no statistically significant difference in the rate of admission to psychiatric hospitals between currently married or never-married women who obtained abortions and those who carried their pregnancies to term. (It should be noted, however, that a sizable proportion of never-married Danish women who deliver are probably living in stable nonmarital relationships.) The highest rate of admission to a psychiatric hospital is found among those women who were separated, divorced or widowed (most were divorced), whether they delivered or obtained abortions. . . . Some were probably terminating a pregnancy that had been intended when the spouses were living together, but which became unwanted after the relationship ended. (David, Rasmussen, and Holst 1981:89, 91)

David, Rasmussen, and Holst recommend that special consideration be given to counsel women separated from their partners and seeking termination of a pregnancy that was originally intended and was conceived in the context of a relationship then intact (cf. David 1985).

## THE MALE PARTNER

Although an unwanted pregnancy is necessarily the result of a heterosexual relationship, little abortion research has considered that relationship. Two early writers (Munford 1963; Walter 1970) cited a few case studies indicative of pathology in the heterosexual relationships of women seeking abortion. Recent research has not confirmed those findings (Shusterman 1979; David, Rasmussen, and Holst 1981; David 1985). A majority of the women in Shusterman's sample had a long-term relationship with their male partner. A high proportion (87 percent) of the male partners knew of the pregnancy and most were supportive of the woman's decision. The post-abortion quality of the relationship with the male partner was not significantly different from the pre-abortion quality.

Rothstein (1977) conducted lengthy interviews with 60 men selected at random at an abortion clinic waiting room. Questionnaire responses were also obtained from 200 women having abortions at the same clinic. Only one-sixth of the women were accompanied by their male partners.

Most of the men cooperated eagerly with the researchers, perhaps because they welcomed something to do during several hours in the waiting room. The males generally reported that their relationships with the aborting women were stable, with a sense of mutual understanding and trust, although only half of the couples lived together.

Respondents of either sex generally perceived themselves to be more in favor of the abortion than their partners, but most felt there had been shared discussion. About one-third of the men said the abortion was predominantly the woman's decision, and one-fifth said it was predominantly the man's decision. Few respondents felt that the abortion had a significant impact on the relationship. Rothstein concluded that the abortion decision did not reflect or provoke pathology in the relationships, and that it "may even have a growth-promoting effect on some couples" (1977:117). This finding is consistent with the research of Gilligan (1982) and her colleagues who found that the development of moral reasoning required the experience of resolving real-life dilemmas.

***Including the male partner in counseling.*** In a second paper

(1977a) Rothstein reported that the male partners he interviewed, although somewhat guarded initially, reacted favorably to the opportunity to participate in the clinic's program of counseling with regard to financial alternatives, contraception, and the abortion procedure. Permitting men increased educational and psychological participation in abortion services appeared advantageous to the men and to the relationship between the couples and may be conducive to more effective contraception after the abortion.

## THE PROVIDERS OF ABORTION SERVICES

In the United States in 1984 over 90 percent of all first trimester abortions (up to 12 weeks after the last menstrual period) were performed on an outpatient basis, usually at walk-in clinics. In such clinics the staff often consists of the physicians who perform the abortion procedure, one or more nurses, a laboratory technician, and counselors who conduct group and perhaps individual counseling sessions before the procedure and who stay with the client during the procedure. Many clinics are franchised, profit-making businesses performing thousands of abortions annually.

The physicians are highly paid, although perhaps not commensurate with other physicians' fees. Typically, the counselors, who interact closely with the clients, receive little more than the legal minimum wage. The counselors are often deeply committed to the women's movement; frequently they are graduate students, medical students, or recent college graduates who work part time at the clinic. Nurses and an administrator trained in a helping profession, and often very concerned about women's health issues, receive slightly higher pay. The rest of the money goes for insurance, supplies, rent, advertising, and profit for the owners.

Those who are concerned about the welfare of women often express dismay at the commercialization of this service, and at the exploitation of counselors motivated by their commitment to women's issues. Yet these critics concede that such facilities provide safe, decent care, usually offer nonjudgmental, nondirective counseling, and have a commendable safety record—fewer than one death per 100,000 abortions. Birth control counseling, both pre-abortion and follow-up, is usually included.

In contrast with the commercialized system that has developed in the United States, many countries provide abortion and other fertility control services as part of a national program of health services available to all residents of the country at little or no cost. The great disadvantage of the American system is that abortion is least available to those who are least able to support the emotional and financial costs of pregnancy. Young women in rural areas, and low-income women in general, have reduced access to good, safe care. But these categories of women are also least well served in many other countries (Rodman and Trost 1986).

**Professional burnout.** Evidence that abortion may cause trauma among health professionals was reported by Baluk and O'Neill (1980). Staff, particularly hospital staff, may suffer negative reactions (Such-Baer 1974). "Burnout" may occur, so that staff may demand transfer, refuse to do any more abortions, or may require counseling (Char and McDermott 1972). Nurses and physicians may perceive a conflict between their commitment to preserve life and their role in relieving a patient of an unwanted pregnancy. Professionals often project severe feelings of anxiety and depression on the aborting women, even though the women themselves rarely report such feelings. Baluk and O'Neill administered

> measures of depression, guilt, and state and trait anxiety to doctors, nurses, and social workers, under two conditions, self-report and role play... all three professional groups expected extreme depression, guilt, and anxiety on the part of the abortion patient, when compared to their own responses. These expectations do not match the experience reported by abortion patients. (1980:67)

A respected professor of obstetrics and gynecology at Cornell Medical School, Dr. Bernard Nathanson played a prominent role in the movement to legalize abortion in this country. In 1971–1972, during the period of "reform laws" in the United States, he ran the nation's largest abortion clinic, in New York City. Later, he wrote, "after a tenure of a year and a half I resigned. The Center had performed 60,000 abortions with no maternal deaths.... However, I am deeply troubled by my own increasing certainty that I had in fact presided over 60,000 deaths" (Nathanson 1979:164).

There are two separate issues involved: (a) the right of the woman to make decisions about her own body and (b) the right of the physician to refuse to perform procedures the physician feels are immoral. In reviewing Nathanson's book, Kristin Luker noted that Nathanson appeared to ignore the first issue. When Nathanson felt that his right to decide what was best for his patients was being infringed upon, he insisted on his right to perform abortion procedures. When he decided that abortion was murder he resigned as director of the abortion clinic, and later wrote a book to explain his belief that abortion is immoral.

Many physicians support the idea that people should have the right to make their own reproductive health decisions. When abortion is legal and easily available, women who choose to have an abortion can find competent physicians who recognize their responsibility to provide safe abortions. Physicians who are uncomfortable about performing abortions can choose not to provide such care, knowing that women can obtain good medical care from other physicians who are willing to perform legal abortion procedures.

A survey of all obstetricians and gynecologists practicing in Maryland in 1975–1976 (Nathanson and Becker 1977) found that a majority of respondents supported the 1973 Supreme Court abortion decisions and supported publicly funded abortions for indigent women, health insurance coverage for abortion and, to a lesser degree, abortions without parental consent for women under 18.

Using Nathanson and Becker's questionnaire, Bonar, Watson, and Koester (1983) surveyed 320 medical students in North Carolina. The male medical students were significantly more anti-abortion than the female medical students. The women students were in much closer agreement with the older cohort of practicing Maryland obstetricians, many of whom had once practiced under restrictive abortion laws. The older cohort, however, more often favored requiring parental consent for minors seeking abortion and more often favored requiring consent of the spouse prior to sterilization.

## The Children of Mothers Denied Abortion

Few studies have considered the emotional development of children born to mothers who had preferred induced abortion to delivery. However, one well-designed longitudinal study has appeared in the literature (David and Matejcek 1981; Matejcek, Dytrych, and Schuller 1985).

In 1957 Czechoslovakia began permitting district abortion commissions to approve abortions requested for medical or social reasons during the first trimester of pregnancy. Over the subsequent decade 2 percent of the requests were denied by the district commissions and by appeal commissions, usually because the woman was beyond the first trimester, or because she had terminated a pregnancy in the immediately preceding six months.

Records were obtained for 110 boys and 110 girls born to mothers who had twice requested abortion and were twice denied. These children were pair-matched, on the basis of age, sex, birth order, number of siblings, school class, mother's age and marital status, and socioeconomic status, with a control group of children whose mothers had not requested abortion.

When they were 9 years old the 440 children were thoroughly examined by a research team unaware of the children's background. Psychological, sociological, medical, and educational records and interviews were collected. Consistent differences between the unwanted children and the control group were found. The unwanted children, particularly the boys and only children, appeared at a disadvantage, with less satisfactory family, school, and social lives.

The best adjustment scores were attained by only children in the control group, whereas only children in the study group had the worst adjustment scores. The study group had a higher incidence of illness and hospitalization, and poorer school performance, although the IQ test scores were not significantly different.

By 14 years of age 28 percent of the study boys and 11 percent of the study girls, compared with 16 percent of the control boys and 11 percent of the control girls, had come to the attention of school psychiatric or counseling centers, which were totally unaware of the children's involvement in the study. Study group children had more serious behavior problems.

At ages 14 to 16 there were no significant differences in intelligence test scores, but school performance continued to deteriorate for the study group and was significantly lower than for the control group. Teachers rated the study children as less sociable; significantly more of the study children did not continue their education.

Many described their mothers as inconsistent emotionally and less warm than their fathers.

At 16 to 18 years, the study boys more frequently rated themselves as more rejected by their mothers than by their fathers (the reverse of the control boys) but there was no significant difference between the two groups of girls. The study boys more often (1) reported that their mothers were dissatisfied with them; (2) perceived the parents' marriage as less happy; (3) felt insufficiently informed about sexual matters, especially contraception, and expressed more conservative views on issues such as resolution of unplanned pregnancy and divorce. The study girls were relatively more liberal than the boys.

At ages 21 to 23, statistically significant differences between the groups persisted and widened. Those born to women who were denied abortions were less satisfied with their mental health, less satisfied with their lives, and less satisfied with personal friendships and love relationships. A search of records revealed that they were more likely to have been sentenced by the courts and to have been involved in alcohol and drug treatment centers (David 1986).

The authors concluded that there are aggregate differences in development between study and control groups, particularly for boys. Though there was compensation in individual cases, group differences tended to increase over time. "Unwantedness" appears to be a risk factor for these children (David 1986; David and Matejcek 1981; Dytrych et al. 1975; Matejcek, Dytrych, and Schuller 1978, 1985).

## Summary

There is little evidence that legal abortion, chosen without coercion, causes lasting emotional trauma for the woman having the abortion. The decision-making process is often accompanied by some anxiety or depression, but these negative feelings seem to resolve once the procedure is accomplished.

Many male partners are supportive of the woman and share with her in making the decision. It appears that women are better able to cope with the abortion experience when they have a supportive relationship with their sexual partner and when they have other positive social relationships.

Both the research literature and the statistics on adoption and abortion indicate that most women faced with the choice prefer to abort the pregnancy rather than give an infant up for adoption.

Nurses and physicians may perceive a conflict between their commitment to preserve life and their commitment to care for a patient in need, in this case, the pregnant woman. Professionals may project severe feelings of anxiety and depression on the aborting women, but the women themselves rarely report such feelings once the abortion is done.

Evidence suggests that children—especially boys—born to mothers who wanted to abort the pregnancy are "at risk" in their social and emotional development.

CHAPTER 6

# THE ROAD TO
# ROE v. WADE

ABORTION LAWS THROUGHOUT THE WORLD vary from highly restrictive ones that allow abortion for few or no reasons to highly permissive laws that permit abortion for any reason. Belgium and Ireland are examples of countries with restrictive laws; Denmark, Hungary, Sweden, and the United States are examples of countries with permissive laws (Rodman and Trost 1986). But the law on abortion is only part of the story. Under restrictive laws, skilled and unskilled "abortionists" perform "criminal" abortions outside of hospitals. They may be permitted to operate by law enforcement agencies and some are well patronized by women seeking abortions. "Reputable" physicians do "therapeutic" abortions in hospitals for selected patients, even though these abortions may be illegal. Under moderate or liberal laws, abortions may be done primarily in certain regions or cities of a country. Thus, depending on where a woman lives, on the attitudes and practices of the woman's physician and hospital, or on who she is and whom she knows, she may find it easy or difficult to obtain an abortion regardless of how restrictive or permissive the laws are.*

The gap between the law and medical practice became an outstanding feature of the abortion controversy, and it was one of the factors that contributed to the liberalization of abortion laws in

---

* For evidence that hospitals in the United States, prior to 1973, were doing abortions that did not comply with the law see Gold et al. (1965); Hall (1965, 1967, 1967a); Simon, Senturia, and Rothman (1967); Spivak (1967); and Tietze (1968).

many countries. Over the past two decades, there has been a pro-
nounced worldwide trend toward more permissive attitudes and
behavior about sexuality, contraception, and abortion. "The trend
toward liberalization involves adults as well as minors, abortion as
well as contraception, and sex education in the schools as well as
counseling centers for family planning" (Rodman and Trost
1986:232). To give a few examples, permissive abortion legislation
was first approved in Hungary in 1956 and in Czechoslovakia in
1957. Limited access to abortion began in Denmark in 1937, culminating in fully permissive legislation in 1973. In France, in 1975,
abortion was legalized for a trial period of five years, and in 1980
the law was renewed without any time limitation. In Italy abortion
was legalized in 1978, in Spain in 1985. Although the major trend
has been toward liberalization, there have also been countertrends
as the political leaders of some countries became concerned about
low birth rates and their implications for economic growth and
political power.

In the United States, the 1973 decision of the United States
Supreme Court, *Roe v. Wade,* changed the legality of abortion overnight from restrictive to permissive. An appendix to this book gives
a detailed history of the legal changes and legal controversy in the
1960s and early 1970s. This is instructive not only to better un-
derstand the current controversy but also as a possible scenario
should the United States return to more restrictive laws.

### The Original Intent of Anti-Abortion Laws

In the United States even the issue of the original intent of anti-
abortion legislation became debatable. To some the historical record
indicates that anti-abortion legislation was intended to protect
women from inept or unscrupulous abortionists or from social pressures to undergo abortion. To others, the record suggests that anti-
abortion legislation was designed to protect the fetus.

These ideological differences about the intent of the original laws
reflect beliefs about when a fetus becomes a person entitled to all of
the rights of those already born. That time can be defined as conception, implantation, quickening, viability, or birth. One's position

on this issue may then color one's view of the intent of the original laws and of the relative weighting the present laws should give to the rights of the fetus and the woman.

## PROTECTION OF THE WOMAN

Until 1971 pro- and anti-abortionists agreed that at common law abortion was not a crime before quickening and was a misdemeanor after quickening. But in 1971 Cyril Means published an article that examined the common law in detail and concluded that a common law right to abortion existed at every stage of gestation. To explain why statute law abolished this right, those who favored lawful access to abortion focused upon the medical conditions of the 1800s. At that time, any surgical procedure was very risky and often fatal. The abortion statutes were therefore intended to protect the woman from the medical dangers of abortion. Once early abortion became safer than childbirth, the restrictive laws were no longer necessary. Means (1968:513–514; 1971:392–396) referred to this as the "relative safety test" since the legislature intended abortion to be unlawful where it was more dangerous than childbirth so that the woman was "forced" to take the least dangerous course. Means described the "unbelievable historical irony" which ensued. "A statute was passed more than a century ago for the purpose of imposing on women the duty of protecting their lives from destruction through wanted but dangerous abortional surgery. Now that the danger has all but disappeared, the State's obstinate persistence in enforcing the law's letter, but not its purpose, denies its intended beneficiaries (pregnant women) the very right to protect their lives from death which the law originally imposed on them as a duty" (1971:388).

A logical reply to this position is: were other laws passed at the same time imposing upon people the duty of protecting their lives from all kinds of surgical procedures? Means answers this question by looking at the history of the United States statutes and concluding that the original intent of the legislation was to protect people from surgical procedures. The English abortion statutes of 1803 and the Connecticut law of 1821 were the first abortion statutes and made abortion of a willing woman before quickening a crime; neither of these statutes contained the therapeutic exception for abortion "necessary to preserve the life of the woman." The New York Revised Statutes of 1829, which went into effect January 1, 1830, contained the first abortion statute in the United States which included the therapeutic exception. Most other state legislatures followed the New York example of including this therapeutic exception, and "in the few cases where the legislatures neglected to do this, the courts have read such an exception into the statutes" (Means 1968:450). This early New York statute is therefore highly significant, and an examination of the meaning of the therapeutic exception hints at the reason for the abortion statutes.

Means quotes a section of the law that was proposed in 1828 but which the legislature did not pass:

> Every person who shall perform any surgical operation, by which human life shall be destroyed or endangered, such as the amputation of a limb, or of the breast, trepanning, cutting for the stone, or for hernia, unless it appear that the same was necessary for the preservation of life, or was advised by at least two physicians, shall be adjudged guilty of a misdemeanor. (1968:451)

Further clarification of the intent of this proposal is provided by the commissioners who formulated the revised statutes for the New York legislature of 1828 and included the following note in their report:

> The rashness of many young practitioners in performing the most important surgical operations for the mere purposes of distinguishing themselves, has been a subject of much complaint, and we are advised by old and experienced surgeons, that the loss of life occasioned by the practice, is alarming. (quoted in Means 1968:451)

Means argued that the purpose of the original abortion statutes, as exemplified by detailed information about the actions of the New York legislature of 1828, was to protect the health and life of the women against the dangers of abortional surgery. He explained that the legislature rejected the sections forbidding the performance of other operations because "only in the case of abortion were both patient and surgeon under strong extramedical pressures to undergo the risks of the operation. In other types of surgery, professional conscience and patients' caution could be relied upon to prevent unnecessary operations without the aid of a new penal law. It can scarcely be said that such a legislative differentiation between abortion and other equally dangerous types of surgery was, in 1828, unreasonable" (Means 1971:389).

PROTECTION OF FETAL LIFE

Those opposed to abortion argued that the states' original anti-abortion statutes were clearly designed to protect the fetus. Louisell and Noonan state that English and American criminal law in the nineteenth century was changed to protect the fetus at all stages of its development. "The purpose of the change was not to protect the life of the mother but the life of the fetus. The response of the legislators and then of the courts...was a response to data which showed the unreality of distinctions based on differences in the stages of fetal development" (1970:226).

Anti-abortionists contend that these abortion laws embody the Judeo-Christian prohibition against the destruction of innocent human life. Thomas O'Donnell expressed the position as follows:

> Since a new and distinct human life may very likely be present from that moment [conception], directly to destroy the products of human conception, even at a very early stage of development, is at least very likely the destruction of an innocent human life.
>
> One who does even this has already discarded from his moral code the inviolability of human life and the human person and falls far short of that regard for the dignity and rights of the individual which is basic to the entire Judeo-Christian theology and tradition. Such an action is identified with the moral malice of murder since it implies a willingness to take a human life (1970:38).

Lest this be labeled only a religious dogma, St. John-Stevas (1964:117) reminds us that "the concept of the right to life has profoundly influenced men throughout the Western world and is accepted by many who would reject the Christian doctrine on which it is based."

PHYSICIAN PROFESSIONALIZATION

Another likely intent of the original abortion laws, from the standpoint of physicians if not state legislators, relates to the development of the American medical profession. Kristin Luker (1984a:11–39) describes a mid-nineteenth-century medical profession besieged by competition from home remedies and a variety of healers, and flooded with graduates from proprietary medical schools. By claiming superior technical skill to do abortions while at the same time offering themselves as appropriate guardians of morality, an elite group of regular physicians campaigned successfully for restrictive abortion laws. Their anti-abortion stance and scientific pronouncements on fetal development aided their claim of superiority, and their successful campaign gave them control over the abortion decision. This effectively removed the abortion decision from women and obscured competing issues "beneath the cloak of an emerging profession's claims, there to rest quietly for almost a century" (Luker 1984a:39).

## Constitutional Issues: Rights of the Woman vs. Rights of the Fetus

The arguments about the intent of nineteenth-century anti-abortion laws became part of the abortion debate in the United States, and soon were intertwined with questions about the constitutionality of these laws.

Prior to 1969, occasional judicial involvement in abortion cases established that the threat to the life of the woman need not be imminent or certain for an abortion request to be justified, and courts in Massachusetts and New Jersey, where the statutes had no therapeutic exception, added life or health provisions (Lucas 1968:740; George 1967:6). The thalidomide scare and the rubella epidemic of the early 1960s, along with the American Law Institute's proposals for legal reform, initiated a dialogue among lawyers on the merits of abortion law reform. The 1965 *Griswold v. Connecticut* Supreme Court decision overturning an anti-contraceptive statute led to speculation on whether this decision applied to the abortion laws.

In 1968, while the reform movement was gathering momentum, Roy Lucas published a landmark article that laid out the grounds for a constitutional attack on the abortion laws. Lucas wrote that "the constitutional issues implicit in the enactment and application of abortion laws have received scant judicial attention." He explained further that "in the constitutional context abortion is a problem bearing few factual similarities to any decisions in the 150-year expanse of pre-*Griswold* history" (Lucas 1968:753, 754). In a very short time the first decisions on the constitutionality of abortion laws were handed down: *People v. Belous* in September 1969 by the California Supreme Court and *U.S. v. Vuitch* in November 1969 by the U.S. District Court for the District of Columbia. Both of these decisions declared parts of the original abortion statutes unconstitutional.

Optimism ran high in the pro-abortion camp, and many looked to the courts to quickly strike down the restrictive statutes and thereby dispense with time-consuming, state-by-state legislative change. As more cases were decided by federal and local courts, however, the hopes of the pro-abortionists were cooled by several decisions that upheld the constitutionality of the original abortion laws. In the fall of 1970, Roemer (1971:502) counted five cases on the U.S. Supreme Court docket, over twenty cases before three-judge federal courts, and eleven states with cases in local courts. By 1972 many cases were still before the courts, and the judicial and legislative situations were unpredictable. As Justice Douglas aptly wrote in his opinion on *U.S. v. Vuitch*: "The subject of abortions— like cases involving obscenity—is one of the most inflammatory ones to reach the Court. People instantly take sides and the public, from whom juries are drawn, makes up its mind one way or the other before the case is even argued." From 1969 to 1972 the phenomenal number of abortion cases brought before all levels of courts across the country singled out several constitutional issues as most salient and dramatized the sharp cleavage in positions between those opposed to abortion and those who favored unrestricted access to abortion.

VAGUENESS

To declare a law unconstitutional because of vagueness rests essentially on the due process requirement of the Fourteenth Amendment. Constitutionally, the law must be specific enough so that individuals know what is and is not a crime. In the case of abortion, physicians faced criminal prosecution if their interpretation differed from that of law enforcement agencies. Lucas argued that no medical agreement exists regarding the meaning of phrases in the original laws like "without lawful justification" and "except to save the life of the mother"; he further noted that the medical community was not in agreement on cases of abortion for physical or mental health, rape, incest, or fetal deformity (1968:767–768). The opposition argued that the original statutes had been in operation for many years "without the court ever before adverting to the difficulty of understanding these words," and "by the standard customarily invoked to measure definiteness, the usual statutory phrase 'necessary to preserve life' is clear enough" (Louisell and Noonan 1970:238, 240).

The initial rulings of several courts on the vagueness argument were mixed. *People v. Belous,* decided by the California Supreme Court in 1969, gives a good example of a court's declaring an original abortion statute unconstitutionally vague. The court ruled that

> the term "necessary to preserve" ... is not susceptible of a construction that does not violate legislative intent and that is sufficiently certain to satisfy due process requirements without improperly infringing on fundamental constitutional rights.... Dictionary definitions and judicial interpretations fail to provide a clear meaning for the words, "necessary" or "preserve." There is, of course, no standard definition of "necessary to preserve," and taking the words separately, no clear meaning emerges.... Various possible meanings of "necessary to preserve life" have been suggested. However, none of the proposed definitions will sustain the statute.

In contrast, the district court rejected the vagueness argument in a 1970 Wisconsin case, *Babbitz v. McCann.* The court declared that they had

> examined the challenged phraseology and are persuaded that it is not indefinite or vague. In our opinion, the word "necessary" and the expression

"to save the life of the mother" are both reasonably comprehensible in their meaning.... In *People v. Belous*, ... the California court found that the words "necessary to preserve her life" in that state's abortion statute were unconstitutionally vague. While the Wisconsin statute uses slightly different language ("necessary to save"), we doubt that the distinction between the words used in the two statutes is significant. However, we do not share the view of the majority in *Belous* that such language is so vague that one must guess at its meaning.

A district court was persuaded that the Wisconsin statute was not "so vague that men of common intelligence must necessarily guess at its meaning and differ as to its application," while the California Supreme Court thought that the interpretation of the statute would require guesswork.

## PRIVACY

The Ninth Amendment, which has infrequently been cited in court cases, holds that the enumeration of certain rights in the Constitution "shall not be construed to deny or disparage others retained by the people" (Mabbutt 1972). One of these unenumerated rights is the right to privacy, and several court cases have established the right to privacy in the area of sexual activity. The essential issue is that these rights are considered of "fundamental" personal interest, and that state law may not infringe upon these individual rights. The most famous of these decisions, *Griswold v. Connecticut,* declared Connecticut's statute forbidding the use of contraceptives unconstitutional and asserted that it violated the right to marital privacy. The right also stems from the Fourteenth Amendment.

The proponents of legalized abortion argued that the rights of parents to plan the number and timing of children falls within the scope of marital privacy, and therefore *"Griswold,* on its facts, protected a general interest in planning a family without state interference" and includes a right to abortion (Lucas 1968:764). The opposition argued vehemently that this overextends the meaning of *Griswold* and other cases. Abortion is not a fundamental personal right, and the state has a "compelling" interest in protecting the fetus. For instance, forbidding the use of contraceptives violates the privacy of husband and wife in the sexual relationship since "enforcement of the statute would have required invasion of the marital bedchamber." But abortion laws do not interfere with the sexual relationship, and their enforcement does not involve "invasion of the conjugal bedroom" (Louisell and Noonan 1970:233).

District court decisions on the abortion laws acknowledged the fundamental individual right to privacy in sexual activity and the right to determine family size, but opinions differed on whether these rights include abortion. If these rights include abortion, the state may not infringe upon them, and statutes regulating abortion are unconstitutional. If abortion is not included in these rights, the state may have a compelling interest in protecting the fetus, and abortion statutes represent this state interest and are not unconstitutional. In 1970 a district court in the case of *Rosen v. Louisiana State Board of Medical Examiners* expressed this problem and the related moral controversy about the value of fetal life.

> We deal in this case, however, not merely with whether a woman has a generalized right to choose whether to bear children, but instead with the more complicated question whether a pregnant woman has the right to cause the abortion of the embryo or fetus she carries in her womb. We do not find that an equation of the generalized right of the woman to determine whether she shall bear children with the asserted right to abort an embryo or fetus is compelled by fact or logic. Exercise of the right to an abortion on request is not essential to an effective exercise of the right not to bear a child, if a child for whatever reason is not wanted. Abstinence, rhythm, contraception, and sterilization are alternative means to this end.... Before the "moment" of conception has occurred, ... the choice whether or not to bear children is made in circumstances quite different from those in which such a choice might be made after conception.... The basic distinction between a decision whether to bear children which is made before conception and one which is made after conception is that the first contemplates the creation of a new human organism, but the latter contemplates the destruction of such an organism already created. To some engaged in the controversy over abortion, this distinction is one without a difference. These men of intelligence and good will do not perceive the human organism in the early part of its life cycle as a human "being" or "person." In their view, the granting to such an organism of the right to survive on a basis of equality with human beings generally should be delayed until a later stage of its development. To others, however, the "moment" of conception or some stage of development very close to this "moment" is the point at which distinctively human life begins. In their view the difference is the point at which distinctively human life begins. In their view the difference between the decision not to conceive and the decision to abort is of fundamental

determinative importance. Thus the root problem in the controversy over abortion is the one of assigning value to embryonic and fetal life.

The court concluded that the abortion laws of Louisiana protected the embryo or fetus and that the state had an interest in protecting life before birth. The law was not declared unconstitutional because the court did "not recognize the asserted right of a woman to choose to destroy the embryo or fetus she carries as being so rooted in the traditions and collective conscience of our people that it must be ranked as 'fundamental.' " In sharp contrast to this ruling, another district court in the 1970 Wisconsin case, *Babbitz v. McCann*, found that "a woman's right to refuse to carry an embryo during the early months of pregnancy may not be invaded by the state without a more compelling public necessity than is reflected in the statute in question. When measured against the claimed 'rights' of an embryo of four months or less, we hold that the mother's right transcends that of such an embryo."

### RIGHTS OF THE FETUS

The opinions in *Rosen* and *Babbitz* set forth the dilemma the courts faced: the firmly established "fundamental" rights of privacy and self-determination guaranteed to the woman versus any "compelling" state interest in abridging these rights. The "compelling" state interest refers to protection of the fetus and formed the core of the anti-abortion position. Against the cases which assert an individual's right to personal privacy in the area of sexual activity without state interference, the anti-abortionists emphasized a series of court decisions that point to the ascendancy of the rights of the fetus. It was argued that these decisions "help establish the intent of legislatures to give [the fetus] a right to life" (Charles and Alexander 1971:160), and abortion, except for "the necessary self-defense of the mother," deprives the fetus of its constitutional right to life (Louisell and Noonan 1970:255–256). To determine if the fetus has constitutional rights, "a court must ascertain what the word 'person' means in the Federal Constitution, in which this word is used many times . . . and in the Bill of Rights in the fourth, and the fifth, amendments" (Means 1971:402). Summarizing the court decisions in favor of the fetus' rights, Louisell and Noonan presented the case for restrictive abortion laws and suggested that any other solution confronts us with serious legal inconsistencies:

> It would be strange if a fetus had rights to support from his parents, rights enforceable by a guardian and sanctioned by the criminal law of neglect, and yet have no right to be protected from an abortion. It would be incongruous that a fetus should be protected by the state from willful harm by a parent when the injury was inflicted indirectly but not when it was inflicted directly. It would be odd if the fetus had property rights which must be respected but could himself be extinguished. The decisions recognize that where a choice must be made between the life of the fetus and the convenience or deep desires of the parent, the law will make the parent subordinate his rights in order to preserve the life in the womb. (1970:246)

The opposition, as exemplified by the ruling on this issue in *People v. Belous,* answered either that "statutes classifying the unborn child as the same as the born child require that the child be born alive for the provisions to apply" or that the statutes "reflect the interest of the parents." The pro-abortionists also argued that no evidence exists that the framers of the original Constitution and Bill of Rights thought of the fetus as a person (Means 1971:403). Anti-abortionists' attempts to establish a fetal right to life were relatively unsuccessful. For instance, anti-abortionists succeeded in being appointed as guardians to represent all unborn fetuses, but the courts ultimately rejected these attempts to establish a fetal right to life.

One possible solution, or at least compromise, of the serious dilemma between the woman's rights and the fetus' rights, is to grant the states the right to exert a compelling interest in the protection of the fetus only after a certain period of gestation. This explains in part why time limits became such an important part of reform and repeal legislation. While this provides a compromise for the courts and the legislatures, it displeases pro- and anti-abortionists alike. Anti-abortionists charge that it places an arbitrary, meaningless date on when a fetus is entitled to its right to life while the pro-abortionists agree about the arbitrary nature of the time limit and claim that "it constitutes an arbitrary limitation on medical practice" and "invites constitutional attack on equal protection grounds" (George 1972).

EQUAL PROTECTION

This argument was used primarily by the pro-abortionists and involves the right to receive proper and lawful medical care. Because of cost, procedural requirements, residency requirements, and differing hospital policies, the same medical services for abortion were not as available to blacks and the poor as to whites and the affluent. This argument does not require that the court assert a woman's right to abortion or a state's interest in regulating abortion, but "expressed as an equal protection right, the interest in receiving an abortion on the same terms as others receive them may more easily be considered 'fundamental' " (Charles and Alexander 1971:162). The opponents of abortion contended "that not every inequality in fact is denial of equal protection of the law" (Louisell and Noonan 1970:237). As a district court said in *Doe v. Bolton* (1970): "the mere fact that physicians and psychiatrists are more accessible to rich people than to poor people, making abortions more available to the wealthy than to the indigent, is not in itself a violation of the Equal Protection Clause." The anti-abortionists further argued that if the state permits abortion for any reason other than to save the woman's life, it constitutes a denial of equal protection to one group—the unborn (Louisell and Noonan 1970:246). The courts were relatively silent in the late 1960s and early 1970s on the merits of the equal protection argument.

These few arguments formed the basis of most constitutional attacks upon the abortion laws between 1969 and 1972–regardless of whether original, reform, or repeal laws were involved, or whether the attacker was pro-abortion or anti-abortion. In the January 22, 1973 decision, *Roe v. Wade,* the U.S. Supreme Court addressed some of the major constitutional uncertainties.

## Roe versus Wade

From 1967 to 1970 twelve states passed reform laws and four states passed repeal laws. It was therefore easy to conclude, in 1970, that state abortion laws throughout the United States would be liberalized rapidly. During 1971, however, not one additional state joined the ranks of those with liberalized laws. And in 1972, while several states became more liberal through judicial or legislative action, Connecticut passed a more restrictive law and New York's repeal law was almost retracted. Several factors contributed to a cooling off in the movement toward liberalization: (1) those supporting reform laws of the Model Penal Code variety realized the inadequacy of these laws; (2) those opposed to any change from restrictive laws became better organized to exert public pressure; (3) the availability of legal abortions in New York relieved some of the pressure for change, while legislatures marked time to observe what happened in states with repeal laws—Alaska, Hawaii, New York, and Washington; and (4) everyone waited for legal clarification from the U.S. Supreme Court.

The long-awaited decision of the U.S. Supreme Court was delivered on January 22, 1973. (There were, in fact, two cases and two decisions, both by the same 7 to 2 majority.) Both an original statute (Texas, *Roe v. Wade*) and a reform statute (Georgia, *Doe v. Bolton*) were declared unconstitutional. The Court ruled that a state could not intervene in the abortion decision between a woman and her physician during the first three months of pregnancy. During the second trimester, when abortion is more hazardous, the state's interest in the health of the woman permits the enactment of regulations to protect maternal health, such as statutes specifying where abortions may or may not be performed. Beyond such procedural requirements, however, the decision rests with the woman and her physician. After the fetus has reached the stage of viability, corresponding to approximately the last three months of pregnancy, the state can exercise an interest in promoting potential human life. It may do so by prohibiting abortion except when it is necessary to preserve the life or health of the mother. The Court's sweeping decision rendered all original and reform laws unconstitutional, and entirely altered the abortion landscape of the United States.

Of the four major constitutional issues that were being debated between 1969 and 1972—the woman's privacy, equal protection, vagueness, and the rights of the fetus—the Court's decision hinged mainly upon the first. The equal protection of the laws was not an issue in the two cases before the Court. The Georgia statute making it a crime for a physician to perform an abortion except when it is "based upon his best clinical judgment that an abortion is necessary" was not considered unconstitutionally vague *(Doe v. Bolton)*. The major ground for the Court's decision was the woman's right to privacy. "This right of privacy, whether it be founded in the Fourteenth Amendment's concept of personal liberty and restrictions upon state action, as we feel it is, or, as the District Court determined, in the Ninth Amendment's reservation of rights to the people, is broad enough to encompass a woman's decision whether or not to terminate her pregnancy" *(Roe v. Wade)*. Thus, based principally upon the due process clause of the Fourteenth Amendment of the U.S. Constitution—"nor shall any State deprive any person of life, liberty, or property, without due process of law"—the United States moved from being one of the most legally restrictive countries (excepting the four states with repeal laws) to one of the most permissive countries on the question of abortion.

What was the Court's position on the rights of the fetus? It rejected the argument that a state could assert a compelling interest to protect life from the time of conception and thus forbid abortion. It thus vindicated Governor Shapp's veto of a 1972 Pennsylvania abortion statute, which sought "to use the force of law for the protection of all human life," including the unborn. It also vindicated Governor Sargent's veto of a 1972 Massachusetts abortion bill, which stated that "every child shall be entitled to life from the moment of conception." These bills were similar to the one signed into law in Connecticut in 1972 and later declared unconstitutional by a federal district court.

The U.S. Supreme Court's reasons for rejecting a state's interest in protecting human life from the moment of conception were: (1) that "the unborn have never been recognized in the law as persons in the whole sense" *(Roe v. Wade)*; (2) that the rights extended to the unborn, in tort law, are contingent upon live birth; therefore (3) a state's interest in protecting fetal life cannot override the woman's right to privacy. The Court, however, did not accept the pro-abortion position that women have an absolute right to abortion regardless of circumstances. It recognized the rights of the fetus in a highly qualified way. These rights stem from the fetus' potential for human life; in the final trimester of its prenatal development the Court recognized a state's possible interest in protecting this potential:

> With respect to the State's important and legitimate interest in potential life, the "compelling" point is at viability. This is so because the fetus then presumably has the capability of meaningful life outside the mother's womb. State regulation protective of fetal life after viability thus has both logical and biological justification. If the State is interested in protecting fetal life after viability, it may go so far as to proscribe abortion during that period except when it is necessary to preserve the life or health of the mother. (*Roe v. Wade*, 1973)

In the face of such a strong position on the woman's right to privacy, other constitutional attacks upon restrictive abortion laws became less germane. For example, the Court struck down the residency requirement of the Georgia law (*Doe v. Bolton*), but since the Court's decision made abortion readily available in all states the residency issue was of limited significance. The Court also struck down Georgia's requirements (see table A.1 in Appendix) for confirming justification from additional physicians and for the approval of a hospital abortion committee as infringing upon the woman's and the physician's rights by placing constitutionally unjustifiable obstacles in their way.

### Reactions to the Court's Decision

The U.S. Supreme Court's instant and dramatic change of the legal situation brought cries of moral anguish and ecstasy from the abortion partisans. Patrick Cardinal O'Boyle called the decision "a catastrophe for America" and emphasized that the Court's ruling that abortion is legal "does not make it morally permissible." Abortion in fact, "remains a hideous and heinous crime" (*Washington Star-News,* January 23, 1973, p. 1–B). Cardinal Cooke pointed out that "judicial decisions are not necessarily sound moral decisions" and said: "I hope and pray that our citizens will do all in their power to reverse this injustice to the rights of the unborn." Cardinal Krol called the Court's action "a monstrous injustice" and added, "One trusts in the decency and good sense of the American people not to let an illogical court decision dictate to them on the subject of morality and human life" (*New York Times,* January 23, 1973, p. 20). Those favoring legalized abortion, with equal fervor, praised the decision of the Court as a wise one that returned the abortion decision to where it belongs—in the hands of the pregnant woman.

The emotional reactions to the U.S. Supreme Court's decision echoed through the state legislatures. A major consequence of the decision was to greatly restrict the area of legal maneuvering left to the states. Each state had the option of writing a new abortion law in keeping with the Court's decision or of operating without an abortion statute. In writing a new law, each state could still exercise some discretion with respect to the second and third trimesters of pregnancy. In some states, the attorney general, the legislature, or the medical establishment moved quickly to implement the Court's decision; in other states, delaying tactics were used, including the passage of new laws that were patently unconstitutional. But there was a limit to what the states could do, or in how long they could delay, because the major questions had been resolved at the federal level, and because the U.S. Supreme Court acted promptly in subsequent abortion cases to affirm its decision.

As a result the major controversy shifted from the state to the federal level. Since restrictive state laws were nullified because they did not conform to the U.S. Constitution, the anti-abortion forces seized upon the possibility of a constitutional amendment as a major way to reverse the Court's decision. As temporary measures, they pressed for legislation and regulations to limit abortions as much as possible within the parameters of the Court's decisions. Moreover, since legislative change depended on the actions of the U.S. Congress, they became politically active to try to elect members of Congress who would support their cause. The abortion question, far from being resolved, was becoming more intense.

CHAPTER 7

# THE LEGAL CONTROVERSY
# SINCE 1973

THE U.S. SUPREME COURT's 1973 decisions, *Roe v. Wade* and *Doe v. Bolton,* answered some of the legal questions on the constitutionality of abortion, but the decisions did not resolve the moral questions. In fact, as suggested by the strong reactions to the Court's decisions, the flames of the controversy were fanned, and the anti-abortionists reacted to their loss by organizing and fighting a more heated and more effective battle to get their message across to the public and to Congress.

The Court's 1973 decisions left a number of subsidiary legal questions unsettled. For example, the questions of husband's consent or parents' consent (in the case of a minor) for an abortion were not addressed since these were not at issue in the two cases before the Court. Nor did the Court deal with the use of public funds for abortions, nor with a number of procedural requirements for an abortion, such as waiting periods. These questions emerged after the 1973 decisions as some states added requirements for husband's consent, parental consent, waiting periods, and a variety of other requirements to try to limit the number of legal abortions. Since the U.S. Supreme Court had not ruled on these issues, the courts and state legislatures played a cat and mouse game as states tried out new restrictions and the courts ruled on them. For the most part, the courts quashed these restrictions, especially since some of them were clearly stepping beyond the constitutional boundary the Court had established in 1973 to protect a woman's right to decide on an abortion. Not all state statutes, however, were ruled unconstitutional; moreover, Congress also entered the fray by challenging the expenditure of federal funds for induced abortions.

The history of the legal controversy, from 1973 to 1986, can be described as one in which the courts generally supported a woman's right to an abortion without outside interference, but did not support the position that the federal government or the states had an obligation to provide funding for abortions. The entire history of these convoluted legal and judicial battles is beyond the scope of this book, but we will deal briefly with several of the key issues: husband's consent for a woman's abortion; parental consent requirements for minors; Medicaid funded abortions for medically indigent women; a variety of procedural requirements; and congressional efforts, through legislation or a constitutional amendment, to "overturn" the U.S. Supreme Court's decisions. Finally, we will discuss the efforts by the Reagan administration to restrict abortion and to find a way of overcoming the Court's 1973 decisions.

## Husband's Consent

In the last footnote to its *Roe v. Wade* decision, the U.S. Supreme Court pointed out that it was not discussing "the father's rights" because this was not an issue presented to the Court. "No paternal right has been asserted in either of the cases, and the Texas and the Georgia statutes on their face take no cognizance of the father." This left the door open for states to pass legislation requiring the pregnant woman's husband's consent to an abortion, and about one quarter of the states passed such legislation within two years of the *Roe v. Wade* decision.

Several arguments have been advanced for requiring the husband's consent. He has a marital and parental interest in the pregnancy and possible birth. Since he has sired the fetus, and may have an interest in its development, it is unfair and deceptive for the woman to be able to terminate the pregnancy without his knowledge or consent. As Wardle and Wood (1982:78) say, "In the case of a married woman, the pregnancy may represent her husband's great hope for and interest in posterity. Indeed, procreation goes to the very heart of the marriage relation."

Contrary arguments have also been advanced. The husband may not have fathered the child; the husband may be strongly opposed to abortion; the husband may be emotionally unstable. Under such circumstances, requiring the husband's consent may subject the woman to physical abuse and may lead to a disruption of the marriage.

The state and federal courts that considered the question had almost all decided that the husband's interest in the pregnancy and potential birth was not strong enough to overcome the woman's privacy right to make a decision about abortion. An exception, however, was the federal court's decision in a case involving a Missouri statute.

Missouri was one of the states that passed legislation requiring the husband's consent before an abortion could be performed. With strong influence from the Roman Catholic Church, this restriction on abortion, among others, was passed in 1974. The statute required the husband's consent unless the abortion was necessary to save the woman's life. The several restrictions of Missouri law were challenged on constitutional grounds by Planned Parenthood of Missouri. Although the federal court invalidated other requirements, it upheld the requirement for husband's consent. On appeal to the U.S. Supreme Court, however, the requirement for husband's consent was held to be unconstitutional.

This case, *Planned Parenthood of Central Missouri v. Danforth,* was decided by the Supreme Court in 1976. Missouri argued that the requirement for husband's consent was justified by several compelling state interests, "including the husband's interest in the future childbearing capacity of his wife, the state's interest in regulating marriage relationships, and the state's interest in seeing that a fundamental change in family membership set in motion by mutual consent should be terminated only by mutual consent" (Wardle and Wood 1982:80).

The U.S. Supreme Court, however, did not accept the state's reasoning. Although it recognized that the husband has a legitimate interest in the pregnancy, and that an abortion can greatly influence the marriage, it did not agree that giving the husband veto power

over his wife's abortion decision would further the goals of mu-
tuality and trust in the marriage, or strengthen the marriage relationship. It held that a state cannot give the husband an absolute
veto when it does not have that authority itself. In effect, the woman
retained the right to make her own decision about the abortion,
free of coercion, but also free to consult voluntarily with her husband or male partner.

### Parental Consent

One of the most controversial questions that emerged after *Roe
v. Wade* was whether minors had the right to make their own
abortion decisions, or whether states could require parental consent.
Should a pregnant 13-year-old be permitted, by law, to have an
abortion without her parents' consent? Does a minor have the social
and psychological competence to make such a decision? Is a minor
competent to care for an infant? If not, should the presumption be
that abortion is her best alternative? Should we make it easier, rather
than harder, for a minor to terminate her pregnancy? Would it help
a minor's decision to require that her parents be informed and
involved? Would it help the parent-child relationship? The major
legal developments pertaining to these issues are covered here (see
Rodman, Lewis, and Griffith 1984, for a detailed discussion).

The U.S. Supreme Court noted in *Roe v. Wade* that some states
had parental consent as well as husband consent requirements. Since
consent questions were not before the Court that day, the last
footnote in *Roe* concludes: "We need not now decide whether provisions of this kind are constitutional."

For anti-abortion partisans, this presented an opportunity to restrict abortions, and many states passed statutes requiring minors
to obtain their parents' consent for an abortion. In view of a long
tradition, under common law, requiring parental consent for medical procedures, such a requirement by a state seemed likely to be
within the Court's constitutional boundaries. There are exceptions,
however, for certain types of medical treatment, and for medical
care for mature minors, emancipated minors, and emergencies.

There were also earlier decisions making it clear that constitutional rights did not suddenly emerge with adulthood. As the U.S. Supreme Court said in *In re Gault* (1967), an important case granting minors constitutional rights in criminal cases, "neither the Fourteenth Amendment nor the Bill of Rights is for adults alone."

There were numerous court decisions on the question of parental consent for a minor's abortion. The vast majority of these decisions ruled against the parental consent requirement (Schell 1977). The issue first presented itself before the U.S. Supreme Court in *Planned Parenthood of Central Missouri v. Danforth* (1976). One of the restrictions passed by the Missouri legislature in 1974 called for parental consent for a minor's abortion, unless the abortion was necessary to save the minor's life. The federal district court upheld this requirement, but the U.S. Supreme Court reversed the decision, invalidating parental consent statutes in thirteen states.

Missouri argued that the law protected minors by insuring parental counsel in an important decision, and that the law was aimed at preserving parental authority within the family. The Court rejected these arguments, expressing doubt "that such veto power will enhance parental authority or control where the minor and the nonconsenting parent are so fundamentally in conflict and the very existence of the pregnancy already has fractured the family structure." The Court held that "the State does not have the constitutional authority to give a third party an *absolute,* and possibly arbitrary, veto over the decision of the physician and his patient to terminate the patient's pregnancy." Mindful of the tradition of parental authority, the Court qualified its decision. "We emphasize that our holding . . . does not suggest that every minor, regardless of age or maturity, may give effective consent for termination of her pregnancy."

The U.S. Supreme Court elaborated its qualification in *Bellotti v. Baird ("Bellotti I"),* a related case that was decided on the same day as *Danforth.* The Court indicated that its objection to the Missouri statute was the statute's blanket requirement for parental consent, for all minors, with no exception for "mature minors" or for minors whose best interest would be served by an abortion without parental involvement. In light of these two decisions, one could conclude

that while a blanket parental veto of the minor's abortion decision
was unconstitutional, something short of a blanket veto might be
acceptable.

In 1979 the U.S. Supreme Court presented a comprehensive
discussion of the parental authority and consent issues raised in
*Danforth* and *Bellotti I*. This occurred when *Bellotti v. Baird* returned
to the Court for a second time *("Bellotti II")*. The Massachusetts
law required parental consent, or a judge's consent if the parents
refused. The district court declared the law unconstitutional, relying
upon *Danforth*. In reviewing the district court opinion, the U.S.
Supreme Court took the opportunity to elaborate its view of the
constitutional status of children's rights within the framework of
the parent-child relationship.

> The Court long has recognized that the status of minors under the law is
> unique in many respects.... We have recognized three reasons justifying the
> conclusion that the constitutional rights of children cannot be equated with
> those of adults: the peculiar vulnerability of children; their inability to make
> critical decisions in an informed, mature manner; and the importance of the
> parental role in child-rearing.
>
> The Court's concern for the vulnerability of children is demonstrated in
> its decisions dealing with minors' claims to constitutional protection against
> deprivations of liberty or property interests by the State.... Viewed to-
> gether, our cases show that although children generally are protected by the
> same constitutional guarantees against governmental deprivations as are
> adults, the State is entitled to adjust its legal system to account for children's
> vulnerability....
>
> Second, the Court has held that the States validly may limit the freedom
> of children to choose for themselves in the making of important, affirmative
> choices with potentially serious consequences. These rulings have been
> grounded in the recognition that, during the formative years of childhood
> and adolescence, minors often lack the experience, perspective, and judgment
> to recognize and avoid choices that could be detrimental to them....
>
> Third, the guiding role of parents in the upbringing of their children
> justifies limitations on the freedom of minors. The State commonly protects
> its youth from adverse governmental action and from their own immaturity
> by requiring parental consent to or involvement in important decisions by
> minors. But an additional and more important justification for state defer-
> ence to parental control over children is that "the child is not the mere
> creature of the State; those who nurture him and direct his destiny have the
> right, coupled with the high duty, to ... prepare him for additional
> obligations.

The Court further points to the belief, "deeply rooted in our nation's
history and tradition," that the parental role "implies a substantial

measure of authority over one's children. Indeed, 'constitutional interpretation has consistently recognized that the parents' claim to authority in their own household to direct the rearing of their children is basic to the structure of our society.' " The Court also indicates that "the tradition of parental authority is not inconsistent with our tradition of individual liberty" and that "legal restrictions on minors, especially those supportive of the parental role, may be important to the child's chances for the full growth and maturity that make eventual participation in a free society meaningful and rewarding."

Despite this ringing endorsement of the doctrine of parental authority, the Supreme Court held the Massachusetts statute unconstitutional. It disapproved of the requirement that a minor seek her parents' consent *before* she was entitled to court relief. The Court ruled that the statute was unconstitutional because (1) it required parental involvement in every instance and (2) it permitted a judge to deny an abortion even if the minor was mature and competent to make the decision.

Some state statutes did not require parental consent, but rather parental notification. Utah required a physician to "notify, if possible" the parents of a dependent, unmarried minor girl before performing the abortion. The statute was challenged in *H.L. v. Matheson,* which was decided in 1981 by the U.S. Supreme Court. The decision provided slightly more clarification of the constitutional question of parental involvement. It upheld the statute on narrow grounds. Since the minor challenging the Utah statute in *Matheson* did not claim to be either mature or emancipated, the Court excluded such minors from its decision. The statute, at least as applied to H.L., was held to be constitutional, and the Court indicated that parental notification was less intrusive upon a minor's right to privacy in the abortion decision than parental consent.

In a 1983 decision, *City of Akron v. Akron Center for Reproductive Health,* the Court reaffirmed its objection to a blanket parental veto over a minor's abortion decision. It held that an Akron statute, requiring parental consent for all minors under the age of 15, was unconstitutional.

Although the issue of parental involvement in the abortion decision has not been fully resolved, the cases decided thus far suggest

roughly how far a state statute may go while still passing constitutional muster. It appears that a state may, if it desires, require
parental consent or notification for a minor's abortion, as long as
it provides for certain exceptions. One exception is for emancipated
minors—minors who are largely independent of their parents, such
as those who are living away from their parents and supporting
themselves. Another exception is to provide an expeditious route
for dependent minors to demonstrate to the courts that they are
mature and hence competent to make the decision on their own.
Failing that, they must have the opportunity to demonstrate to the
courts that obtaining an abortion without parental involvement is
in their best interest.

Do these decisions, which permit an important procedure without parental involvement, suggest that the U.S. Supreme Court has
abandoned its strong concern for parental autonomy and authority?
The answer is no. As pointed out elsewhere:

> the possibility must be considered that the *Danforth* line of cases are direct
> responses to what the Court saw as deliberate attempts to thwart the effect
> of *Roe v. Wade,* and that the Court has merely carved out a special exception
> to the doctrine of parental autonomy in the reproductive rights area. This
> interpretation would not be inconsistent with the Court's previous decisions
> in the family planning/abortion area, where one finds repeated examples of
> the Court's impatience with legislative policies that are antagonistic to family
> planning efforts. (Rodman, Lewis, and Griffith 1984:68–69)

At present, more than one-third of the states have laws requiring
either parental consent or notification, although some of these laws
have been enjoined on constitutional grounds. These laws create
obstacles and delays for minors seeking an abortion (Rodman,
Lewis, and Griffith 1984). In Massachusetts, for example, which
required either parental or judicial consent for unmarried minors
beginning in 1981, the number of abortions for minors declined
by nearly 50 percent. The total number of abortions obtained by
Massachusetts minors, however, was only slightly reduced. Many
minors obtained an abortion in nearby states that did not have
parental consent requirements (Cartoof and Klerman 1986).

## *Public Funding of Abortions*

After the 1973 decisions one of the most bitter battles revolved around the use of public funds to pay for abortions. Some anti-abortion partisans expressed outrage that their tax money was being used in support of a procedure that they equated with murder, and strong efforts were made to forbid the expenditure of public funds for abortion. For example, federal legislation was passed to prohibit the use of foreign aid money in support of abortion and to prohibit lawyers working for the federally created Legal Services Corporation from helping any clients secure an abortion.

The major area of controversy, however, was over the Medicaid program, Title XIX of the Social Security Act. It provides federal matching funds to the states for the medical care of indigent women. In 1976, about $45 million in federal Medicaid funds helped to pay for more than 250,000 abortions. This represented more than 25 percent of all the abortions in the United States during the year.

The extent of the legal controversy is emphasized by Wardle and Wood: "Public funding of abortions has been the subject of more litigation since *Roe v. Wade* was decided than any other abortion issue. The funding question has also produced the sharpest conflict among the federal judges who have decided abortion cases" (1982:55). The central question faced by the courts was whether the Constitution or federal Medicaid law required state or federal government to provide free abortions to medically indigent women.

Under the Medicaid program, the states must follow the require-ments of federal law to be eligible for federal funds. Some states tried to restrict funding under the Medicaid program to medically necessary abortions. A federal court found that such a restriction, in Pennsylvania, did not conform to federal Medicaid law. That law, passed in 1965, called for a state plan with "reasonable stand-ards" to determine eligibility for medical assistance. The U.S. Su-preme Court upheld the restriction in the Pennsylvania law, in *Beal v. Doe,* decided in 1977. The Court ruled that restricting the state plan to medically necessary abortions was reasonable and in com-pliance with federal law. In effect, a state has the discretion to include or exclude coverage for elective abortions. According to the majority opinion, the Court had earlier accepted, in *Roe v. Wade,* that "the State has a valid and important interest in . . . encouraging childbirth. . . . Respondents point to nothing in either the language or legislative history of Title XIX that suggests that it is unreasonable for a participating State to further this unquestionably strong and legitimate interest."

A companion case, *Maher v. Roe,* decided the same day, also dealt with medically necessary abortions, but focused on a constitutional question rather than on the interpretation of Medicaid legislation. The Court upheld a Connecticut Medicaid regulation requiring a physician to certify that an abortion was medically or psychiatrically necessary. The constitutional challenge, on equal protection grounds, that a state must pay for elective abortions if it pays for childbirth expenses, was turned down. The Court held that a state's Medicaid policy favoring childbirth over elective abortion did not interfere with a woman's fundamental right of privacy to have an abortion, since she could turn to other sources of support for her abortion without state interference.

Further steps were taken against the use of federal funds for any abortion, whether therapeutic or elective. Starting soon after *Roe v. Wade,* plans were made within the anti-abortion group to attach amendments to federal health bills to bar the use of federal funds for abortion. Each year since *Roe v. Wade,* such an amendment has been introduced to appropriation bills. Although earlier efforts failed, such an amendment was successfully introduced by Representative Henry J. Hyde (R., Ill.) in 1976 and went into effect in 1977. It barred the use of federal funds for any abortion under the Medicaid program, "except where the life of the mother would be endangered if the fetus were carried to term." Similar amendments were successfully introduced each year thereafter, and generated tremendous controversy and media attention. They led to bitter debates within each House and also within the Senate-House conference committee and delayed the annual appropriation bills for the federal departments of labor and health. Each year the exceptions under which federal Medicaid funds could be spent on an abortion differed, with the disagreement centered on exceptions similar to those introduced in the pre-1970 reform laws. The usual exception, however, was for abortions necessary to save the woman's life, and under such a restriction it became very difficult for indigent women to obtain abortions under the Medicaid program. By 1978, fewer than 2,500 abortions were covered by federal Medicaid funds, a decline of about 99 percent from the 1976 figure.

The federal restriction on Medicaid funding for abortion, referred to as the Hyde amendment, was challenged in the courts. The courts took different positions on the question. Judge Dooling, a federal district court judge, had issued a restraining order against the implementation of the Hyde amendment in 1976, and on remand from the Supreme Court after *Beal* and *Maher* in 1977, he held an extensive hearing on the questions involved in the case. His decision, in 1980, held the Hyde amendment to be unconstitutional. The case was appealed to the U.S. Supreme Court, which was presented with a brief signed by 238 members of Congress arguing that Judge Dooling's decision infringed upon Congressional authority over the federal budget.

The U.S. Supreme Court, in *Harris v. McRae,* overturned Judge Dooling's decision and ruled that the Hyde amendment was constitutional. In a 5 to 4 decision, the Court held that the restrictions on federal funding do not infringe on a woman's freedom to decide whether to terminate her pregnancy. As in *Beal* and *Maher,* the Court stressed that a woman does not have a constitutional entitlement to financial assistance for an abortion. Therefore, the Medicaid restrictions by the federal government, and by any states that follow the lead of the federal government, do not violate the due process clause or the equal protection clause of the Fifth Amendment. Although the decision was split, the majority in the Court distinguished between an unconstitutional bar to abortion through placing direct obstacles in a woman's path, and a constitutionally permissible bar to the expenditure of public funds for abortion.

Typical of the abortion issue, policy decisions stimulate the contenders to further action. Those on the losing side of *Harris v. McRae* were highly critical of the Court's decision and of the political pressure that Congress and the religious New Right exerted on the Court. At the state level, the legal controversy continues. For example, arguments that a particular state's constitution protects a poor woman's right to funding for abortion have met with success in some states, as in California and Massachusetts. Moreover, since most states have discretion over whether to use their funds to support abortions for indigent women, the battleground has shifted to the state level.

## Procedural Requirements

Other kinds of restrictions on abortion that are available to state legislatures are procedural requirements. States have passed laws specifying who may perform abortions, what procedures they may use, where abortions may be performed, when they may be done, and under what conditions. For example, states require abortions to be performed only by licensed physicians, and the U.S. Supreme Court has upheld such a requirement, even during the first trimester. Some states, in addition, have required the physician performing the abortion to be involved in the pre-abortion counseling of the pregnant woman. These requirements are attempts by states or cities "to give reality to the supposition made by the Supreme Court that the abortion decision would be made by the pregnant woman and her physician after carefully counseling together" (Wardle and Wood 1982:102). For the most part, in actual practice, non-physician abortion counselors in clinics do the counseling, and the physician specializes in performing abortions. In *City of Akron v. Akron Center for Reproductive Health* (1983), the U.S. Supreme Court struck down such a requirement; it accepted a procedure in which "a physician delegates the counseling task to another qualified individual."

The use of procedural requirements is a throwback to the 1960s and early 1970s, when some states were reforming or repealing their criminal abortion laws (see appendix). States that reformed their laws, making abortion legal under such conditions as fetal deformity, rape or incest, and threats to the woman's health, often added procedural requirements. Almost without exception, the reform statutes required abortions to be performed by physicians in hospitals. Some states set gestation time limits beyond which the abortion could not be performed, or could only be performed if the abortion were necessary to preserve the woman's life. In general, the procedural requirements of the original laws were greatly elaborated in the reform laws. This included a variety of requirements for physician consultation and medical committee approval of abortions. These procedural requirements provided protection to physicians against prosecution in a situation where there was no clear line between a legal and illegal abortion, and where there were many differences about how to interpret the laws. The procedural requirements of that time are summarized in appendix table A.1.

These procedural requirements, by acting as a brake on the indiscriminate performance of therapeutic abortions, helped to ease the passage from a restrictive to a more permissive system. Interestingly, after the U.S. Supreme Court legalized abortion in 1973, many states added procedural requirements that interfered with the abortion decision. Whether these requirements are the forerunner of a change from a permissive to a restrictive situation remains to be seen.

It is not surprising that some states and cities turned to a variety of procedural restrictions on abortion. This was a clear way for anti-abortionists to display their displeasure and to try to limit women's access to abortion. Most restrictive procedural requirements have been overturned by the courts because they were held to interfere with a woman's fundamental right to make her own decision about childbearing and abortion in consultation with her physician. Not all procedural requirements, however, were struck down. Nor were they all established merely to hobble access to abortion. Some legislators have acted out of mixed motives; some have acted out of a belief in fetal rights; some have acted to safeguard the pregnant woman's health.

We will examine a few of the key procedural requirements, providing the basic legal arguments and the outcome of the courts' decisions. Our major focus will be on U.S. Supreme Court decisions, since the controversy typically hinges on difficult questions of constitutional interpretation for which federal district courts have come up with differing decisions. We will discuss the question of whether states can require that all abortions performed after the first trimester must be done in hospitals; the question of whether a waiting period can be mandated before an abortion is performed; and whether a state can require that certain types of information be provided to a pregnant woman before the abortion procedure is performed. Finally, we will discuss *City of Akron v. Center for Reproductive Health,* because this case typifies the kinds of procedural restrictions that have been placed on abortion and provides a comprehensive response of the U.S. Supreme Court to these restrictions.

### HOSPITAL REQUIREMENTS

Several requirements of the reform law in Georgia were overturned by the 1973 U.S. Supreme Court decision in *Doe v. Bolton.* One of the requirements was that abortions be performed only in hospitals accredited by the Joint Commission on Accreditation of Hospitals (JCAH). The Court pointed out that there were no such restrictions on non-abortion surgery; that JCAH accreditation could not be obtained until after a hospital's first year of operation; that model legal codes contain no such requirement; and that some courts had held that such a requirement "is an overbroad infringement of fundamental rights." The Court therefore held that the requirement was unconstitutional. On the question of whether the state could require that abortions be performed in a licensed hospital, leaving aside the issue of JCAH accreditation, the Court, referring to its decision in *Roe v. Wade,* stressed that "the hospital requirement of the Georgia law, because it fails to exclude the first trimester of pregnancy," is invalid. The Court left open the question of hospital licensing requirements after the end of the first trimester.

Many states, subsequent to the 1973 decisions in *Roe* and *Doe,* required that all abortions after the first trimester be performed in a licensed hospital. For the most part, federal courts affirmed such requirements for several years after 1973. But by 1980, with improved abortion techniques, it was becoming clear that a dilatation and evacuation (D&E) abortion procedure in the early part of the second trimester could be performed safely and inexpensively in abortion clinics. At that time, some federal district courts were affirming state requirements that all abortions after the first trimester be performed in approved hospitals, and some were striking down such requirements. In 1983, the U.S. Supreme Court ruled on this question in *City of Akron,* striking down such a requirement. It held that the Akron requirement "unreasonably infringes upon a woman's constitutional right to obtain an abortion."

The Court based its decision on several factors. First, that second trimester abortions are far more expensive in hospitals than in clinics. Second, that Akron hospitals rarely performed second trimester abortions, so that a woman might have to travel elsewhere, incurring "both financial expense and additional health risk." Third, that "the safety of second-trimester abortions has increased dramatically" due to the use of the D&E procedure between the twelfth and sixteenth weeks of pregnancy. Fourth, that there is evidence to support the safety of the D&E procedure carried out in abortion clinics. As the Court said, "by preventing the performance of D&E abortions in an appropriate nonhospital setting, Akron has imposed a heavy, and unnecessary, burden on women's access to a relatively inexpensive, otherwise accessible, and safe abortion procedure."

## WAITING PERIODS

Another route that some legislative bodies have taken to restrict abortions is through requiring a waiting period before an abortion can be performed. Such a waiting period has typically been associated with a requirement for informed consent. The woman must be provided with information about the abortion procedure; after that she must wait 2 hours, or 24 hours, or 48 hours for the abortion. This presumably makes it possible for her informed consent to be based on good information about the abortion procedure. Those who support a waiting period argue that it gives the woman an opportunity to consider carefully her decision based on new information that she may learn while being counseled about the nature of the abortion procedure. Those who are against a waiting period argue that it is intended to dissuade a woman from having an abortion by placing psychological pressure on her after she has already decided to have an abortion.

The city of Akron required a 24-hour waiting period. This requirement was upheld by the district court, reversed by the court of appeals, and the latter court's decision was affirmed by the U.S. Supreme Court in *City of Akron* (1983). In overturning the requirement for a waiting period the Court noted the following arguments: that a waiting period increases the cost of obtaining an abortion, that scheduling difficulties may increase the delay beyond the mandated time, "and that such a delay in some cases could increase the risk of an abortion." The Court concluded that: "Akron has failed to demonstrate that any legitimate state interest is furthered by an arbitrary and inflexible waiting period. There is no evidence suggesting that the abortion procedure will be performed more safely. Nor are we convinced that the State's legitimate concern that the woman's decision be informed is reasonably served by requiring a 24-hour delay as a matter of course. . . . If a woman, after appropriate counseling, is prepared to give her written informed consent and proceed with the abortion, a State may not demand that she delay the effectuation of that decision."

### INFORMATION-DISPENSING REQUIREMENTS

As we have said, waiting periods were typically presented as part of the process of informed consent. They were justified as a time for the woman to consider carefully her decision to abort. Another type of state statute, also phrased in terms of informed consent, is a requirement to provide information to the woman intending to have an abortion. Some of these statutes are very general, and permit physicians to use their professional judgment about what to tell the woman. Other statutes are quite specific and are intended to hobble the abortion decision.

Information-dispensing requirements phrased in general terms were held to be constitutional by the courts. Missouri, for example, requires that a woman's consent "is informed and freely given and is not the result of coercion"; the woman has to certify to that effect in writing. Appellants argued that the requirement interposed the state between the woman and her physician, a situation that was unconstitutional during the first trimester, according to *Roe* and *Doe*. They also argued that the provision was vague—that the word "informed" could be variously interpreted.

The U.S. Supreme Court rejected these arguments in *Danforth*, in 1976. It held that "the imposition . . . of such a requirement for termination of pregnancy even during the first stage, in our view, is not in itself an unconstitutional requirement." Emphasizing that the abortion decision is important and often stressful, the Court stated that "it is desirable and imperative that it be made with full knowledge of its nature and consequences. The woman is the one primarily concerned, and her awareness of the decision and its significance may be assured, constitutionally, by the State to the extent of requiring her prior written consent."

The Court dispensed with the argument that the requirement for "informed consent" is vague by accepting the meaning given to the phrase by the federal district court—"the giving of information to the patient as to just what would be done and as to its consequences. To ascribe more meaning than this might well confine the attending physician in an undesired and uncomfortable straitjacket in the practice of his profession."

The U.S. Supreme Court seems willing to accept some degree of specificity in an informed consent requirement, as long as it gives physicians considerable discretion to exercise their judgment about what information to provide before performing an abortion (see Wardle and Wood 1982:92). The Court, however, is not willing to accept detailed information-dispensing requirements for informed consent, since these would interfere with the physician's professional judgment. The city of Akron, in passing one of the most stringent pieces of legislation to limit abortion, included an informed written consent requirement that called for the woman to be told about the physical development of the fetus, the stage of her pregnancy, the date of possible viability, and her loss of parental rights if the fetus were born alive, among other things. She also had to be told that "the unborn child is a human life from the moment of conception." Several states used the Akron law as a model. The Court rejected these requirements as unconstitutional, in *City of Akron,* in effect holding that "it is primarily the responsibility of the physician to ensure that appropriate information is conveyed to his patient, depending on her particular circumstances."

In developing its argument, the Court points out that "the validity of an informed consent requirement . . . rests on the State's interest in protecting the health of the pregnant woman." Thus, the state may require that an abortion decision be made with appropriate information about the physical and emotional circumstances that are relevant to the patient. "This does not mean, however, that a

State has unreviewable authority to decide what information a woman must be given before she chooses to have an abortion." According to the Court:

> [Akron] attempts to extend the State's interest in ensuring "informed consent" beyond permissible limits. First, it is fair to say that much of the information required is designed not to inform the woman's consent but rather to persuade her to withhold it altogether.... An additional, and equally decisive, objection to [the requirement] is its intrusion upon the discretion of the pregnant woman's physician. This provision specifies a litany of information that the physician must recite to each woman regardless of whether in his judgment the information is relevant to her personal decision.

The state of Pennsylvania, in enacting legislation in 1982 to control abortion, included several "informed consent" requirements. The woman was to be provided with the following information at least 24 hours before giving her consent: the "fact that there may be detrimental physical and psychological effects which are not accurately foreseeable"; the "particular medical risks associated with the particular abortion procedure to be employed"; that the father of the child is legally obligated to assist in the child's support; and that printed materials were available to her. These printed materials, supplied by the state, included detailed descriptions of fetal development, information about agencies offering alternatives to an abortion, and a statement that "the Commonwealth of Pennsylvania urges you to contact [these agencies] before making a final decision about abortion."

Referring to its earlier *Akron* decision, the U.S. Supreme Court, in *Thornburg v. American College of Obstetricians and Gynecologists,* held all of the information-dispensing requirements to be unconstitutional. The majority opinion stated that the printed materials required by the state "seem to us to be nothing less than an outright attempt to wedge the Commonwealth's message discouraging abortion into the privacy of the informed-consent dialogue between the woman and her physician." The Court further stated that "the requirements ... that the woman be advised that medical assistance benefits may be available, and that the father is responsible for financial assistance in the support of the child similarly are poorly disguised elements of discouragement for the abortion decision...."

Under the guise of informed consent, the Act requires the dissemination of information that is not relevant to such consent, and, thus, it advances no legitimate state interest." Further, the Court's majority opinion, referring to required information about the detrimental effects and medical risks of an abortion, stated that these "compound the problem of medical assistance, increase the patient's anxiety, and intrude upon the physician's exercise of proper professional judgment. This type of compelled information is the antithesis of informed consent."

It is noteworthy that *Roe* was decided in 1973 by a 7 to 2 majority, *Akron* was decided in 1983 by a 6 to 3 majority, while *Thornburgh* was decided in 1986 by a 5 to 4 majority. All of these were pro-choice decisions, but the margin has been narrowing. The changing composition of the Court, with new appointments being made by an anti-abortion president, makes the future of legal abortion in the United States somewhat shaky.

In summary, states may require, in general terms, that information be provided to the woman about the physical and psychological aspects of the abortion procedure as they relate to the patient's well-being. The extent to which specific information-dispensing requirements may be mandated is unclear, but if these requirements place constraints upon the physician's judgment then they would presumably be ruled unconstitutional. The *Akron* and *Thornburgh* decisions may not be the last word on the issue, but they set limits on what a state can do.

CITY OF AKRON

Akron's legislation on abortion, passed in 1978, was perhaps the most severe attempt to place restrictions on legal abortion. The Akron law served as a model for anti-abortion partisans who sought restrictions on abortion in other jurisdictions. The Akron restrictions were substantive and procedural, and several have already been discussed. The requirement that all abortions be performed in a hospital after the first trimester was struck down. The parental consent requirement for all abortions on minors under the age of 15 was also struck down. So, too, were the 24-hour waiting period and the detailed information-dispensing requirement for informed consent. Another requirement, not heretofore discussed, to dispose of the fetal remains in a "humane and sanitary manner" was struck down as impermissibly vague.

The statutes passed by Akron and by some states, and subsequently struck down by the U.S. Supreme Court, illustrate the political and judicial battles that are taking place. Some state, county, and city legislative bodies, supporting the anti-abortion or pro-life position, passed legislation that attempted to restrict abortion by adhering to the Supreme Court's guidelines; some of the statutes tested guidelines that were unclear, and some merely indicated legislative hostility and opposition to the guidelines. Most of these statutes were nullified by court decisions, but some, such as health reporting records and general information-dispensing requirements, survived.

In addition to the battles at the state level, battles at the federal level still rage and include the struggles over the Hyde amendment. Also at the federal level, anti-abortionists agitate for legislation and a constitutional amendment that might overturn the Court's decisions in *Roe* and *Doe* and once again outlaw abortion.

### Overturning Roe v. Wade

Despite strenuous efforts by the pro-life movement to restrict abortion, the number of legal abortions in the United States now exceeds 1.5 million per year. States that have passed anti-abortion statutes have generally had these statutes struck down by the courts. As a result, the anti-abortion movement has placed more emphasis in recent years on a constitutional amendment or a federal statute that would overturn the 1973 abortion decisions of the U.S. Supreme Court. Such attempts began in 1973, but only since 1980, with the election of a president who supported these efforts, was any progress made in Congress.

The many different constitutional amendments that have been offered fall into two major types. One is a states' rights amendment that would return control over abortion to the fifty states. Another is a "human life" amendment that would ban abortion through redefining a person to include a fetus. This classification oversimplifies the nature of some proposals, but it captures their essence and intent.

Since there are substantial differences between a constitutional amendment and a federal statute, and also substantial differences between a states' rights approach and a human life approach, the various anti-abortion groups have had difficulty in developing a common agenda. None of the approaches have had much success, but they have occupied considerable Congressional time and public attention, and they dramatize the high stakes of the abortion controversy.

CONSTITUTIONAL AMENDMENTS

In *Roe*, the Court ruled that there is a constitutional right to privacy that "is broad enough to encompass a woman's decision whether or not to terminate her pregnancy." The merits of the Court's decision and whether the Court has usurped legislative authority have been sharply contested by legal scholars and abortion partisans. The Court, however, has thus far maintained its constitutional interpretation. It therefore became important for abortion foes to consider the passage of a constitutional amendment that would undo the Court's decision.

A states' rights amendment would authorize the states to deal with abortion. One bill says that "the power to regulate the circumstances under which pregnancy may be terminated is reserved to the States." Another says that nothing in the Constitution would prevent any state "from allowing, regulating, or prohibiting the practice of abortion." With the passage of such an amendment, some states would undoubtedly ban abortion except to save the mother's life; others would adopt exceptions similar to those in the reform laws of 1967 to 1973; and others would permit abortion in terms similar to those now in existence. Such a situation, however, would be highly unstable. It would invite continuing battles in each state as anti-abortionists and pro-abortionists vie for position. Nor is this kind of federal amendment satisfactory to any of the partisans. The pro-life groups want to ban abortions everywhere; the pro-choice groups want to maintain the right to an abortion everywhere. As a result, states' rights amendments have lost their popularity.

A "human life" amendment is one that includes a fetus under the definition of a person. The phrasing varies. For example: "The paramount right to life is vested in each human being from the moment of fertilization without regard to age, health, or condition of dependency." Other proposed amendments grant personhood "from the moment of fertilization" or "at every state of biological development." Legal scholars have warned of a serious problem with a human life amendment. It could lead to chaos and uncertainty in many areas of law having nothing to do with abortion (Pilpel 1976; Robertson 1983; Westfall 1982). Would fetuses be counted as persons in determining Congressional representation? Would women be monitored for abuse and neglect of the fetus? Might capital punishment be banned by the wording of some of the proposed amendments? Would popular contraceptives, such as birth control pills and IUDs, be prohibited? Would job discrimination against women increase under the guise of a constitutional need to protect fetuses?

These legal questions make it difficult to gain widespread support for a human life amendment. In attempting to prohibit abortion by indirection, these amendments threaten to overwhelm the judicial system with confusion and litigation. Why not, therefore, pursue a constitutional amendment that would directly ban abortion? The intent of such a prohibition amendment would be clear, and it would avoid the chaos of a human life amendment. But it simply does not have much Congressional or public support. Some anti-abortion partisans favor a straightforward prohibition approach, despite its dismal chances; others favor a human life approach, despite its potential for confusion; yet others favor a states' rights approach, despite the fact that it compromises the goal of completely banning abortion.

The only constitutional amendment that reached the Senate floor for debate was essentially a states' rights amendment, although it did not start out that way. Initially introduced by Senator Orrin Hatch, in 1981, it called for both federal and state control over abortion, and for the more restrictive law, whether federal or state, to govern. It was, however, subsequently amended to read, "A right to abortion is not guaranteed by the Constitution." In this guise it was reported to the Senate and voted down in 1983, 50 to 49. Since it needed 67 votes to pass (a two-thirds majority), it failed by 18 votes. Despite the controversy it generated among pro-life partisans, it came closer than any other amendment.

## FEDERAL LEGISLATION

Since a constitutional amendment is difficult to pass, abortion foes have tried to accomplish their purpose through federal legislation. A constitutional amendment requires a two-thirds majority vote by both the Senate and the House and subsequent ratification by three-fourths of the states; federal legislation requires a simple majority in both the Senate and the House. The legislative bills on abortion, aimed at overturning the Court's 1973 decisions, typically combine a human life approach and a states' rights approach.

Several of the proposed anti-abortion bills state that human life begins at conception, contradicting *Roe v. Wade*. Their intent is to enable or to require states to protect human life from the moment of conception. One such bill, S. 158, was introduced by the late Senator John East, who held lengthy subcommittee hearings during 1981 on the question of when human life begins. These hearings, as with many debates about abortion, sparked much controversy and media attention but shed little new light on the question. The bill was recommended to the full Judiciary Committee but was not acted on.

A federal statute to overturn the U.S. Supreme Court's decision in *Roe v. Wade* is not popular, and Congress probably lacks the authority to do so. Twelve constitutional scholars sent a joint letter to Senator East's subcommittee:

> Our views about the correctness of the Supreme Court's 1973 abortion decision vary widely, but all of us are agreed that Congress has no constitutional authority either to overturn that decision by enacting a statute redefining such terms as "person" or "human life," or selectively to restrict the jurisdiction of federal courts so as to prevent them from enforcing that decision fully.

Six former attorneys general also took the same position (Milbauer 1983). So did the American Medical Association and the National Academy of Sciences, among other professional and scientific organizations. It is not surprising, with this kind of opposition, that the legislative route to overturning *Roe v. Wade* has not been successful.

### THE REAGAN ADMINISTRATION

The election of Ronald Reagan in 1980, and his reelection in 1984, gave hope to those seeking to restrict and to criminalize abortion in the United States. Reagan ran for the U.S. presidency on a Republican platform that endorsed a constitutional amendment to ban abortion. He has placed pro-life partisans in several key positions, including Dr. C. Everett Koop as surgeon general. In 1985 and 1986 he spoke against abortion to thousands of pro-life partisans at the annual demonstration against the U.S. Supreme Court's 1973 decisions. He has voiced his anti-abortion sentiment on numerous occasions. For example, in 1982, in support of Senator Jesse Helms' anti-abortion efforts, he wrote to nine senators asking them to provide "an opportunity for the Supreme Court to reconsider its usurpation of the role of legislators and state courts" and to affirm "the humanity of the unborn." He has also said, before a convention of the Knights of Columbus in 1982, that "the national tragedy of abortion on demand must end." In his administration the Justice Department, in 1985, filed an *amicus* brief in support of Illinois and Pennsylvania statutes seeking to control abortion, and it asked the Court to reconsider and overturn its *Roe v. Wade* decision and to give each state the authority to set its own policy on abortion. Although the Justice Department's effort was not successful, it provided the Reagan administration a highly visible opportunity to restate its opposition to abortion. Speaking to the National Right-to-Life Convention in 1986, Reagan referred to abortion as the "ultimate human rights issue."

Although President Reagan has not placed abortion at the top of his agenda, he has given consistent support to efforts to restrict abortion through withdrawing federal funds for abortion services, and to efforts to ban abortion outright except when the mother's life is in danger. Congress has been willing to ban the use of federal funds for abortion services for Medicaid recipients, Peace Corps volunteers, Native Americans, and federal employees and their dependents. Efforts to ban abortion, however, either through a federal statute or a federal constitutional amendment, have so far not been successful.

Pro-choice partisans, faced by threats from the Reagan administration and from some quarters in Congress to make abortion illegal once again, have increased their organizational strength and political clout to protect the legality of abortion. The Reproductive Health Equity Act, first introduced in Congress in 1984 and subsequently reintroduced, would require that all medical services related to pregnancy, including abortion, be treated in the same way. The intent was to eliminate all previously enacted restrictions on the use of public funds. Educational, political, and public relations efforts on the part of pro-choice and anti-abortion groups are about equally matched in the mid-1980s, and the uneasy Congressional compromise limits the use of federal funds for abortion while accepting the legality of abortion.

During the presidential election campaign in 1984 the president's power to appoint U.S. Supreme Court justices became an important issue. Might it be possible for Reagan, in a second term, to appoint new justices to the Court who would change the minority opposed to *Roe v. Wade* into a majority? Might the 1973 abortion decisions be overturned by the U.S. Supreme Court itself?

## THE COMPOSITION OF THE U.S. SUPREME COURT

There are differences among Court members about how the Constitution applies to various questions about abortion. *Roe v. Wade* and *Doe v. Bolton* were both decided in 1973 on 7 to 2 votes. *Harris v. McRae* and *Thornburgh* were decided by a 5 to 4 majority. The *Matheson* and *City of Akron* votes were both 6 to 3. Some cases have several concurring and dissenting opinions, indicating the diversity of opinion in the Court. Clearly any changes in the composition of the Court could lead to changes in the Court's decisions. Sandra

Day O'Connor, appointed by President Reagan in 1981, wrote the dissenting opinion in *City of Akron;* she was joined in that opinion by Justices White and Rehnquist, the two justices who dissented in *Roe* and *Doe* in 1973. That minority opinion is studded with challenges to *Roe v. Wade*. The resignation of Chief Justice Warren Burger in 1986, his replacement by Associate Justice William Rehnquist, and the appointment of Justice Antonin Scalia, have made the Court more conservative and may have moved it a bit closer to decisions that are less tied to the philosophy expressed in *Roe v. Wade*.

Many of the justices on the Court are elderly. A couple of them are in ill health. This suggests that President Reagan may have the opportunity of appointing additional justices to the Court. Many conservatives, both inside and outside government, have relished the idea of further Court appointments by President Reagan. Reagan has already given many federal courts a more conservative cast through his ideologically screened appointments. Numerous reports have surfaced in the media regarding the strict and extensive screening that prospective judges undergo, including screens for their position on abortion. Jerry Falwell, who has often spoken about the appointment of pro-life justices to the U.S. Supreme Court, predicted on a trip to North Carolina in 1985 that President Reagan will be able to appoint up to four pro-life justices. In 1986, the president appointed Justice Scalia. None of the other justices, at least late in 1986, are talking about retirement. But there is certainly the possibility of further change in the Court's composition during President Reagan's second term, and the possibility of Court decisions that would alter the legal landscape of abortion in the United States.

Appointments to the Court are made by the president with the advice and consent of the Senate. Laurence H. Tribe has reminded us that almost one-fifth of presidential nominations to the Court have not been confirmed by the Senate. He stresses that the Senate has an important role to play in maintaining balance on the Court:

> Picking judges is too important a task to be left to any President: unless the Senate, acting as a continuing body accountable to the nation as a whole,

plays an active and thoughtful part—something we have seen it do through much of our history—the way we and our children live and die will be shaped more powerfully by a single official's vision than any electoral mandate on any Tuesday in November could possibly justify. (Tribe 1985:141)

## THE NEAR FUTURE

The likelihood of a resolution of the abortion question, in the not-too-distant future, is discussed in the last chapter. In the near future, unfortunately, the prospects for taming the controversy are not good. As one side loses ground it fights with greater vigor. Neither side is willing to compromise, at least not in terms of what they view as the basic moral and legal issues. When the groups fighting for the legalization of abortion achieved a series of victories, culminating in the 1973 U.S. Supreme Court decisions, the anti-abortion groups grew stronger. When the anti-abortion groups succeeded in placing some restrictions on abortion, and in banning the use of federal funds in support of abortion, the pro-choice groups fought harder to maintain the legality of abortion. Pictures of aborted fetuses were met with pictures of women who died of an illegal abortion. *The Silent Scream,* an ultra-sound film showing greatly enlarged images of a suction abortion, with imaginative and effective anti-abortion narration by Bernard Nathanson, was countered with a publicity campaign to highlight the inaccuracies of the film and the narration, and to emphasize the fact that women's screams are not silent.

The near future holds the possibility of change and the certainty that such change will be met with bitter opposition. Further restrictions on abortion will undoubtedly be met with stronger attempts to eliminate all restrictions. An easing of restrictions will be met with stronger attempts to prohibit all abortions. Should abortion again be criminalized, there would be outright defiance and an acrimonious campaign to eliminate the new prohibition.

Prohibition would strengthen the pro-choice groups (as the anti-abortion groups were strengthened by the 1973 decisions), and we would observe a bitter seesaw battle, at the federal and state levels, about the legality of abortion. Because of the high stakes involved, including millions of people, billions of dollars, and fervently held beliefs, a protracted battle—with several back-and-forth changes in policy—could have devastating consequences for American society.

CHAPTER 8

# ABORTION ATTITUDES: POLLS, POLITICS, AND PREJUDICE

THE KNOWLEDGE THAT INDIVIDUALS have about abortion and their attitudes and behavior are greatly influenced by the social and cultural context. If one wants to predict whether someone has favorable or unfavorable attitudes toward abortion, or whether a woman experiences relief or guilt after an abortion, the most important item of information would be the sociocultural interpretation of abortion. Nationality, social class, race, religion, age, place of residence, education, and marital status are among the social variables that influence a person's access to, use of, and attitudes toward abortion services and alternatives to abortion. The rapid changes that have taken place in the United States over the past two decades also emphasize the importance of historical time as a variable.

We will explore public attitudes toward abortion in the United States since the early 1960s, when attempts to liberalize state abortion laws were beginning to gain momentum. Attitudes and values influence abortion behavior and public policy, and are in turn influenced by behavior and policy. That is why the various partisan abortion groups have been working so assiduously to change public attitudes or, as they would say, to educate the public. We will focus on the changes in abortion attitudes that have taken place since the early 1960s, and on the relationship between these attitudes and religion and gender.

Since the 1960s, public attitudes have generally supported the legality of abortion for medical reasons, such as danger to the mother's health and possible fetal deformity. There has been less public support of abortion for nonmedical reasons. The differences between the "hard" medical reasons and the "soft" nonmedical reasons are clearly illustrated in table 8.1. Looking at 1985 attitudes, the favorable percentages range from 79 to 89 percent for medical reasons involving health, rape, and fetal deformity, and from 36 to 44 percent for nonmedical reasons such as the woman being unmarried or the woman being married but not wanting any more children. Although pregnancy due to rape is arguably a social reason, it is viewed by the public as a "hard" medical reason.

During the 1960s, attitudes did not change much. National polls by the Gallup organization indicate that people became only slightly more favorable toward abortion during the decade (Blake 1971; Sarvis and Rodman 1974). For example, in asking whether abortion "should or should not be legal . . . where the family does not have enough money to support another child," 74 percent disapproved of abortion in both 1962 and 1965, 72 percent and later 68 percent disapproved in two surveys taken in 1968, and 68 percent disapproved in 1969.

Attitudes became considerably more favorable during the early 1970s, in conjunction with the U.S. Supreme Court's legalization of abortion. During the second half of the 1970s, the increase in favorable attitudes was arrested and there was no discernible trend. By the 1980s, however, favorable attitudes were declining (see table 8.1). Again, using the question about a family that cannot afford more children as an example, percentages that are favorable to abortion rise from 22 percent in 1965 to 55 percent in 1974, and decline to 44 percent in 1985.

What has led to a decline in attitudes favorable to legal abortion? Although no one has a definitive answer we can speculate about some major influences during the first half of the 1980s. One such influence is a president who has been outspoken in opposition to abortion. Another is a pope, who has been outspoken in his opposition. Yet another opponent is a Roman Catholic nun, who was awarded the Nobel Peace Prize in 1979. President Reagan, Pope John Paul II, and Mother Teresa have been uncompromising in

Table 8.1
**Percentage of U.S. Adults Approving of Legal Abortion Under Various Circumstances**

| Circumstance | 1965 | 1972 | 1974 | 1977 | 1980 | 1982 | 1984 | 1985 |
|---|---|---|---|---|---|---|---|---|
| If the woman's health is seriously endangered by the pregnancy | 73 | 87 | 92 | 90 | 90 | 92 | 90 | 89 |
| If the woman became pregnant as a result of rape | 59 | 79 | 86 | 84 | 83 | 87 | 80 | 81 |
| If there is a strong chance of a serious defect in the baby | 57 | 79 | 85 | 85 | 83 | 85 | 80 | 79 |
| If the family has a very low income and cannot afford any more children | 22 | 49 | 55 | 53 | 52 | 52 | 46 | 44 |
| If the woman is not married and does not want to marry the man | 18 | 43 | 50 | 50 | 48 | 49 | 44 | 41 |
| If the woman is married and does not want any more children | 16 | 40 | 47 | 46 | 47 | 49 | 43 | 40 |
| For any reason* | | | | 38 | 41 | 41 | 39 | 36 |
| Average approval for the six specific reasons | 41 | 63 | 69 | 68 | 67 | 69 | 64 | 62 |

SOURCE: Information is based on NORC General Social Surveys. Granberg and Granberg (1980); *Family Planning Perspectives* (1983); Tom W. Smith, NORC, personal communication, June 25, 1985.
NOTE: Percentages are based on the number of respondents answering yes or no to each question. Respondents who said they did not know or who did not give a yes-or-no answer were excluded from the analysis.
* This question was first asked in 1977.

their opposition and have received much media attention. It is likely that some of the decline in attitudes favorable to abortion stems from their staunch and widely publicized opposition. In addition, the political climate in the United States has become more conservative, and most conservatives have adopted an anti-abortion position. Several conservative religious leaders with large television audiences have also condemned abortion. It is therefore not surprising that public attitudes have become less favorable to abortion. Projecting recent changes into the near future, we would expect that overall support for the legality of abortion in the United States would remain firm, that differences in attitudes between hard and soft reasons would remain wide, and that there would be a continuing, but very slight, decline in support for abortion. Such projections seem reasonable and probable. It must be emphasized, however, that abortion is a highly controversial and sharply contested issue, and that public attitudes may change quickly, as demonstrated in the early 1970s.

## Attitudes and Religion

While the overall percentages provide an important indication of how the U.S. adult population as a whole is changing in abortion attitudes, it is also instructive to make some focused comparisons within that population. How do attitudes differ by religion? Given the condemnation of abortion by officials of the Roman Catholic Church, how do Catholics differ from non-Catholics?

Catholics are slightly less favorable toward abortion than non-Catholics, but the differences are small. The Gallup organization has polled Americans over the years on their attitudes to abortion, and a breakdown of attitudes by religion is presented in table 8.2. The comparison is made between Catholics and Protestants, the two religious groups with adequate numbers in the sample.

The figures in table 8.2 indicate that there has not been a great deal of change from 1975 to 1983. But the data do show some convergence in the attitudes of Catholics and Protestants; from about 1980 on, there is very little difference between the attitudes of Catholics and Protestants. In 1983, for example, 22 percent of

Table 8.2.
Attitudes of U.S. Adults Toward the Legality of Abortion, by Religion: Percentages

| Abortion should be: | 1975 Cath. | 1975 Prot. | 1977 Cath. | 1977 Prot. | 1979 Cath. | 1979 Prot. | 1980 Cath. | 1980 Prot. | 1981 Cath. | 1981 Prot. | 1983 Cath. | 1983 Prot. |
|---|---|---|---|---|---|---|---|---|---|---|---|---|
| Legal under any circumstances | 17 | 18 | 20 | 18 | 17 | 20 | 22 | 23 | 21 | 20 | 22 | 20 |
| Legal only under certain circumstances | 50 | 58 | 53 | 58 | 52 | 59 | 55 | 55 | 49 | 55 | 57 | 62 |
| Illegal in all circumstances | 32 | 21 | 23 | 19 | 25 | 17 | 21 | 18 | 25 | 22 | 19 | 15 |
| No opinion | 1 | 3 | 4 | 5 | 6 | 4 | 2 | 4 | 5 | 3 | 2 | 3 |

SOURCE: *The Gallup Opinion Index*: Report No. 121, July 1975, p. 12; Report No. 153, April 1978, p. 26; Report No. 166, May 1979, p. 21; Report No. 178, June 1980, p. 7. *The Gallup Report*: Report No. 190, July 1981, p. 21; Report No. 215, August 1983, p. 18.

Catholics say that abortion should be legal under any circumstances, compared to 20 percent of Protestants; 19 percent of Catholics and 15 percent of Protestants say that abortion should be illegal in all circumstances.

The Gallup organization has also presented the following question to a representative sample of adult Americans: "The U.S. Supreme Court has ruled that a woman may go to a doctor to end her pregnancy at any time during the first three months of pregnancy. Do you favor or oppose this ruling?" In 1981, 37 percent of Catholics and 45 percent of Protestants favored the ruling. In 1983, 47 percent of Catholics and 50 percent of Protestants favored the ruling. In 1986, 41 percent of Catholics and 42 percent of Protestants favored the ruling. Once again, we see some degree of convergence of Catholic and Protestant attitudes.

Although the abortion attitude differences between Catholics and Protestants have not disappeared, they have narrowed and they are small. These developments indicate the limited influence that the official Roman Catholic position on abortion has had, and they lend weight to Reverend Andrew Greeley's (1985:86) observation that the abortion attitudes of American Catholics are "at odds with the position of the official church" (1985:86). Moreover, many Catholic theologians and scholars also hold attitudes that differ from the church's anti-abortion stance and have publicly proclaimed their dissenting views (Anderson 1985; Stan 1986).

## Attitudes and Gender

Women become pregnant; women bear children; women have abortions. Would the history of abortion legislation differ if men had these experiences? Since men predominate in state and federal legislatures, many have speculated that abortion would have been legalized earlier if men became pregnant and wanted abortions. Some feminists view attitudes, laws, and regulations opposed to abortion as key examples of men's continuing attempt to control and oppress women. In stark contrast, anti-abortion partisans speculate about the harm being done to women and to society by legislation that permits over 1.5 million induced abortions per year in the United States. These contrasting ideological positions are part of the debate about abortion and they make it difficult to resolve the policy issues raised by the abortion question.

Leaving aside unanswerable "what if" questions—what if men had abortions, what if women had legislative power—let us turn to gender differences in abortion attitudes. Do women and men differ in their attitudes toward abortion?

Although men do not have abortions, many men become actively involved in the abortion decisions of their partners. The evidence is rather clear that a very large majority of women inform their husbands and partners about their pregnancies and abortions (McCain 1985). In one study of 2,337 women who obtained abortions at a clinic in Illinois (Plutzer and Ryan 1985), 93 percent of married women told their husbands about the pregnancy and 89 percent of never-married women told their partners. Many men share the abortion experience with their partners and accompany them to the abortion clinic (Shostak and McLouth 1984; Shusterman 1979). It is therefore difficult to know what to expect when comparing women's and men's attitudes to abortion.

On the whole, from the early 1960s to the mid-1980s, national polls have reported that slightly higher percentages of men than women express favorable attitudes to abortion. Some questions in some polls have drawn virtually similar responses from men and women, or have drawn more favorable responses toward legal abortion from women. For example, in 1980, the Gallup Poll asked a national sample of adults, "Do you think abortions should be legal under any circumstances, legal only under certain circumstances, or illegal in all circumstances?" More women than men answered "legal under any circumstances" by 26 to 24 percent, and "legal under certain circumstances" by 54 to 51 percent; more men than women answered "illegal under all circumstances" by 20 to 16 percent. The remaining women and men had no opinion.

In a sample of 320 medical students (Bonar, Koester, and Watson 1983), women were significantly more likely to support a pro-choice position of unrestricted access to abortion than were their male colleagues. Among medical students, 90 percent of the women favored unrestricted access to abortion, compared to 80 percent of the men; 80 percent of the women students thought unmarried

142

*Abortion Attitudes*

**Table 8.3.**
**Attitudes of U.S. Adults Toward the U.S. Supreme Court Ruling on Abortion, by Sex (Percentages)**

|  | 1974 | | 1981 | | 1983 | | 1986 | |
| --- | --- | --- | --- | --- | --- | --- | --- | --- |
|  | Male | Female | Male | Female | Male | Female | Male | Female |
| Favor | 51 | 43 | 47 | 43 | 56 | 46 | 45 | 45 |
| Oppose | 38 | 49 | 44 | 49 | 37 | 48 | 43 | 46 |
| No opinion | 11 | 8 | 9 | 8 | 7 | 6 | 12 | 9 |

SOURCE: *The Gallup Opinion Index*: Report No. 106, April 1974, p. 24. *The Gallup Report*: Report No. 190, July 1981, p. 20; Report No. 215, August 1983, p. 17; Report Nos. 244–245, January-February 1986, p. 18.

women under age 18 should not be required to obtain parental consent for abortion, a position supported by only 60 percent of the men. The women also had more equalitarian sex role attitudes than the men. Similar findings were reported by a national survey (Weisman et al. 1986) of practicing obstetrician-gynecologists who received their medical degrees between 1974 and 1979. Questioned on whether women should have the legal right to an abortion, 90 percent of the female respondents and 76 percent of the males strongly agreed. Questioned on whether unmarried minors should be required to obtain parental consent for an abortion, 64 percent of the females strongly disagreed, compared to 48 percent of the males. It seems that medical professionals are more favorably disposed to legal abortion than the general population, and that the women in this group are more favorable toward legal abortion than the men.

In most national polls, however, men's attitudes are more favorable to abortion. In table 8.3 we present data from four polls conducted in 1974, 1981, 1983, and 1986. The question asked was: "The U.S. Supreme Court has ruled that a woman may go to a doctor to end her pregnancy at any time during the first three months of pregnancy. Do you favor or oppose that ruling?" In three of the four polls, men were more favorable toward the Court's liberalized ruling than women.

Men's and women's attitudes toward abortion seem to be influenced by different factors, with women's attitudes being influenced by a larger number of factors. Finlay (1981) reports that men's abortion attitudes vary primarily with their conventionality, whereas women's attitudes are more complex, and are related to a broader set of attitudes, including the value they place on children, attitudes about the equality of men and women (Granberg 1981; Luker 1985), and ideological issues about abortion. Bonar, Watson, and Koester (1983) also report a more complex structure determining women's attitudes, as does McCain (1985). The more complex structure of women's attitudes may be due to their greater ability to empathize with women facing unintended pregnancies under a wide variety of circumstances and subject to multiple pressures about how to resolve the problem; it may also reflect women's socialization as the childbearers and chief caretakers of children.

## Ambivalence

Protestants are somewhat more favorable toward abortion than Catholics, and men are somewhat more favorable than women, but the differences are small, and in some attitude polls they are nonexistent. One striking feature of the attitudes of the American public, cutting across religion and gender, is ambivalence. Polls that ask respondents whether they are for or against something can mask the ambivalence that lurks behind the high percentages that are either for or against. This situation stems from the usual polling method, in which questions are phrased to determine whether respondents favor or oppose something. Respondents with a slight leaning in one direction (and some who are in dead center) will usually reply in terms of the choices presented by the question. They are not likely to reveal their uncertainty or ambivalence. Unless survey questions are formulated to reveal ambivalence, it may be necessary for the analyst to take an indirect approach to ferret it out. For example, when the reasoning behind an answer is elicited by asking "why do you feel that way" or "explain your answer," the ambivalence may be brought out as the respondent says "it depends on the situation" (Gilligan 1982).

Although there are many pro-choice and pro-life groups in the United States, and although these groups dominate the attention of the media, only a small percentage of the American population belongs to these highly partisan and highly polarized groups. The vast majority of the population is not polarized and does not hold starkly partisan attitudes. Most people fall between the two extremes and demonstrate considerable ambivalence of attitudes (Blake and Del Pinal 1981; Silber 1980).

Most people would prefer that unwanted pregnancy did not occur, but they recognize that the real world is rarely perfect and that pregnancy does occur in the context of poverty, destructive relationships, gross congenital anomaly, or simply immaturity and lack of foresight. Even among members of partisan groups, such as the National Right to Life Committee (NRLC) and the National Abortion Rights Action League (NARAL), there is considerable variation about the conditions under which they accept or reject abortion, and also considerable variation in whether they would act as single-issue voters on the question of abortion (Granberg 1981).

The abortion debate among Roman Catholics provides an example of a context that fosters ambivalence. The pope and the bishops, representing the official Church position, are strongly opposed to abortion and have been overtly critical of public officials, especially Catholic officials, who express personal opposition to abortion but accept its legality. The running debate between Archbishop (now Cardinal) O'Connor and Governor Cuomo provides a vivid example of the conflicting pressures facing Catholics and others. These debates provide fertile ground for the growth of ambivalent attitudes and sow the seeds of difficulty for the Roman Catholic Church (Greeley 1985; see also Maguire 1986).

A clear example of Americans' ambivalent attitudes toward abortion is provided by a survey conducted in 1981 by Yankelovich, Skelly, and White for *Life* magazine. They interviewed a representative national sample of adult American women: 92 percent state that abortion should be legal for "a woman whose health is at risk," 88 percent for "a woman who has been raped," and 87 percent for "a woman who is carrying a fetus with a severe genetic defect" (Henshaw and Martire 1982). These percentages are almost identical to the 1982 percentages reported in table 8.1 for similar questions.

But this survey, unlike others, also asked women about the morality of abortion. "Despite the high level of support for legal abortion, many American women believe it to be morally wrong" (Henshaw and Martire 1982:55). In fact, 56 percent of American women say that abortion is morally wrong; nevertheless, half of these women "believe that any woman who wants an abortion should be able to obtain it legally. Thus the belief that abortion is morally wrong does not necessarily lead to the conclusion that women should be prevented by law from obtaining abortions" (Henshaw and Martire 1982:55).

The distinction many people make between morality and legality reveals a profound ambivalence in attitudes and a profound commitment to tolerance on the part of a sizable percentage of the American public. It parallels the distinction made by Roman Catholic politicians, such as Governor Cuomo of New York, between private morality and public policy. It should be noted that this need not reflect ambivalence, but may reflect a carefully reasoned distinction between morality and policy.

Several investigators document ambivalence about abortion among women who experience abortion (Francke 1978; Freeman 1978). In her study of women who experienced abortion, Zimmerman (1977) reports that only 30 percent were "completely favorable to abortion prior to their own experience." Some women were strongly opposed to abortion, even though they later chose to have an abortion: "I decided I would never have an abortion. I was entirely against it. I felt that it was murder, first degree, and that I would never have one. I felt like that up until I got pregnant. ...My feelings on abortion were so intense that I always felt that even if I did get pregnant, I would go ahead and have the baby" (quoted in Zimmerman 1977:64). As Watters (1976:180) has noted, women's belief that abortion is morally wrong may dissipate "when the realities of unwanted pregnancy overtake them."

This ambivalence is also reflected by other studies where many women report that they were generally opposed to abortion and did not think of themselves as potential candidates for abortion. When they were faced with the fact of pregnancy, however, they decided that abortion was the best solution, given their particular circumstances (Cameron 1985; Freeman 1978; Gilligan 1982).

Ambivalence about abortion is not surprising. Gilligan (1982) noted that when a woman considers abortion, she contemplates a decision that affects herself and others. As she confronts the reality of an unwanted pregnancy she realizes that there is no choice she can make that will not hurt someone—herself, the child she may deliver, her sexual partner, her other children, or her family as a whole. An abstract principle of morality is not helpful in her situation; she must make her decision within a network of relationships and responsibilities.

Those who view abortion in terms of an abstract moral principle may ignore the social context in which the pregnancy occurs. When considering moral dilemmas—the actuality of conflicting claims—Gilligan stated:

> The essence of moral decision-making is the willingness to accept responsibility for choice.... In our society, women have traditionally been denied choice.... For centuries women's sexuality anchored them in passivity ... where the events of conception and childbirth could be controlled only by a withholding in which their own ... needs were either denied or sacrificed. ... When birth control and abortion provide women with effective means for controlling their own fertility ... moral judgments no longer flow inevitably from their reproductive capacity but become matters of decision over which they have control.... The conflict between self and other thus constitutes the central moral problem for women. (1982:67–69)

Gilligan argues that true morality is the willingness to accept responsibility for the choices one makes. Those opposed to abortion argue that true morality is found in a woman's self-sacrifice, in her renouncement of induced abortion as a possible choice.

## Language, Ideology, and Politics

Culture strongly influences our values and behavior, and language is part of culture. Advocates for change therefore may try to reshape language use. For example, those who perceive the English language as biased in support of male dominance are trying, with some success, to eliminate its sexist features (Philips 1980). Contending abortion partisans are also trying to influence language, as a way of supporting an ideological and political position. Are you pro-choice or pro-life? Are you terminating pregnancies or killing unborn children? Shall we refer to a fetus as a child and to a pregnant woman as a mother? In most instances, language use is unconscious. But where there is controversy and competing terminology, language use is more likely to be deliberate. Abortion partisans are very deliberate in their use of language and are trying to shape the language to support their ideological position and further their political cause.

The media sometimes find it difficult to steer a neutral course between the language shoals built by the partisans. A news headline in the June 14, 1982, issue of the *New York Times* (p. B–10) stated, "Pro-Abortion Group Sets a Major Political Drive." A later critique from the editors, concerned about impartial reporting, reacted: "Such groups consider themselves neither 'pro' nor 'anti'—merely advocates of a woman's ability to decide. We use the neutral phrase 'abortion rights group' " (*Winners & Sinners,* 1982).

Abortion partisans consistently use their preferred terminology to try to shape the language and to reinforce their values. Such language use is part of a public relations effort to propagandize their position and to influence public attitudes. It is also part of a continuing campaign to exert political pressure and to affect public policy on abortion.

During the 1950s and most of the 1960s, when abortion was illegal, those favoring the legalization of abortion were well organized and were gaining momentum. Since 1973, with abortion legal, the tables have been turned and groups opposed to legal abortion have been gaining momentum. They have won a few battles, but the legality of abortion has not been derailed.

One indication of the strength of abortion opponents is the stronger language and stronger symbols they are using. They are pro-*life;* being pro-*choice,* as a symbol, is weaker. They are opposed to the murder of 1.5 million unborn children per year; being for a woman's right to privacy, as a symbol, is weaker. They have *The Silent Scream,* a sonogram film purporting to show an "unborn child" reacting in pain to the abortion knife. The "Silent No More" reaction, by the women's movement, in which women recount their experiences with abortion, as a public relations effort, is weaker.

Gaylor (1979) acknowledges that the anti-abortion forces have succeeded in getting the media to refer to them as "pro-life," a term she describes as ridiculous and inaccurate. She would prefer that the media refer to the "Human Life" amendment as the "Women's Death" amendment, but that has not happened. The conservative, anti-abortion groups have also captured the term "pro-family," and the efforts of Geraldine Ferraro and Walter Mondale to recapture the term during the 1984 presidential elections were not successful. Ann Landers steadfastly remains pro-choice, but she continues to receive (1985) questions about aborted babies being ground into beauty products. Such tales, concocted by some individuals in the anti-abortion movement, make up in drama what they lack in veracity. The anti-abortion rhetoric seems more strident and more powerful.

An example of the effectiveness of the anti-abortion movement in getting the media to adopt pro-life language comes from the pages of the *New York Times*. On June 3 and July 31, 1981, stories referred to Congressional action aimed at barring the use of federal funds to pay for abortions "except when they are necessary to save the life of the mother" or "except for when the mother's life is endangered." A later editorial critique stated: "Is a woman a 'mother' before the birth of her child? Opinions differ, often heatedly. We had best stick to the undisputed expression *woman* or *pregnant woman*" (*Winners & Sinners*, 1981).

Leadership is an influential factor in the popularity of the anti-abortion moral position. Anti-abortion spokespersons such as Ronald Reagan and Jerry Falwell are media experts who spend large amounts of time communicating and selling their beliefs. To this expertise they owe much of their personal popularity as well as the presumed popularity of their beliefs, including their anti-abortion sentiments.

Journalist Ellen Goodman writes perceptively about the media role in the abortion story. The momentum is with the anti-abortion faction partly because of the media's insatiable appetite for newness and change. This has made a woman's unwanted pregnancy old, dull news and the fetus in the womb newsworthy. Goodman says of media morals in creating the current climate: "Most of us in the media are uneasy with this, uneasy providing—even grooming— an emotional battleground of such intensity. But as surely as the pendulum swings, we lean toward the new story, go where the action is, build the momentum" (1985:111).

A similar reason for the forcefulness of the anti-abortion position is that the "death drama" of abortion is on the side of whichever position does not prevail in law. Under restrictive laws the death drama is on the side of the women who die from illegal abortions and, indeed, there were ample pro-abortion demonstrations during the 1960s and early 1970s featuring the shrouded coffin of a dead woman. With permissive laws, the death drama shifts to the anti-abortion camp and coincides with the expert media use of several national figures. Thus far, despite these forceful efforts, the anti-abortion forces have merely been able to erect several barriers that make access to legal abortions somewhat more difficult. Abortion's basic legality endures as a beacon of light to the pro-choice forces and as a shadow of darkness for the pro-life forces.

## Prejudice and Discrimination

Prejudice and discrimination against blacks and the poor are long-standing problems of American society and indeed throughout many parts of the world (Rodman 1965, 1971; Rodman and Trost 1986). As a result, access to social, economic, and political advantages have been hampered for these groups. As with access to medical services generally, those who are young, poor, and members of minority groups do not have equal access to legally induced abortions. Several states do not permit minors to have an abortion unless parents are notified or give their consent; while there are exceptions to this requirement, it can present a formidable barrier to minors whose parents are vehemently opposed to premarital sexual intercourse or to abortion. Except under limited circumstances, the poor have had access to federal funds blocked by the Hyde amendment. And minority group members, with disproportionate numbers who are young and poor, are particularly hard hit by lack of equal access.

Discrimination and unequal access were especially severe when most abortions were illegal. Sarvis and Rodman (1974) summarized the evidence documenting such discrimination against the poor, blacks, and other minority groups. Higher rates of legal abortion were reported for private patients than for public patients and for white patients than for nonwhites. These differences, documented for the years 1952 to 1970, reflect the fact that women who were affluent and white had greater access to hard-to-get legal abortions.

For example, in the state of Georgia, the legal abortion rate for single white women in 1970 was twenty-four times greater than the rate for single black women.

Most of the studies that reported differential abortion rates by social class or race were based on experiences during the 1950s and 1960s. During those years, legal (therapeutic) abortion was generally available only to save the pregnant woman's life, and medical indications for a therapeutic abortion were declining. It therefore became more difficult to obtain a legal abortion. At the same time, however, pressure was mounting to incorporate threats to a pregnant woman's health, including her mental health, as justification for a therapeutic abortion. Most of the liberalized abortion laws passed between 1967 and 1970 included mental health factors as an indication for therapeutic abortion. This led to a great deal of pressure on psychiatrists to provide legal justification for requested abortions.

> The information needed to locate the most liberal hospitals and psychiatrists, the money for psychiatric consultation as well as for the abortion, and the experience needed to deal with a large array of largely white and often hostile medical personnel in order to get approval for an abortion were generally less available to black women and poor women; consequently, the abortion rate differentials between whites and blacks and between private patients and ward patients increased during the 1950s and 1960s. (Sarvis and Rodman 1974:162)

Facing discrimination in access to legal hospital abortions, the poor and black could have turned to illegal abortion. Although good data on illegal abortions are lacking, the existing evidence suggests that affluent and white women also had preferential access to illegal abortions, especially those carried out by physicians. Blacks and the poor turned disproportionately to nonmedical, unskilled abortionists for dangerous and illegal abortions. This led to higher rates of maternal mortality due to abortion. Drawing on several studies, Sarvis and Rodman (1974) reported that the black maternal mortality rate for abortion, between the years 1940 and 1970, ranged from about 2.4 times to 9 times higher than the white rate.

### BLACKS

Discrimination against blacks casts a long shadow across the pages of American history. At times blacks have had difficulty in gaining access to sterilization and abortion, and at times they have faced coercive sterilization and abortion. Such discrimination and oppression have also been visited on poor people generally. In the years before abortion in the United States was legalized, blacks found it difficult to obtain therapeutic abortions in hospitals. Such procedures were reserved for white, well-connected women who could have strings pulled and favors done. Later, when the abortion laws were liberalized in some states, and physicians were empowered to make abortion decisions, forced sterilization was practiced. Some women were presented with a "package deal"—the physician would agree to do the abortion if the woman would agree to be sterilized. Compulsory sterilization was not an isolated occurrence. One survey reported that 53.6 percent of teaching hospitals insisted on sterilization for some of their abortion patients (Eliot et al. 1970). Black women were especially vulnerable to such coercion. These package deals were rationalized as being for the benefit of the patient.

During a 1970 symposium at Wayne State University, the following exchange took place between a black woman student in the audience and a white woman gynecologist on the panel:

> BLACK STUDENT: The real reason that many low-income women and minority group women are refusing to have abortions or other operations is that they are afraid of what will happen to them. I know one woman who died needing an appendix operation, and she was afraid to go for the operation. Women are afraid they will come out sterilized or with parts of their body missing.
>
> WHITE GYNECOLOGIST: We call that superstition.

In heated words, the physician denied any basis for fear while the student claimed she knew of women who were sterilized against their wishes. Mutual respect and understanding were absent in the fiery exchange, which revealed a wide gap between the student and the physician. Women's fears about missing body parts seem rational when we recognize that some hospitals were advocating hysterectomy rather than tubal ligation as the procedure of choice for indigent women requesting sterilization. Sarvis and Rodman (1974) document considerable concern among blacks about compulsory sterilization, as well as about the general question of black genocide. As Weisbord has said, "In response to white racist brutality over the centuries blacks have evolved antennae highly sensitive to potential dangers" (1975:176).

As knowledge about the practice of compulsory sterilization spread, many in the medical profession voiced their strong opposition. Further, once abortion was legalized, women became less vulnerable to physicians who rationalized prejudice and justified coercive medicine under the guise of the patient's best interest. As a result the issues of limited access, coercive treatment, and family planning as black genocide—although they have not disappeared—have receded into the background.

Until recently, black attitudes have been less favorable to abortion than white attitudes. Several reasons help to explain the earlier difference. One is the lower educational, occupational, and income position of blacks, factors that are predictive of less favorable attitudes to abortion. A second is a stronger Southern, rural, and religious influence among blacks, also factors associated with less support for abortion (see Combs and Welch 1982). Another reason, less often discussed, are the different abortion experiences that blacks have had. Before legalization, they had less access to hospital abortions or to skillfully done illegal abortions and they had to rely on self-induced abortions and illegal abortions by unskilled practitioners. This contributed to knowledge about the dangers of abortion and had a negative influence on black attitudes.

In studying unmarried pregnant black girls, Prudence Rains found that "whenever abortion was mentioned spontaneously or in answer to a question of mine, girls spoke only in terms of self-induced abortions and the dangers involved" (1971:37). These more negative attitudes by blacks persisted through the early 1980s. In 1983, for example, the Gallup Poll put the following question to a national sample: "The U.S. Supreme Court has ruled that a woman may go to a doctor to end her pregnancy at any time during the first three months of pregnancy. Do you favor or oppose this ruling?" Among whites, 52 percent were in favor, 42 percent were opposed, and 6 percent had no opinion. Among nonwhites, 44 percent were in favor, 45 percent were opposed, and 11 percent had no opinion. In 1986, however, blacks had more favorable attitudes than whites. Asked the same question, 44 percent of whites were in favor, 45 percent were opposed, and 11 percent had no opinion. Among blacks, 53 percent were in favor, 41 percent were opposed, and 6 percent had no opinion.

Given the earlier, less favorable attitudes to abortion, one would expect blacks to make less use of abortion than whites. While this was the case before abortion was legalized, due to a lack of access to abortion by blacks, the figures changed rather quickly once abortion was legalized. With access to safe, legal abortions, blacks took advantage of the availability of services previously denied them. Changes in states that liberalized their abortions laws before the 1973 U.S. Supreme Court decisions were dramatic: in both California and New York, for example, abortion ratios moved very quickly from being much lower than white ratios to being much higher. Black women continue to face proportionately more unintended pregnancies than white women, and they continue to make proportionately more use of abortion than white women. In 1981, based on reported data from thirty-four states, black (and other) women had approximately 240,000 abortions and white women approximately 580,000. The abortion ratio (number of legal abortions per 1,000 live births) was 549 for black women and 329 for white women (CDC 1985; Hani K. Atrash, personal communication, May 30, 1986).

Compared to the recent past, black women are currently exercising more reproductive control by using legally induced abortions. As a result, earlier cries that family planning was black genocide have been drowned by cries to maintain access to contraceptive and abortion services. Significantly, in Congressional voting on the Hyde amendment (to bar the use of federally funded abortions for poor women), members from districts with a higher proportion of nonwhites were more likely to vote against the amendment (Schneider and Vinovskis 1980). In short, the votes of Congressional representatives more closely reflected the abortion behavior of their constituents than their abortion attitudes.

SOCIAL CLASS

Since blacks are disproportionately poor and of lower educational and occupational status, the discrimination faced by the poor parallels the discrimination faced by blacks. Thus, poor women had less access to abortion before legalization and were more subject to coercive medical treatment during the years of state reform and repeal laws. Private hospitals during the 1950s and 1960s, for example, carried out many more legal abortions than public hospitals. In New York, between 1960 and 1962, the abortion rate (per 1,000 live births) was 3.9 at private hospitals and 0.1 at municipal hospitals, a rate that was thirty-nine times greater at private hospitals. As Theodore Irwin (1970) pointed out, surveys indicated that four out of five therapeutic abortions were done on private patients, those who were affluent and white. When abortion was illegal under virtually all circumstances, it was extremely difficult to get a legal, therapeutic abortion. Without question, among women who sought a therapeutic abortion, higher social class status was a distinct advantage.

Poor women also faced more coercive and less considerate medical care. For example, some physicians once advocated hysterectomy as the procedure of choice for poor women. Major hospitals in California, Colorado, Kentucky, and Massachusetts justified hysterectomy for resident training (Kozol 1973). Van Nagell and Roddick offered this justification: poor women are "most susceptible to the future development of benign and malignant uterine disease and ... probably will not return for adequate postoperative follow-up" (1971:70). This is similar to removing a patient's finger now because he may get it infected later and not come in to have it treated.

From the time that abortion was legalized in 1973, anti-abortion groups have chipped away at its accessibility. Expressing outrage that federal tax funds were supporting abortion, these groups fought to end federal support. One effort that eventually proved successful was the attempt to bar the use of federal funds for abortion in the Medicaid program. Since that program enables states to provide medical services for medically indigent women, the attack on Medicaid support for abortion provides an illuminating sidelight on the treatment of the poor. Initially, in 1977, federal Medicaid funding was eliminated for abortions that were not "medically necessary"; subsequently, in 1980, the elimination of federal Medicaid funding for all abortions was upheld by the U.S. Supreme Court in *Harris v. McRae*. These cases were discussed in chapter 7.

The moral and political clash over Medicaid-funded abortions has ridden roughshod over poor women. As Justice William Brennan, Jr. said in his 1977 dissent, the Court showed "distressing insensitivity to the plight of impoverished pregnant women." And Justice Harry A. Blackmun, in his dissent, found the majority opinion—telling the "indigent and financially helpless" woman to "go elsewhere for her abortion"—"almost reminiscent of 'let them eat cake.' "

The reactions to the U.S. Supreme Court decision in 1980 were equally pointed and poignant. Congressman Hyde, who sponsored the amendment that was upheld by the Court, was "exultant, delighted, and pleased and happy." Eleanor Smeal, president of the National Organization for Women (NOW), began her letter to NOW members with: "Shock. Disbelief. Anger. Outrage. Fear." And once again, the dissenting opinions of the justices emphasized the plight of poor women. Justice Brennan, in his dissent in *McRae*, stated that the Hyde amendment was a "transparent attempt" to impose the majority's view of what was morally desirable:

> Worse yet, the Hyde Amendment does not foist that majoritarian viewpoint with equal measure upon everyone in our Nation, rich and poor alike; rather, it imposes that viewpoint only upon that segment of our society which because of its position of political powerlessness, is least able to defend its privacy rights from the encroachment of state-mandated morality. . . . When elected leaders cower before public pressure, this Court, more than ever, must not shirk its duty to enforce the Constitution for the benefit of the poor and powerless.

And Justice Marshall, in his *McRae* dissent, referred to the denial of Medicaid payments for medically necessary abortions as "a form of discrimination repugnant to the equal protection of the laws guaranteed by the Constitution."

The hope of anti-abortion groups and the fear of pro-choice groups that restrictions of federal Medicaid funding for abortion would greatly reduce the number of abortions by poor women have not been borne out. One estimate, for a thirty-month period between 1977 and 1980, is that 94 percent of women eligible for Medicaid who would otherwise have obtained a legally induced abortion did in fact do so despite federal restrictions (Cates 1981). About one-third of the abortions were financed by the private rather than the public sector; in many cases poor women used their own meager resources to pay for the abortion. In two-thirds of the cases, state funds paid for the abortion, either because of a voluntary state program or because of a court order. The early results were therefore not devastating, but they were not entirely benign. About 5 percent of the women who desired an abortion were unable to get one and bore a child; other estimates are much higher (see Henshaw and Wallisch 1984). About 1 percent turned to an illegal abortion. Many who did get an abortion were delayed in the process, with an increased risk to their health (Henshaw and Wallisch 1984). In short, the restrictions increased the obstacles already faced by poor women in obtaining an abortion, but the increase was not dramatic. Poor women continue to face prejudice and discrimination in medical and reproductive health institutions and they also receive poorer service as a result of their limited resources (see Petchesky 1984, 1985).

# CHAPTER 9

# WHERE DO WE GO
# FROM HERE?

O PPOSING POSITIONS ON THE ABORTION QUESTION are so sharply different and so strongly held that it is difficult to develop a satisfactory abortion policy. The abortion laws in many countries represent an attempt at compromise between opposing positions, but the compromises do not please the partisans on either side of the abortion debate. The controversy therefore continues in the media, in the legislatures, in the courts, in the streets, and sometimes in the abortion clinics.

Although we often refer to pro-choice and pro-life positions as though they are monolithic, the situation is far more complex. Some people, for example, want to prohibit abortion except when the woman's life is threatened by the pregnancy. Some also accept one or more other justifications for a legal abortion—e.g., threats to the woman's physical or mental health, a pregnancy resulting from rape or incest, the likelihood of fetal deformity, and the woman's social and economic circumstances. Some want to accept abortion without the requirement of justifications, and hence would like to see the repeal of all laws pertaining to abortion (see Callahan 1977).

Partisans sometimes feel so strongly about their positions that communication is impossible because they are on completely different wavelengths. Research and clinical findings are often shaped to conform to preconceived beliefs. One psychiatrist assures us that guilt never accompanies abortion and another that it always does (Sarvis and Rodman 1974:106). The dark and choppy waters surrounding the abortion question make for difficult sailing. Shaping abortion policy is difficult and seems endlessly controversial. In recent years, however, a few glimmers of light have appeared. One hope for calmer waters, as this chapter will make clear, stems from several developments that lead toward greater acceptance of early abortion and lesser acceptance of late abortion. Another hope on the horizon is the development of new contraceptive and abortifacient drugs.

## Underlying Moral Differences

The major opposing groups in the abortion controversy have adopted terms that aptly summarize their position and the irresolvable essence of their moral differences. One side is pro-choice. Its cohorts insist they are not pro-abortion. They often make it clear that they are against abortion and would like to reduce the number of abortions through improved sex education and family planning programs. But since they recognize that there will still be unwanted pregnancies, they accept abortion as a last resort, and they deplore any attempt to eliminate that choice from a pregnant woman.

The other side is pro-life. Its supporters recognize the difficulty of the woman with an unwanted pregnancy. Although they are ambivalent in their support of improved sex education and family planning programs, they want to prevent unwanted pregnancies or to help women with unwanted pregnancies. But they are not prepared to accept abortion because they believe that it is the killing of human life. It is only when the pregnant woman's life is endangered that they may be willing to accept abortion.

Although the above attempt to summarize opposing positions is oversimplified, it is a reasonable account of the principal arguments. The pro-choice groups decry the enlarged pictures of human fetuses that pro-lifers sometimes show. And the pro-life groups understandably pay less attention to the trials and tribulations of women with unwanted pregnancies, and decry the pictures of women who have died at the hands of illegal abortionists.

In the United States, until the early 1970s, restrictive abortion laws forced many woman into illegal abortion and its attendant

Where Do We Go From Here?159

dangers. As a result, there were dramatic appeals to change the laws, including exaggerated estimates of the number of illegal abortions and deaths resulting from them. This led to revised laws that made abortion legal, at least under some conditions.

Currently, the legal status of abortion has made possible a growing number of abortions and leads to occasional cases of an aborted fetus that lives for a while and that may have been viable (Tunkel 1979). As a result, there are now dramatic appeals to restrict abortions, including exaggerated accounts of the human characteristics of the embryo and fetus and exaggerated estimates of the number of late abortions.

## Law and Private Morality

By separating private morality from the law it becomes possible to accommodate differing moral positions and to respect (or at the least not to prosecute those who adhere to) these positions. The Wolfenden Report of 1957, which dealt with homosexuality in Britain, strongly urged the separation of law and private morality: "There must remain a realm of private morality and immorality which is . . . not the law's business" (Wolfenden Report 1957). This argument, of ancient vintage, produced major changes in British law in 1967, including a liberalization of the abortion law. The argument was also influential in bringing about passage of the revised Canadian abortion law in 1969. Although the percentage of Roman Catholics in Canada is much higher than in the United States, the voice of the Catholic hierarchy in Canada has been muted and has better accepted the separation of law and private morality (de Valk 1974).

If we could clearly and consensually distinguish universal values from group-specific values, or public morality from private morality, we might have a route toward a resolution of the abortion controversy. Thus, the 1957 Wolfenden Report accepted the idea that homosexuality was in the domain of private rather than public morality. Similar ideas in many countries influenced the liberalization of laws on birth control and divorce, and in these areas the Roman Catholic Church has accepted the distinction between moral law and civil law (de Valk 1974:29–32). There has been a general movement in the Western world to sever the tie between traditional religious morality and the law on sexual behavior. As a result we commonly hear that "the state has no business in the bedrooms of the nation" (Pierre E. Trudeau, quoted in de Valk 1974:57), and there is a growing—but certainly not universal—acceptance of sexual behavior as private morality.

On abortion, however, it is much more difficult to get moral consensus. The Roman Catholic hierarchy is not prepared to deal with abortion in the same way that it deals with birth control and divorce. In most developed nations, birth control and divorce clearly are in the realm of private morality, but there is no such moral consensus on abortion. This is due to a fundamental difference. For pro-life partisans, human life is at stake when we deal with abortion. Thus a pro-choice statement that abortion reduces maternal mortality or morbidity, or reduces the suffering of unwanted children, has a hollow sound when it strikes against the idea that each abortion represents the killing of an innocent human life. The abortion controversy therefore persists, and the separation of law and private morality does not seem to be a route that is available to resolve the controversy.

## Attempted Compromises

Given the absolute position that abortion is the killing of a human being and the absolute position that a woman has a right to control her own body and her own childbearing, there can be no compromise and no debate—only opposing partisans who talk past each other. But although the moral debate is irresolvable, the legal and judicial worlds have had to make policy decisions about abortion.

Some suggest that the best way out of the legal and moral difficulty is to write no law regarding abortion, and to deal with it like any other medical procedure. In that way no legal justifications (such as health or eugenic indications) that might be objectionable to Roman Catholics or others are specifically acknowledged. This was the American situation prior to the mid-nineteenth century.

Such a solution is, of course, tantamount to placing abortion in the realm of private morality, and separating private morality from the law. It effectively treats abortion in a permissive fashion, without any need for special justifications or procedures. In consequence, this approach is not acceptable to pro-life partisans and it does not resolve the legal and moral controversy.

Legislatures and courts have used two kinds of compromises in deciding difficult abortion questions: (a) permitting abortion only for certain reasons and forbidding all other abortions; (b) permitting abortions up to a certain gestation time and forbidding later abortions. We shall briefly discuss each of these compromise solutions, and indicate how they point the way toward future directions in abortion policy.

## Justifications for Abortion

Under this compromise, abortion is forbidden unless there are certain reasons or justifications for it. The moral principle that underlies this compromise is that the embryo and fetus have rights, but not the right to life in the same sense that a human being has. As a result, abortion is not legally available unless it can be justified. One widely accepted justification is the preservation of the pregnant woman's life. Other justifications are illustrated by the British law, passed in 1967: justifications for abortion include danger to the woman's life or health, pregnancy due to criminal assault, a threat of fetal deformity, and socioeconomic reasons. According to proposals made by the American Law Institute (1962:189–190) justifications include danger to the woman's physical or mental health, the threat of severe fetal deformity, and pregnancy due to rape, incest, or other felonious intercourse. Several states in the United States adopted some of these legal justifications between 1967 and 1970, and an account of these developments is presented in the appendix. The law in Canada, passed in 1969, is a good example of the "justifications" compromise. It bans abortion unless justified on the grounds of protecting the woman's life or health. There is no time limit in the gestation period after which abortion is forbidden, and thus the Canadian law is a pure case of a "justifications" approach.

## Gestation Time

Another compromise is to permit abortion up to a particular time in the gestation process and to forbid abortions after that time. The principle that underlies this compromise is that the embryo and fetus represent developing human life. Up to a certain point the embryo or fetus is judged not to be sufficiently developed to warrant protection, and no justification for abortion is needed. Beyond that point, however, the embryo or fetus is judged to have developed sufficiently to be worthy of protection, and abortions are not permitted after that time (except to save the pregnant woman's life). Alternatively, a justifications approach may be applied during a time period between permissive early abortion and prohibited late abortion.

The process of biological development, from the zygote at conception to the baby at birth, is conceptualized and subdivided in many ways. Distinctions are made by days or weeks of gestation, by months or trimesters, or by using conception, implantation, quickening, viability, and birth as anchoring points. One can refer to the development of various organs or to the development of the cerebral cortex as the critical processes.

There is no absolutely clear point in the development process at which we can agree that biological development has reached the point where the fetus should be protected from an abortion. Legal policies on abortion are therefore somewhat arbitrary and often contentious. Some insist that the uncertainty calls for a moral choice in favor of human life, with abortion prohibited from the earliest possible time in the gestation period. Others insist that the moral imperative of a woman's right to make decisions about reproduction and childbearing call for a policy that permits legal abortion until the latest possible time in the gestation period. The earliest possible time in the gestation period is fertilization and the latest possible time is birth, and there are opposing partisans in the abortion debate who have adopted these radically different points as the cornerstone of their policy. Research findings in medicine, however, and new technological developments, are narrowing the range of policy choices about abortion.

## Medical Advances

Advances in medical technology have been increasing the survival rate of premature infants of low birth weight. These techniques, used before and during labor, and after delivery (Beard, 1981; Campbell 1985), are having an impact on medical and ethical thinking about fetal viability. Neonatal intensive care units, with respirators and drug treatment, have lowered the age of viability to about 24 weeks, and infants of even lower gestational age* have a chance of surviving with aggressive medical intervention. These advances have changed the possibilities for fetal viability and have become part of the debate on abortion law and policy. From the 1960s to the 1980s the point of viability decreased from about 28 weeks to about 24 weeks gestational age (Stubblefield 1985). More than 50 percent of the premature infants at these gestational ages are able to survive with state-of-the-art medical care.

The neurological outcome for these infants is not always favorable; many premature infants kept alive through aggressive treatment survive with major handicaps such as mental retardation or cerebral palsy. But the outcome is often positive, with normal functioning or only minor handicaps. Strong (1983) summarizes several reports on infants weighing 500 to 1,000 grams at birth. The reports range from approximately 5 to 30 percent with a normal neurological outcome among infants who survive, and they range from 7 to 30 percent who survive with a major handicap. Aggressive medical treatment is expensive and the outcome for very low birth weight and very low gestational age infants is not very good. These medical advances therefore raise difficult ethical and social policy questions about whether to pursue aggressive care, when to do so, and for how long (Milligan, Shennan, and Hoskins 1984).

---

\* In this chapter, we use gestational age and weeks of gestation to refer to the time since the last menstrual period (LMP) This is in accord with conventional use—for example, Stubblefield (1985:161) and Centers for Disease Control (1985:35)

### Legal Considerations

Medical advances lowering the threshold of fetal viability have implications for the legal situation in the United States. The U.S. Supreme Court, in its *Roe v. Wade* decision, refers to the developing fetus and its potential life; viability is the critical point at which a state may prohibit abortion (unless the woman's life or health is threatened). Medical advances in caring for premature infants have influenced many hospitals and physicians to eschew late abortions. The occasional birth of a live infant resulting from a late abortion, and criminal charges brought against a few physicians for contributing to the subsequent death of the infant, have also made late abortions more difficult to obtain. Approximately half of all abortions take place during the first 8 weeks of gestation (i.e., 8 weeks since the last menstrual period), and approximately 85 to 90 percent during the first 12 weeks LMP. Only about 1 percent take place at 21 weeks or later (CDC 1985).

Amniocentesis, to determine numerous fetal diseases, cannot be carried out until the sixteenth week of gestation. Amniotic fluid is withdrawn and fetal cells are cultured, providing a prenatal diagnosis by the eighteenth to twentieth week. If the threshold of fetal viability were lowered to 18 or 20 weeks, many abortions based on information from amniocentesis would be denied. If the threshold were lowered further, a larger number of abortions would be denied. Many medical researchers, however, are not hopeful about the prospects for lowering the threshold of viability below 22 to 23 weeks, unless some sort of artificial womb were developed. Medical developments in neonatal care therefore do not rule out legal abortions performed up to about 21 weeks' gestation. Moreover, recent advances in prenatal testing are making it possible to diagnose fetal abnormalities much earlier in pregnancy.

Justice O'Connor's dissenting opinion in *Akron* (1983) has drawn much attention. She questions the reliance on "stages" of pregnancy that was adopted in *Roe* and believes that the trimester approach "cannot be supported as a legitimate or useful framework for accommodating the woman's right and the State's interests." This is because of changing medical technology and because "the Roe framework is inherently tied to the state of medical technology that exists whenever particular litigation ensues." O'Connor's *Akron* dissent, however, is more fundamental than the problem posed by advancing medical technology:

> In *Roe,* the Court held that although the State had an important and legitimate interest in protecting potential life, that interest could not become compelling until the point at which the fetus was viable. The difficulty with this analysis is clear: *potential* life is no less potential in the first weeks of pregnancy than it is at viability or afterward. At any stage in pregnancy, there is the potential for human life. . . . Accordingly, I believe that the State's interest in protecting potential human life exists throughout the pregnancy.

Justice O'Connor's dissent in *Akron* has increased speculation that *Roe* will eventually be overturned. However, we should not conclude that O'Connor wants to overturn *Roe.* True, she does stress the existence of potential life throughout the pregnancy and she states that medical science is pushing the point of viability toward conception. When she says that the *Roe* framework "is clearly on a collision course with itself," she is referring to a collision between a principle that limits states' rights to regulate abortion and a principle that extends states' rights. O'Connor states the first principle in her *Akron* dissent. "As the medical risks of various abortion procedures decrease, the point at which the State may regulate for reasons of maternal health is moved further forward to actual childbirth." The second principle—prohibiting abortion from the time of fetal viability—pushes the potential ban on abortion "further back toward conception." The first principle has curtailed state regulations for reasons of maternal health through the sixteenth week of gestation. The second principle has extended prohibitions due to fetal viability to 21–23 weeks.

The O'Connor collision is not as serious as it has at times been portrayed. First, there is still a good deal of space between 16 and 21 weeks. Second, it is likely that one principle will take precedence over the other, thereby avoiding a collision. Will the first principle or the second principle take precedence?

### First Solution

One possible solution to the abortion question, a solution that may eventually dampen the controversy, will be the easy acceptance of early abortions and the prohibition of late abortions. The outlines of such a solution are already visible in many countries throughout the world. Although there is still much controversy in the United States about induced abortion at any stage of pregnancy, most abortions take place early, and it is now virtually impossible to obtain an abortion during the last trimester of pregnancy or even during the latter part of the second trimester.

The solution we are predicting assumes that most nations will permit abortion during the early weeks of gestation without a need to justify the abortion. It also assumes that abortions will be forbidden or will be difficult to obtain later on during pregnancy. Evidence of such developments can be found in many nations. For example, Czechoslovakia, Denmark, and Hungary have permissive abortion policies during the first 12 weeks of gestation, with more stringent requirements afterwards. The dividing line is 18 weeks in Sweden, 90 days in Italy, and 10 weeks in France (Rodman and Trost 1986).

In Canada, even early abortions must be justified, and each abortion must be approved by a hospital abortion committee. This procedure, however, is not working well (Badgley Report 1977). As Rodman says:

> The members of therapeutic abortion committees do not see the woman whose abortion is at issue; they rely strictly upon the written record. Thus, depending upon the willingness of the woman's physician to tailor the record to the justifications permitted by law, and the willingness of the therapeutic abortion committee to interpret the law broadly, the woman may or may not be approved for an abortion. As a result of this bureaucratic procedure, there are great inequities in how the law is implemented from province to province, from locality to locality, and from hospital to hospital. (1981:234)

These procedures contribute to very substantial delays in obtaining an abortion in Canada, adding to the risk of an abortion. They are not likely to survive for much longer. Their survival thus far has been aided by physicians who circumvent the legal requirements for abortion (Badgley Report 1977; Rodman 1981).

Another reason for moving away from a justifications approach is found in the U.S. experience under reform laws, during the 1960s and early 1970s (see appendix). Making judgments about whether an abortion is legally justified on medical or psychiatric grounds is subjective and difficult. Physicians often make these judgments based on their ideological beliefs. They may grant permission for otherwise illegal acts or withhold permission for legal acts based on deeply held values rather than on legal considerations. Under such circumstances, the medical role is uncomfortable; some physicians become the mechanism for circumventing restrictive laws. It is demeaning to patients and to physicians to go through the charade of paying lip service to the law while circumventing it.

Along with developments in a more permissive direction for early abortions, there are developments toward greater restriction for later abortions. Technological advances making it possible to sustain a fetus outside the mother's body at earlier gestational ages are contributing toward these restrictions. Further, improvements in contraceptive technology and in the delivery of contraceptive information and services will very likely reduce the number of unwanted pregnancies and the demand for abortion. Once a monthly or a post-coital pill is developed, the demand for induced abortion as presently practiced will decrease still further. Finally, advances in embryology and fetology, including advances in diagnosing and treating fetal disease, will increase the pressure for early abortion and against later abortion.

Whether through changes in law or in medical practice, abortion policy is heading toward our predicted "first solution": easy-to-get early abortions, hard-to-get late abortions. The dividing line between early and late abortion, of course, is critical. Because of the present inability of prenatal testing to diagnose many fetal abnormalities until about the eighteenth to twentieth week of gestation, there are reasoned suggestions to draw the line at about 20 or 21 weeks.

> Not only would such a voluntary limit respond to the sense of repugnance generated by late abortions, it would also take account of the growing ability of medicine to push the point of viability back below 24 weeks. That latter point is not trivial. As many commentators have noted, any significant change in the time of viability could seriously challenge an important aspect of the *Roe v. Wade* decision. (Callahan 1985:163)

There are also reasoned suggestions to sever the tie between fetal viability and a woman's right to an abortion. "We need to refocus the right to abortion as one not defined by the fetus or by technological advances, but rather one that is tied to women's constitutional right to privacy, autonomy and bodily integrity" (Benshoof 1985:163). In many countries, however, the direction of abortion policy is toward finding a compromise between a woman's right to an abortion and the state's right to provide some degree of protection to the developing fetus.

New prenatal techniques are making it possible to diagnose fetal abnormalities much earlier than heretofore. This will relieve some of the pressure that is generated by tying the legality of abortion to fetal viability. One technique, chorionic villus sampling, makes diagnosis possible by 9 or 10 weeks' gestational age. A catheter, guided by ultrasound, is inserted into the uterus through the cervix, and it aspirates a small amount of the tissue surrounding the fetus. Many medical centers are undertaking clinical trials with the technique, comparing its accuracy and safety with amniocentesis. Initial reports suggest that the technique is more likely to lead to spontaneous abortion than is the case with amniocentesis, but that complication rates decrease with physicians' experience (Hogge, Schonberg, and Golbus 1986; Elias et al. 1986). If the risks are eventually shown to be low, chorionic villus sampling may replace amniocentesis as the diagnostic procedure of choice (see McGovern, Goldberg, and Desnick 1986). Such a development would greatly reduce the need for late abortions in cases of fetal abnormality.

We predict that the dividing line between early and late abortion will eventually turn out to be approximately 12 weeks. Induced abortion prior to that time will be readily accepted by a very large majority of the public; after that time, abortion will be severely restricted, and perhaps legally available only to preserve the pregnant woman's health or life.

### Second Solution

A second possible solution to the abortion controversy will stem from the development of new contraceptive technology. New drugs, still under investigation, offer promise of a once-a-month pill or of a post-coital pill. Like menstrual extraction and IUDs, these new drugs would offer protection before it can be determined whether the woman is pregnant. They hold out the promise of menstrual regulation or of abortifacient action in the first few days of pregnancy, thus fitting neatly into the movement toward early abortion. These drugs, taken once a month, or taken by the woman after sexual intercourse, could become the preferred method of the future. They would be simple, safe, and effective; they would not require continuous use; they would not interfere with the act of coitus; and they would be available for the woman to use at her own convenience. Unfortunately, such drugs are still experimental. But current research efforts suggest that such an ideal contraceptive, or at least improved contraceptives, will be available for widespread use by the first decade of the twenty-first century.

One morning-after pill, currently available for use in England and Germany, indicates the possibilities for the future. The pill, developed by A. Albert Yuzpe of the University of Western Ontario, contains norgestrel and ethinyl estradiol. Four pills are taken over a 12-hour period, and treatment must begin within 72 hours after intercourse (Johnson 1985). The method apparently works by interfering with the implantation of the fertilized ovum. Because of short-term side effects, such as vomiting and nausea, and the possibility of long-term side effects, it is not used on a regular basis. It is recommended for emergencies—for example, if a hole is found in a diaphragm or condom, if withdrawal is mistimed, or under other circumstances that lead to an unprotected act of sexual intercourse. In addition to its use in England and Germany, some use is also made of the method in other European countries. In the United States it is used as a treatment for rape and in some pilot projects at college health centers. This postcoital pill is not the ideal contraceptive of the future and it is not the solution to the abortion controversy, but it is a harbinger of drugs yet to come.

One drug that offers promise for the future, known as RU 486, was developed by scientists at Roussel Uclaf, a pharmaceutical company in Paris. It inhibits the action of progesterone in the uterus, thus interfering with implantation and contributing toward the onset of menstruation. An account of the development of this drug is provided by Spitz and Bardin (1985). Initial research suggests that the drug is effective in inducing menses even after implantation has occurred. Several organizations are carrying out research in France, Sweden, the United States, and other countries to determine the most effective method of treatment. One possibility being explored is a once-a-month pill that would induce or assure menses, but the optimal dose and timing has not yet been determined. As Spitz and Bardin (1985:261) say, "RU 486 is still in early clinical trials. Although the results are promising, a once-a-month contraceptive pill using RU 486 is still far from reality. Many problems remain to be resolved." Among other things, the seriousness of side effects must be carefully evaluated. Whether RU 486 actually turns out to be an ideal or useful monthly pill remains to be seen. But it is an example of a new type of drug that will ultimately have major implications for contraceptive and abortion practice and policy.

One result of the widespread use of such a drug, with either contraceptive action preventing fertilization or with contragestive action during the first few days after fertilization, could be a substantial reduction in the fiery controversy engendered by the abortion debate.

## Conclusion

Abortion policy has been plagued by rancorous controversy. The controversy did not end during 1966 to 1973, when various states enacted reform and repeal laws (see appendix). Nor did the controversy end with the U.S. Supreme Court's *Roe* decision of 1973. Rather, with each major change, the controversy increased. Partisans who lost one battle sought other areas in which to press their fight. Thus, after *Roe*, anti-abortion advocates chipped away at various programs and policies in an effort to block access to abortion. Attempts to pass a federal anti-abortion statute or constitutional amendment failed. Efforts to end the use of public funds to subsidize abortions for medically indigent patients were successful at the federal level and showed considerable success at the state level. The battles continue, with much intensity, and with new efforts to sway public opinion and legislators' votes. Thus we have bombings of abortion clinics and vigils to protect them. We have local referenda on abortion. We have a variety of media and publicity campaigns.

Hopes and fears about what may happen are at an all-time high. When it comes to abortion policy, one person's solution is another person's problem. We are going to see new weapons in the abortion war and new arenas in which battles are fought.

In the face of rising tension and controversy, how can one predict that peace will eventually settle on the land? The "definitive" *Roe* decision did not end the war. How can we be so sanguine as to believe that the end is now in sight?

The answer, we believe, can be seen in developments already taking place. One single event will not end the war; rather, a series of developments will gradually quell the intensity of the controversy. Intense debates about alcohol and contraception have diminished, with only pockets of resistance to a public policy that permits the sale of alcohol and contraceptives and the delivery of contraceptive services. We predict that abortion will eventually share the same fate.

In sum, we predict that ultimately U.S. policy will permit early abortions and prohibit late abortions, and that the intensity of the abortion controversy will subside by the first decade of the twenty-first century. It is difficult to predict what the dividing line may be between early and late abortion, and we may find that the dividing line (in medical practice if not also in law) changes over time. Our prediction is that, ultimately, early abortions up to approximately 12 weeks' gestation will be readily available without the need for justification. Beyond that time, abortions would be legally available only when continuing the pregnancy threatens the pregnant woman's life or health, or perhaps also for severe problems of fetal development. This policy would confirm the reasoning of *Roe v. Wade* and it would acknowledge and anticipate medical advances by changing the dividing line between readily available abortions and hard to get abortions from approximately 21 weeks gestational age to 12 weeks.

We also predict (as do many others) that new contraceptive or contragestive drugs will substantially decrease the number of un-intended pregnancies and the need for surgical abortion. Moreover, medical advances will make it possible to diagnose many fetal ab-normalities earlier. These developments fit neatly into the movement toward early abortions. With the development of a once-a-month or morning-after pill, women will be able to regulate their menstrual cycle without knowledge of whether a pregnancy has occurred.

Perhaps we need to emphasize that we are making a prediction about the direction in which abortion policy is heading; we are not making a policy recommendation. We are not saying that 12 weeks' gestation is the ideal dividing line between early and late abortions. Rather, based on medical advances and legal developments, we predict that the eventual dividing line in the United States will be approximately 12 weeks' gestation. Although such a resolution may not appear satisfactory from the current perspective of either pro-choice or pro-life groups, we think that by the first decade of the twenty-first century it will be accepted as reasonable and relatively noncontroversial public policy.

# A HISTORICAL TALE?

THE HISTORY OF THE ABORTION LAWS in the United States ends with a question mark. If anti-abortion forces are successful in implementing more restrictive laws and practices, then the historical tale may be a scenario for the future. One of the goals of the anti-abortion movement is to return abortion policy to the states. Should that happen, history may repeat itself. We may once again see some states with original (restrictive) laws, some with reform laws, and some with repeal laws. This appendix provides a historical view of the original laws, reform laws, and repeal laws and some of the associated medical practices.

## The Original Laws

"Original" laws refer to the first state statutes passed along with any revisions up to 1966, since many abortion statutes went through one or several revisions over the years. But the legislative changes that occurred between 1967 and 1970 were more dramatic than the changes in the prior one hundred years and "original" has therefore become synonymous with "restrictive." Indeed, a glance at Part A of table A.1 shows that, with little variation, the original U.S. abortion laws strictly forbade abortion except for one "therapeutic" exception. The typical wording of this exception, from the Michigan statute, is: "unless the same abortion shall have been necessary to preserve the life of such woman." Original statutes not following this pattern were few: Alabama, the District of Columbia, and

Oregon included life and health; Colorado and New Mexico contained life and serious or permanent bodily injury; the Maryland statute's only exception was "that no other method will secure the safety of the mother"; and the Massachusetts, New Jersey, and Pennsylvania laws gave no therapeutic exception.

In addition to stating a therapeutic exception which provided a justifiable reason for abortion, some of these statutes also set certain conditions or procedural requirements to regulate abortion. Although consultation requirements and procedural requirements regarding who performs abortions appeared in only a few of the original laws, they came to play a key role in the administration of the original laws and in the post-1966 legislation. Eleven of the pre-1966 statutes specified that a physician or surgeon do the operation, and sixteen states required that "prior consultation with one or more physicians is necessary before a claim of justification can be made" (George 1967:7, 9).

Harper (1958) pointed out variations on who had the burden of proof in abortion cases, the state or the defendant, but only a few statutes were specific on this point. Either the state assumed the burden of "proving non-compliance with law beyond a reasonable doubt" or the doctor-defendant had to establish the medical necessity of the abortion (George 1972). When the statutes were silent on this matter, it became a question of judicial interpretation, and George (1972) found that the courts most often placed the burden "on the state to plead and prove the want of medical justification, provided the defendant is shown to be a licensed medical practitioner." These rulings in favor of physicians help to explain why no prosecutions resulted even though physicians wrote and talked about hospital-performed abortions that did not comply with the law. As George said: "If the prosecutor has to attack the medical judgment of a doctor, particularly one who performs an abortion in a hospital or public clinic under the supervision of his peers on a special committee, and sustain that attack in court subject to a burden of proving non-compliance with law beyond a reasonable doubt, it is unlikely that he will proceed at all" (1972:733).

A few of the original statutes held the woman guilty of a crime if she aborted herself or submitted to an abortion, and at least one state, Vermont, in considering new abortion legislation in 1972, debated a provision for punishing the woman who aborts herself (George 1967; Means 1968; *Burlington Free Press,* February 2, 1972). George discussed the legal effect of these provisions:

> ...the fact that the woman is deemed to have committed a criminal act means that the woman may claim privilege against self-incrimination when she is summoned to testify for the state. However, because of the importance, in many instances, of the woman's testimony in establishing the abortionist's guilt, ... immunity against prosecution is conferred upon the woman when she testifies for the state. This brings the matter around full circle to about where it would be if the woman were not considered a criminal in the first place. (1967:13–14)

Although these provisions to punish the woman led to a rather ridiculous legal situation, they symbolically fulfilled the need of some to punish the aborting woman for her moral transgression against society.

Abortion can also be regulated by what George called "administrative sanctions." This refers to the control of licensed medical personnel and hospitals through licensing statutes. George found that performance of or participation in a "criminal" or "unlawful" abortion constituted grounds for license revocation in most states (1967:17–18). Even where no statutory provision existed for revocation of license, "there is statutory authorization for revocation based on conviction of a felony or unprofessional conduct in general" and "since abortion has been declared a form of unprofessional conduct, it is clear that there is no state in which a proven abortionist can continue to practice without his license being subject to revocation" (1967:18). Although the loss of license for performing criminal abortions was a relatively rare occurrence, the fear inspired up until 1973 by labeling the practice of unlawful abortion as unprofessional conduct should not be underestimated.

One of the reasons for the small number of license revocations due to abortion stemmed from a liberalization in medical thinking that accompanied the growing gap between the law and medical practice. Although the original abortion laws were restrictive, they came to be administered liberally by some members of the medical profession.

A study published in 1959 illustrates the variable administration of restrictive laws. Packer and Gampbell investigated "medical

## Table A.1.
### Abortion Laws in the United States (January 1, 1973)

| | Ala. | Ask. | Ariz. | Ark. | Cal. | Colo. | Conn. | Del. | D.C. | Fla. | Ga. | Ha. | Id. | Ill. | Ind. | Iowa | Kan. | Ky. | La. | Me. | Md. | Mass. | Mich. | Minn. | Miss. |
|---|---|---|---|---|---|---|---|---|---|---|---|---|---|---|---|---|---|---|---|---|---|---|---|---|---|
| | 1970 | | | 1969 | 1967 | 1967 | 1972 | 1969 | 1972 | 1968 | 1970 | 1970 | | | | | 1969 | | | | 1968 | | | | 1966 |
| **Part A. Original Laws** | | | | | | | | | | | | | | | | | | | | | | | | | |
| *Grounds* | | | | | | | | | | | | | | | | | | | | | | | | | |
| life | x | x | x | x | x | x | x | x | x | x | x | x | x | x | x | – | x | x | x | x | | x | x | x | x |
| health | x | | | | | | | | | | | | | | | | | | | | | | | | |
| other | | | | | | | | | x | | | | | | | | | | | | x | | | | |
| **Part B. Reform Laws** | | | | | | | | | | | | | | | | | | | | | | | | | |
| *Grounds* | | | | | | | | | | | | | | | | | | | | | | | | | |
| life | x | | | x | x | x | x | x | x | x | x | | | | | | x | | | | x | | | | x |
| health | x | | | | x | | | | x | x | x | | | | | | | | | | | | | | |
| physical health | | | | x | x | x | | x | | | | | | | | | x | | | | x | | | | |
| mental health | | | | x | x | x | | x | | | | | | | | | x | | | | x | | | | |
| fetal deformity | x | | | x | x | x | | x | x | x | | | | | | | x | | | | x | | | | |
| forcible rape | x | | | x | x | x | | x | x | x | | | | | | | x | | | | x | | | | |
| statutory rape | 15 y. | | | 16 y. | | | | | | 14 y. | 14 y. | | | | | | 16 y. | | | | | | | | |
| incest | x | | | x | | x | | x | | x | | | | | | | x | | | | | | | | |
| *Procedural requirements* | | | | | | | | | | | | | | | | | | | | | | | | | |
| time limit | | | | 20 w. | 16 w. | | 20 w. | 20 w. | | | | | | | | | | | | | 26 w. | | | | |
| residency | 4 m. | | | | | | | 4 m. | | | | | | | | | | | | | | | | | |
| M.D. approval | 3C | | | 2–3B | 3B | | 1C-RA | 1C-RA | 1C | 2C-3B | | | | | | | 3C | | | | RA | | | | |
| other consent | | | | | x | | | | x | | | | | | | | | | | | | | | | |
| **Part C. Repeal** | | x | | | | | | | | | | x | | | | | | | | | | | | (x) | (x) |

| | Mo. | Mont. | Neb. | Nev. | N.H. | N.J. 1969 | N.M. 1970 | N.Y. 1967 | N.C. | N.D. | Ohio | Okla. | Ore. 1969ᵃ | Penn. | R.I. | S.C. 1970 | S.D. | Tenn. | Texas | Utah | Vt. | Va. | Wash. 1970 | W.Va. | Wisc. 1970 | Wyo. |
|---|---|---|---|---|---|---|---|---|---|---|---|---|---|---|---|---|---|---|---|---|---|---|---|---|---|---|
| **Part A. *Original Laws*** | | | | | | | | | | | | | | | | | | | | | | | | | | |
| *Grounds* | | | | | | | | | | | | | | | | | | | | | | | | | | |
| life | x | x | x | x | x | | | | x | x | x | x | x | x | x | x | x | x | x | x | x | x | x | x | x | x |
| health | | | | | | | | | | | | | x | | | | | | | | | | | | | |
| other | | | | | | x | x | | | | | | | x | | | | | | | | | | | | |
| **Part B. *Reform Laws*** | | | | | | | | | | | | | | | | | | | | | | | | | | |
| *Grounds* | | | | | | | | | | | | | | | | | | | | | | | | | | |
| life | | | | | | | | x | | | | | x | | | x | | | | | | | | | x | |
| health | | | | | | | | x | | | | | | | | | | | | | | | | | | |
| physical health | | | | | | | | | | | | | x | | | x | | | | | | | | | x | |
| mental health | | | | | | | | | | | | | x | | | x | | | | | | | | | x | |
| fetal deformity | | | | | | | | x | | | | | x | | | x | | | | | | | | | x | |
| forcible rape | | | | | | | | x | | | | | x | | | x | | | | | | | | | x | |
| statutory rape | | | | | | | | 16 y. | | | | | 16 y. | | | | | | | | | | | | | |
| incest | | | | | | | | x | | | | | x | | | x | | | | | | | | | x | |
| *Procedural requirements* | | | | | | | | | | | | | | | | | | | | | | | | | | |
| time limit | | | | | | | | | | | | | 150 d. | | | | | | | | | | | | | |
| residency | | | | | | | | 4 m. | | | | | x | | | 90 d. | | | | | | | | | 120 d. | |
| M.D. approval | | | | | | 2B | | 3C | | | | | 1C | | | 3C | | | | | | | | | B | |
| other consent | | | | | | | | x | | | | | x | | | x | | | | | | | | | x | |

## Table A.1 (continued)

| | Mo. | Mont. | Neb. | Nev. | N.H. | N.J. | N.M. | N.Y. | N.C. | N.D. | Ohio | Okla. | Ore. | Penn. | R.I. | S.C. | S.D. | Tenn. | Texas | Utah | Vt. | Va. | Wash. | W.Va. | Wisc. | Wyo. |
|---|---|---|---|---|---|---|---|---|---|---|---|---|---|---|---|---|---|---|---|---|---|---|---|---|---|---|
| | | | | | | 1969 | 1970 | 1967 | | | | 1969[a] | | | | 1970 | | | | | | | 1970 | 1970 | | |

**Part C. *Repeal Laws***

| | Mo. | Mont. | Neb. | Nev. | N.H. | N.J. | N.M. | N.Y. | N.C. | N.D. | Ohio | Okla. | Ore. | Penn. | R.I. | S.C. | S.D. | Tenn. | Texas | Utah | Vt. | Va. | Wash. | W.Va. | Wisc. | Wyo. |
|---|---|---|---|---|---|---|---|---|---|---|---|---|---|---|---|---|---|---|---|---|---|---|---|---|---|---|
| Procedural requirements | | | | | | | | | | | | | | | | | | | | | | | | | | |
| physician | | | | | | | | x | | | | | | | | | | | | | | | x | | | |
| hospital | | | | | | | | | | | | | | | | | | | | | | | x | | | |
| time limit | | | | | | | | 24w. | | | | | | | | | | | | | | | 4 m. | | | |
| residency | | | | | | | | | | | | | | | | | | | | | | | 90 d. | | | |
| other consent | | | | | | | | | | | | | | | | | | | | | | | x | | | |

SOURCES: Harper (1958:188–92); George (1967:5–7); Means (1968:429); Association for the Study of Abortion; and National Association for Repeal of Abortion Laws.

KEY: A date under a state indicates the year a new law passed; Part B or C indicates the principal contents of the new law.

   *y.* = years and refers to the legal age of consent for statutory rape.

   *d.* = days; *w.* = weeks; *m.* = months; *n.v.f.* = non-viable fetus.

   *C.* = consultant and number required; *B* = therapeutic abortion board and number required; *RA* = hospital review authority required.

[a]The Oregon statute contains the additional explanatory phrase: "In determining whether or not there is substantial risk [to the woman's physical or mental health] account may be taken of the mother's total environment, actual or reasonably foreseeable."

standards and practices viewed in the light of current legal norms" (1959:422). They mailed a two-part questionnaire to the chiefs of the obstetrical services of twenty-nine representative hospitals in the San Francisco and Los Angeles areas. The first part of the questionnaire collected information about such things as the hospital's procedures in deciding which abortions to do, the number of abortions performed, and the attitudes of the physicians. The second part of the questionnaire described eleven hypothetical cases of women requesting abortions and asked each hospital to treat the cases as if they were actually being presented for approval. Twenty-five of the twenty-nine hospitals answered part two, and twenty-two gave a hospital decision on the hypothetical cases. Table A.2 summarizes six typical cases from the eleven, evaluates each case's legal standing, and shows the decisions of the hospitals. Clearly in many cases the indications for abortion accepted by the hospitals did not coincide with the therapeutic exception of California's law at that time.

Until the 1940s "therapeutic abortion was a relatively common procedure, well accepted by the majority of physicians as properly indicated for the preservation of the mother's life or immediate health in certain complicated pregnancies" (Russell 1953:108). Subsequently an "extensive realignment of indications for therapeutic abortion" took place within the medical community, and as the Packer-Gampbell cases illustrate, physicians disagreed about acceptable indications for an abortion. Guttmacher summed up the reasons for such disagreement when he wrote in answer to the question "Who should be aborted?": "Two authors of equally good intent could give different answers, since their judgment in large measure would be affected by their training, experience and social background, and by the institutions in which they have worked" (1967:16).

The net effect of this disagreement and confusion, especially up until 1973, was the establishment of separate therapeutic abortion policies and procedures by each hospital. In the absence of agreement within the larger medical community and in view of increasing discrepancies between the law and medical practice, each hospital set up its own regulations. Various approval systems developed, and the therapeutic abortion committee, started in 1945 by Alan

Table A.2.
The Packer-Gampbell Hypothetical Cases

| Indication | Medical Description | Legal Standing | Number of Hospitals Approve | Number of Hospitals Disapprove |
|---|---|---|---|---|
| Medical | "Rheumatic heart disease with aortic stenosis and insufficiency and mitral stenosis. Auricular fibrillation and moderate heart failure are secondary to her rheumatic heart disease." | Legal—"appears to us to qualify under the strict legal standard." | 21 | 1 |
| Medical-Fetal | Hodgkins Disease | Questionable—"Although the accepted forms of X-ray therapy may have a most deleterious effect on the fetus, the indicated disease does not present any special hazard to it, nor does the continuation of the pregnancy appear to influence the course of the maternal disease.... The legality of a therapeutic abortion in this case is, at best, questionable. The danger to the fetus from X-ray treatment is irrelevant to any justification based on averting a threat to the life of the mother. However, the presence of the fetus may well inhibit the vigor of the measures required to combat the mother's disease; and on this basis, it might be concluded . . . that the pregnancy should be terminated in order to permit effective therapy in the interest of preserving the life of the patient." | 10 | 11(6)[a] |
| Psychiatric | Suicide threats and one suicide attempt since pregnancy was diagnosed. Psychiatrist sees suicide threats as "genuine." | Questionable—"A genuine threat of suicide probably comes as close to presenting a justification under the existing legal standard as is possible for a psychiatric indication. Nonetheless, if the patient is kept under restraint in a mental institution, the possibility of a suc- | 17 | 4(2)[a] |

| | | | | |
|---|---|---|---|---|
| | | under these circumstances is, at best, questionable." | | |
| *Psychiatric* | "Severe anxiety neurosis with hysterical physical manifestations (vomiting, dehydration)." | Illegal—"This case presents a psychiatric indication for termination of pregnancy which, in our judgment, is plainly unjustifiable under the provisions of the California Penal Code. There is no suggestion that the patient's life is endangered. The prospect that an existing neurosis may be intensified by the birth of another child is one which probably characterizes a substantial proportion of all such pregnancies. The threat to mental health, while very real, appears to be irrelevant to the considerations underlying the narrow legal justification provided for termination of pregnancy." | 10 | 12(7)[a] |
| *Fetal* | Tay-Sachs Disease (amaurotic family idiocy); 3 children, first 7 yrs. and apparently healthy, second child died aged 2 of Tay-Sachs, third 1½ yrs. diagnosed as having Tay-Sachs. | Illegal—"The indication presented is purely fetal and consequently does not afford a justification for termination of pregnancy under the current legal standard." | 8 | 14(7)[a] |
| *Socioeconomic* | 5 children, one with fibrocystic disease; husband tubercular and about to be readmitted to sanatorium; woman working and has become "tense and apprehensive" since discovery of pregnancy; family physician recommends abortion; obstetrician willing to operate if approved. | Illegal—"we think that [an abortion] is plainly outside the existing legal justification." | 1 | 20(3)[a] |

SOURCE: Packer and Gampbell (1959).

NOTE: Quotation marks indicate direct quotes from the article. See Packer and Gampbell (1959:431–44) for the full case descriptions, authors' comments, and hospital decisions, including individual responses.

[a]Numbers in parentheses indicate those who thought "the case would stand a good chance of approval at another reputable hospital."

Guttmacher, soon became the most popular method of deciding who received an abortion. Russell enumerated the "manifold values" of a review committee: "1) they serve as deterrents to the indiscriminate use of therapeutic abortion; 2) they act in the best interests of the patient; 3) they are a medicolegal safeguard for the physician; and 4) they serve as repositories for the accumulation of data concerning the utilization and outcome of cases submitted for the therapeutic interruption of pregnancy" (quoted in Hammond 1964:353).

Although many physicians objected to the committee system, Russell's evaluation represents the prevailing attitude of the early to mid-1960s. The committees controlled the number and kind of cases approved and thereby were "deterrents to the indiscriminate use of therapeutic abortion" by those physicians considered to be too liberal in dispensing abortions. In addition, by sharing the responsibility for the decision, rather than placing it in the hands of the individual physician, the committees provided a "medicolegal safeguard" against the ever-present threat of legal action. That committees acted "in the best interests of the patient" is questionable. Phelan and Maginnis gave one of the shortest and most critical descriptions of the purpose and workings of the committee system: "The hospital abortion committee is a completely unnecessary medical precaution, and is simply a smokescreen behind which sexual discrimination flourishes and individual doctors protect themselves against criticism by having this anonymous committee sanction their dereliction of duty towards their female patients" (1969:91).

Whether one approved or disapproved of the committee system probably depended upon one's belief about who should have the ultimate decision-making power. But abortion committees clearly served a purpose for hospitals and physicians in a situation where little consensus could be achieved and where the law left the decision in medical hands. Discussing the composition and workings of committees, Karl Schaupp, Jr., noted that a committee could be set up to "make it do anything you want" resulting in an abortion rate "all the way from zero up to almost no restrictions" (quoted in Hammond 1964:353). Committee decisions were influenced by physicians who wanted legal changes and reasoned that changes would come about only by showing legislators that the incidence of abortion would not soar and could be controlled by the medical profession's committee system. In 1964 Hammond concluded a paper and discussion on hospital committees with the remark: "I hope that the presentation of a paper like this will help Dr. Overstreet in his testifying before the legislature to show a conservative trend and a responsible trend among the medical profession so that the lawyers and the legislature will turn the problem back to doctors where it belongs" (1964:355).

## Reform Laws

To start with an oversimplification, while the original laws generally permitted abortions only to save the pregnant woman's life, the reform laws added health, fetal deformity, and felonious intercourse as indications for a legal abortion. The reform laws were passed between 1966 and 1972 and attempted to clarify or expand the pre-1966 original laws. In all instances where we refer to reform laws without further qualification, we are referring to these liberalized laws as documented in table A.1, Part B.

The reform laws went beyond the original laws, almost without exception, to expand the indications for a legal abortion. But there were also pressures in some states to go beyond the original laws by strengthening their restrictive features against constitutional attack. The first anti-abortionist reform law came with the passage of the 1972 Connecticut law. Shortly after a U.S. district court declared the original Connecticut abortion law unconstitutional, the state legislature passed a new law that contained the same therapeutic exception—to save the woman's life—as the original law, provided a tougher penalty for performing or advising an unlawful abortion than the original law, and stated in a preamble to the new law that "it is the intent of the Legislature to protect and preserve human life from the moment of conception" (*New York Times,* June 28, 1972, p. C21). This preamble was carefully prepared to prevent further court debate about the intent of the legislature and to reform the original law by strengthening its constitutional basis. But this strengthened law was also ruled unconstitutional by a federal district court.

Reform legislation, especcially from 1966 through 1969, was typically based on a moderate law proposed in the American Law Institute's Model Penal Code. The Code states that,

> A licensed physician is justified in terminating a pregnancy if he believes there is substantial risk that continuance of the pregnancy would gravely impair the physical or mental health of the mother, or that the child would be born with grave physical or mental defect, or that the pregnancy resulted from rape, incest, or other felonious intercourse. All illicit intercourse with a girl below the age of 16 shall be deemed felonious for purposes of this subsection. Justifiable abortions shall be performed only in a licensed hospital except in case of emergency when hospital facilities are unavailable. (American Law Institute, 1962:189–90)

Mississippi quietly altered its abortion law in 1966 by adding a provision for rape, without specifying whether statutory or forcible rape or both was meant. The first big, noisy wave of legal changes came in 1967 when California, Colorado, and North Carolina passed laws based upon the American Law Institute recommendations.

As Part B of table A.1 shows, these reforms expanded the grounds for abortion along the lines suggested by the American Law Institute and added procedural requirements or conditions for abortions that were not mentioned by the American Law Institute. The reform laws all included life, health, and either rape or incest or both as justifiable grounds for abortion, but these statutes were far from uniform. Some statutes used the words "life and health" while others specified life and physical and mental health. Statutes having no provision for fetal deformity presented a problem because "before reform many [physicians] did an abortion if the woman had rubella in the first trimester. Now, unless danger of 'fetal defect' is specifically mentioned in their state law, they do not always grant an abortion" (Irwin 1970:80).

The procedural requirements apparent in the original laws were greatly elaborated in the reform laws. Almost without exception, the reform statutes required abortions to be performed by physicians in hospitals. The concept of treating the fetus differently according to the period of gestation appeared in some original laws as a distinction between a quickened and unquickened fetus, but the reform laws made more extensive and specific use of the time limit.

Some statutes set a time limit beyond which abortion was not permitted or was permitted only if necessary to preserve the woman's life (Delaware and Maryland, for example). Or, as another example, in Colorado the time limit applied only to cases of rape and incest. In addition to these conditions, two new procedural requirements appeared in some of the reform laws—residency regulations and consent clauses. A residency requirement meant that a woman could not obtain an abortion in the state until she had been a resident for a specified period of time. Consent referred to statutory requirements of consent from a husband, parents, or guardian and was connected with the age or marital status of the woman. For example, Alaska required consent from a parent or guardian if the woman was under 18 and unmarried.

The greatest elaboration of previous provisions and the key to the administration and interpretation of the reform laws resided in the medical approval systems set up in the statutes. A certain number of consultants *(C)*, a therapeutic abortion board *(B)*, or a hospital review authority *(RA)* was mandatory (see Part B, table A. 1). These approval systems were highly variable. A hospital review authority for instance could consist of one, two, three, or more members, and the approval bodies differed as to whether a unanimous or majority decision was required for approval. One official from California told how the manipulation of the committee system could result in a restrictive policy:

> The law . . . stipulates that for committees of three or less a unanimous vote is required, though for larger committees a majority vote is sufficient. Hence, some hospitals will limit the committee to three members and permanently instate one dissident physician, effectively giving him permanent veto power." (quoted in Plagenz 1969:82–83)

Changes in committee procedures sometimes led to a more liberal policy. Marder reported on one California hospital where initially only "overtly psychotic or highly suicidal" patients were even referred to the abortion committee which resulted in the "rejection of a large proportion of early applications" (1970:1232).

> The growing awareness that we were excluding patients who might be more favorably reviewed by the full committee led to a change in procedure that

enabled all applications, regardless of the initial evaluation recommendation, to be presented to the committee for consideration. This liberalized philosophy brought about a more reasonable definition of mental illness for use by the committee: "A disorder of thinking, feeling or behavior producing a breakdown in living so that the individual cannot deal with reality or cannot function in dealing with daily problems of living." (1970:1232–1233)

Many physicians and observers of the abortion scene saw the effect of these reform laws as making physicians "feel more secure in that what they were doing as a matter of course for years has now been sanctified by the legislature" (Walker and Hulka 1971:444). In essence even before the reform laws were passed many physicians performed abortions to preserve the life or health of women as well as in cases of rape, incest, and fetal deformity; thus, the approval systems that evolved informally within the medical community were formally written into the law. By this reasoning, the legislatures that passed reform bills wanted physicians to continue the medical practices that had evolved and gave them the formal authority, through medical approval systems, to make decisions and set the policy.

Some found this kind of law satisfactory, but most observers noted the difficulty of interpreting the laws and thus attacked the operation of the approval systems. Physicians charged that no common definitions existed for phrases like "gravely impair," "substantial risk," or "mental health." The approval systems set up in law to interpret these legal provisions were "cumbersome, time-consuming, and expensive," and the "operation of the committee itself is highly vulnerable to individual prejudice on the part of members, and the process is far from scientific or rational" (Whittington 1970:1228). The burden placed upon hospital committees to interpret the law when judging abortion requests has brought the system under attack in other countries, too. In Canada, since 1969, an abortion committee is required at each hospital. The system has been analyzed and criticized because it is arbitrary and capricious in its operation, because appeal procedures are lacking, because the variations among committees in their interpretations of the law has a discriminatory impact, and because it produces undue delay (Smith and Wineberg 1969–70; Badgeley Report 1977; Rodman 1981).

In spite of the criticisms leveled against the reform laws, they initiated the trend toward liberalization and for a while they were seen as the most politically feasible course of action since they embodied a compromise between retaining the original restrictive laws and passing permissive repeal laws.

## Repeal Laws

By 1970 twelve states had passed reform laws, but these laws did not eliminate the abortion problem as seen by the pro-abortionists— many women wanting abortions were being delayed or denied. Legislators in some states that passed reform laws, as well as legislators in states with original laws, therefore introduced repeal legislation. The legislatures of Alaska, Hawaii, and New York passed repeal bills in 1970, while the Washington state legislature passed a repeal referendum, which the voters approved.

The "repeal" in these laws refers to the elimination of required grounds for abortion and therefore eliminated the need for physicians to agonize over what constitutes an "indication" for abortion that is medically sound and at the same time legal. Instead, as Part C of table A.1 shows, these laws concentrated on procedural requirements to regulate abortion. In consequence, as long as they adhered to the procedural requirements, a woman could request and a physician could perform an abortion without having to give any reasons or justifications for it.

The passage of these laws caused a considerable stir among the opposing forces. Most anti-abortionists received them as signals of the beginning of the end of respect for life in the United States. Some pro-abortionists celebrated their passage as a major breakthrough. Other pro-abortionists called them "reform" bills or "fake repeal" bills. In reference to a "licensed hospitals" requirement, one critic wrote:

> Hawaii's new law has this kind of restriction, and hospitals there are already busy setting up a new catechism of "guidelines," none of which insure that women will get more abortions and all of which insure that they will have to ask a lot of strangers for "permission" before they are allowed to spend the considerable amount of money that hospitalization inevitably costs.

Maryland's recent bill [which was vetoed] and the legislation and "guidelines" proposed in several other states—like New York—contain the same
provisions that essentially shift the locus of control over women's decisions
from the state to the hospital bureaucracies and their quasi-legal "regulations." (Cisler 1970:20)

This is a more accurate description of the reform statutes than it is
of the repeal laws. The committee procedures written into the reform statutes turned the abortion decision over to hospital bureaucracies. This criticism of the repeal laws did, however, highlight a
major issue with respect to the repeal laws—the role of health agencies in controlling abortion.

The two major opposing points of view are: 1) Having succeeded in getting
criminal laws repealed, the imposition of any restrictions by health agencies
is a step backward in making abortion freely available, and the introduction
of innovative techniques in a fast moving field is likely to be inhibited; 2)
the legislatures that have taken the most radical steps in removing the prohibition against abortion from their criminal laws have done so by narrow
margins. They have allowed matters relating to abortion to be handled in
much the same way other health matters are handled in the community.
The use of official health agency mechanisms to protect the health and safety
of the population in its jurisdiction is responsible public health practice and
is likely to minimize the chance of "backlash" among legislators. (Harting
and Hunter 1971:2091)

Instead of merely shifting the locus of control over women's
decisions from the state to the hospital bureaucracies:

The action of the State Legislature in removing entirely the restrictions of
the past on abortions has created an entirely new and unprecedented situation. These local health departments have acted in the face of this vacuum
of control. Was it the intention of the legislature that such controls not be
exercised? Was it their intention that any licensed physician [in New York]
should be allowed to perform an abortion for any reason at any place as
long as it was during the first 24 weeks? (Curran 1971:624)

In Alaska and Hawaii the statutes restricted abortion to hospitals,
in Washington to hospitals or approved facilities, and in New York
no restrictions were enumerated in the legislation. In Washington
and New York local health agencies stepped in to fill the "vacuum
of control" and issued regulations for abortion facilities. Abortion
became an important public health issue. Curran voiced the opinion:

Health departments should be given the authority unmistakably to enact
regulations to control abortion practice in the interest of the public health.
The lack of precedent or tradition in such fields should not be an obstacle.
In fact, it is the very lack of clear, acceptable, common practices in medicine
and public health concerning abortion which makes it essential that the
public agencies charged with protecting the people's health take proper
action to establish and to enforce adequate standards. (1971:624–625)

Generally, fear that one's state would become an abortion mecca
was the first reaction to a new law. Residency requirements in states
with repeal laws and combined residency restrictions and hospital
policies in states with reform laws discouraged out-of-state patients.
Along with the "abortion mecca" emotionalism, the medical community very practically asked how they were going to deal with an
expected flood of abortion patients. This was particularly dramatic
in New York City (New York's repeal statute did not have a residency requirement), where estimates of the annual number of requests from local women ranged from 50,000 to 100,000 and
estimates of requests from out-of-state women ranged up to
400,000. The possibility of half a million abortion requests annually
for New York City staggered the imagination, especially when compared with the 850 abortions done citywide in 1969. The gloomy
predictions made after the passage of New York's repeal law expressed a concern that was voiced in every state that passed a new
abortion law.

There were dire prophecies that the state and, more particularly, an unpre-
pared New York City would be subjected to social and medical catastrophe.
...Women from all over the country would seek abortions in New York
City hospitals and clinics in the first year, monopolizing precious hospital
beds and the time of scarce medical manpower, with the result that medical
care for other urgent health problems—particularly of New York City's poor
population—would suffer. It was predicted that overburdened medical facilities and physicians would be unable to handle the hordes of abortion
applicants, whose abortions would be dangerously delayed because of
crowded operating room schedules, only to be hastened finally through the
procedure by pressured and weary practitioners. The resultant high costs of
abortion and high rates of morbidity and mortality associated with the
procedure could well create a situation, it was said, as bad as, if not worse
than, the one women found themselves in when the old law restricting
abortions to life-threatening situations forced women into the hands of
illegal abortionists. (Pakter and Nelson 1971:5)

After the first five months under the New York law, Pakter, Harris, and Nelson could report that "on the whole, hospitals have been most cooperative in developing in an amazingly short time the necessary services and staff to care for women requesting abortions. However, anxiety and concern engendered by the large influx of nonresidents and the possibility of overtaxing facilities are not entirely dispelled" (1971:196). Nowhere was the strain on facilities and staff as severe as a lot of people predicted, but the uneven application of services, the attitudes of personnel, and the cost of abortion continued to be problematic for most states.

In a hardhitting attack upon physicians' attitudes, Hall charged that "the major effect of abortion liberalization on the medical community has been not to broaden its views but to polarize them. On the obstetrical service of every hospital, no matter how large the staff, there seem to be two or three doctors who do more than half of the abortions" (1971:517). For the first few months under the Hawaii repeal law, Smith and his colleagues found that 23 percent of the abortions were done by three physicians and 60 percent were done by fifteen physicians (1971:534). Similar distortions, in terms of which hospitals performed abortions, occurred in other states with new laws, and these distortions frequently meant that poor women, rural women, and women from more conservative regions found it more difficult to obtain an abortion. These are problems in the delivery of services that apply today as well as in the 1960s and 1970s, and that also afflict most other countries (Rodman and Trost 1986).

## Criminal Abortions

Restrictive laws and a strong demand for abortion brought about a flourishing trade in criminal abortions. A large part of the estimated $350 million once spent annually for criminal abortions in the United States ended up in the crime syndicate, and until 1970 abortion ranked as the "third largest criminal racket in the United States" (Bell 1971:142).

Criminal (or some might prefer "extralegal") abortions also took place in hospitals. There was almost no legal interference with hospital abortions while abortion was illegal in the United States: "it is virtually unknown for an abortion performed in a hospital under proper jurisdiction to be questioned" (Theodore Lidz, quoted in Calderone 1958:40). The aura of respect that surrounds physicians and hospitals worked to the advantage of those who broke the laws.

The communication network surrounding illegal activities, such as abortion, is largely by word of mouth. In the United States, until the mid-1960s, neither the abortionist nor the patient had access to formal channels of communication. Both relied upon physicians, druggists, former patients, taxi drivers, bellhops, and their own acquaintance networks for information (Bates and Zawadzki 1964:54–55; Lee 1969). It took knowledge, money, and persistence to find a competent abortionist, and though a poor woman had a far more difficult time, even a wealthy woman sometimes had to "endure a difficult and humiliating search, fear, and despair in being forced to deal with unknown, inconsiderate abortionists, severe pain, and the risk of serious injury or even death" (Lee 1969:167–168).

One aim of liberalized laws is to eliminate criminal abortions and the health dangers associated with them. The changes in the U.S. abortion situation since 1970 have virtually eliminated criminal abortions. This is reflected in the decline of abortion-related maternal mortality rates and septic and incomplete abortion rates (Stewart and Goldstein 1971; CDC 1985; see chapter 4). If the world trend toward greater availability of legal abortion continues, the prevalence of criminal abortions will diminish still further throughout the world.

# References

Abernathy, James R. 1976. Abortion data collection under varied legal settings. In Abdel R. Omran, ed., *Liberalization of Abortion Laws,* pp. 61–73.

Ahmad, M. M. 1984. Epidemiology of induced abortion in the Middle East. In Elsayed S. E. Hafez, ed., *Voluntary Termination of Pregnancy,* pp. 11–24.

*Akron v. Akron Center for Reproductive Health et al.,* U.S. Supreme Court, Nos. 81–746 and 81–1172 (June 15, 1983).

American Law Institute. July 30, 1962. *Model Penal Code,* 2d ed. Philadelphia: American Law Institute.

Anderson, David E. Catholic scholars express varied abortion views. *Washington Post,* February 9, 1985.

Andolsek, Lidya. 1985. Abortion services in Slovenia. In Ciba Foundation Symposium 115, *Abortion: Medical Progress and Social Implications,* pp. 21–25.

Arias, Fernando. 1984. Efficacy and safety of low-dose 15-methyl prostaglandin $F_2$ for cervical ripening in the first trimester of pregnancy. *American Journal of Obstetrics and Gynecology* 149:100–101.

Aristotle. 384–322 B.C. *Politics.*

*Babbitz v. McCann,* 310 F. Supp. 293 (E.D. Wis. 1970).

Badgley Report. 1977. *Report of the Committee on the Operation of the Abortion Law* (Robin F. Badgley, Chairman). Ottawa: Minister of Supply and Services.

Baird, David T. and Iain T. Cameron. 1985. Menstrual induction: Surgery vs. prostaglandins. In Ciba Foundation Symposium

115, *Abortion: Medical Progress and Social Implications,* pp. 178–191.

Baluk, Ulana and Patrick O'Neill. 1980. Health professionals' perceptions of the psychological consequences of abortion. *American Journal of Community Psychology* 8:67–75.

Barnabas. 1952. The Epistle of Barnabas. In Ko Lake, tr., *The Apostolic Fathers,* vol. 19. London: Heinemann.

Bates, Jerome E. and Edward S. Zawadzki. 1964. *Criminal Abortion.* Springfield, Ill.: Charles C. Thomas.

Baulieu, Etienne E. 1985. Contragestion by antiprogestin: A new approach to human fertility control. In Ciba Foundation Symposium 115, *Abortion: Medical Progress and Social Implications,* pp. 192–210.

*Beal v. Doe,* 432 U.S. 438 (1977).

Beard, R. W. 1981. Technology in the care of mother and baby: An essential safeguard. In R. Chester, Peter Diggory, and Margaret B. Sutherland, eds., *Changing Patterns of Childbearing and Child Rearing,* pp. 1–12. London: Academic Press.

Bell, Robert R. 1971. *Social Deviance: A Substantive Analysis.* Homewood, Ill.: Dorsey.

*Bellotti v. Baird,* 428 U.S. 132 (1976).

*Bellotti v. Baird,* 443 U.S. 622 (1979).

Belsey, Elizabeth M., H. S. Greer, Shirley Lal, Stella C. Lewis, and R. W. Beard. 1977. Predictive factors in emotional responses to abortion. King's termination study-IV. *Social Science and Medicine* 11:71–82.

Benshoof, Janet. 1985. Late abortion and technological advances in fetal viability: Reasserting women's rights. *Family Planning Perspectives* 17:162–163.

Berger, Charlene, Dolores Gold, David Andres, Peter Gillett, and Robert Kinch. 1984. Repeat abortion: Is it a problem? *Family Planning Perspectives* 16:70–74.

Berger, Gary S., William E. Brenner, and Louis G. Keith, eds. 1981. *Second-Trimester Abortion: Perspectives After a Decade of Experience.* Boston: John Wright.

Berger, Kathleen. 1980. *The Developing Person.* New York: World.

Binkin, Nancy, Julian Gold, and Willard Cates, Jr. 1982. Illegal abortion deaths in the United States: Why are they still occurring? *Family Planning Perspectives* 14:3.

Blake, Judith. 1971. Abortion and public opinion: The 1960–1970 decade. *Science* 171:540–549.

Blake, Judith and Jorge H. Del Pinal. 1981. Negativism, equivocation and wobbly assent: Public 'support' for the pro-choice platform on abortion. *Demography* 18:309–320.

Blake, Judith and Jorge H. Del Pinal. 1980. Predicting polar attitudes toward abortion in the United States. In James T. Burtchaell, ed., *Abortion Parley,* pp. 27–56.

Bolton, Martha B. 1979. Responsible women and abortion decisions. In Onora O'Neill and William Ruddick, eds., *Having Children: Philosophical and Legal Reflections on Parenthood,* pp. 39–51. New York: Oxford University Press.

Bonar, Joy W., James A. Watson, and Lynn S. Koester. 1983. Abortion attitudes in medical students. *Journal of the American Medical Women's Association* 38:43–45.

Brewer, Colin. 1977. Incidence of post-abortion psychosis: A prospective study. *British Medical Journal* 1:476–477.

Burtchaell, James T. 1982. *Rachel Weeping.* Kansas City: Andrews and McMeel.

Burtchaell, James T., ed. 1980. *Abortion Parley.* Kansas City: Andrews and McMeel.

Butts, Robert Y. and Michael Sporakowski. 1974. Unwed pregnancy decisions: Some background factors. *The Journal of Sex Research* 10:110–117.

Bygdeman, Marc. 1981. Prostaglandins. In Jane E. Hodgson, ed., *Abortion and Sterilization.* pp. 333–358.

Calderone, Mary S. 1958. *Abortion in the United States.* New York: Hoeber-Harper.

Califano, Joseph A., Jr. 1981. *Governing America.* New York: Simon and Schuster.

Callahan, Daniel. 1985. Late abortion and technological advances in fetal viability: Some moral reflections. *Family Planning Perspectives* 17:163–164.

Callahan, Daniel. 1977. Abortion: A summary of the arguments. In Robert M. Veatch, ed., *Population Policy and Ethics: The American Experience.* New York: Irvington.

Callahan, Daniel. 1972. Ethics and population limitation. *Science* 175:487–494.

Callahan, Sidney and Daniel Callahan. 1984. *Abortion: Understanding Differences*. New York: Plenum Press.

Campbell, Alastair V. 1985. Viability and the moral status of the fetus. In Ciba Foundation Symposium 115, *Abortion: Medical Progress and Social Implications*, pp. 228–243.

Campbell, B. Kay and Dean C. Barnlund. 1977. Communication patterns and problems of pregnancy. *American Journal of Orthopsychiatry* 47:134–139.

Cartoof, Virginia G. and Lorraine V. Klerman. 1986. Parental consent for abortion: Impact of the Massachusetts law. *American Journal of Public Health* 76:397–400.

Cates, Willard, Jr. 1982. Legal abortion: The public record. *Science* 215:1586–1590.

Cates, Willard, Jr. 1981a. Abortion for teenagers. In Jane E. Hodgson, ed., *Abortion and Sterilization: Medical and Social Aspects*, pp. 139–154.

Cates, Willard, Jr. 1981b. The Hyde amendment in action: How did the restriction of federal funds affect low-income women? *Journal of the American Medical Association* 246:1109–1112.

Cates, Willard, Jr. and David Grimes. 1981a. Morbidity and mortality of abortion in the United States. In Jane E. Hodgson, ed., *Abortion and Sterilization: Medical and Social Aspects*, pp. 155–180.

Cates, Willard, Jr. and David Grimes. 1981b. Deaths from second trimester abortion by dilatation and evacuation: Causes, prevention, facilities. *Obstetrics and Gynecology* 58:401–408.

CDC (Centers for Disease Control). 1985. *Abortion Surveillance: Annual Summary, 1981*. Atlanta: U.S. Department of Health, Education, and Welfare, Public Health Service.

CDC. 1983. *Abortion Surveillance, Annual Summary, 1980*.

CDC. 1981. *Abortion Surveillance, Annual Summary, 1978*.

Char, Walter F. and John F. McDermott. 1972. Abortion and acute identity crisis in nurses. *American Journal of Psychiatry* 128:952–957.

Charles, Alan and Susan Alexander. 1971. Abortions for poor and nonwhite women: A denial of equal protection? *Hastings Law Journal* 23:147–169.

Ciba Foundation Symposium 115. 1985. *Abortion: Medical Progress and Social Implications.* London: Pitman.

Cisler, Lucinda. 1970. Abortion reform: The new tokenism. *Ramparts* (August), 9:19–21.

Combs, Michael W. and Susan Welch. 1982. Blacks, whites, and attitudes toward abortion. *Public Opinion Quarterly* 46:510–520.

Cook, Rebecca J. 1985. Legal abortion and human life. In Ciba Foundation Symposium 115, *Abortion: Medical Progress and Social Implications,* pp. 211–227.

Curran, William J. 1971. The legal authority of health departments to regulate abortion practice. *American Journal of Public Health* 61:621–626.

Cvejic, Helen, Irene Lipper, Robert Kinch, and Peter Benjamin. 1977. Follow-up of 50 adolescent girls two years after abortion. *Canadian Medical Association Journal* 116:44–46.

Daling, Janet R. and Irvin Emanuel. 1977. Induced abortion and subsequent outcomes of pregnancy in a series of American women. *New England Journal of Medicine* 297:1241.

David, Henry P. 1981. Abortion policies. In Jane E. Hodgson, ed., *Abortion and Sterilization,* pp. 1–40.

David, Henry P. 1985. Post-abortion and post-partum psychiatric hospitalization. In Ciba Foundation Symposium 115, *Abortion: Medical Progress and Social Implications,* pp. 150–164.

David, Henry P. 1986. Unwanted children: A follow-up from Prague. *Family Planning Perspectives* 18:143–144.

David, Henry P. and Zdenek Matejcek. 1981. Children born to women denied abortion: An update. *Family Planning Perspectives* 13:33–34.

David, Henry P., Neils Kr. Rasmussen, and Erik Holst. 1981. Postpartum and postabortion psychotic reactions. *Family Planning Perspectives* 13:88–91.

Davis, Kingsley. 1967. Population policy: Will current programs succeed? *Science* 158:730–739.

Dedek, John F. 1975. *Contemporary Medical Ethics.* New York: Skeed and Ward.

de Valk, Alphonse. 1974. *Morality and Law in Canadian Politics: The Abortion Controversy.* Montreal: Palm.

Devereux, George. 1976. *A Study of Abortion in Primitive Societies.* New York: International Universities Press.

Dixon, Garrett W., James J. Schlesselman, Howard W. Ory, and Richard P. Blye. 1980. Ethinyl estradiol and conjugated estrogens as postcoital contraceptives. *Journal of the American Medical Association* 244:1336–1339.

*Doe v. Bolton.* 319 F. Supp. 1048 (N.D. Ga. 1970).

*Doe v. Bolton* 410 U.S. 179 (1973).

Drinan, Robert F. 1970. Should there be laws against abortion? *U.S. Catholic,* April 15–19, 1970.

Dytryck, Zdenek, Zdenek Matejcek, Vratislav Schiller, Henry David, and Herbert Friedman. 1975. Children born to women denied abortion. *Family Planning Perspectives* 7:165.

Edelman, D. A. and Gary S. Berger. 1981. Menstrual regulation. In Jane E. Hodgson, ed., *Abortion and Sterilization: Medical and Social Aspects,* pp. 209–224.

Ekblad, M. 1955. Induced abortion on psychiatric grounds: A follow-up study of 479 women. *Acta Psychiatrica et Neurologica Scandinavica, Supp. 99.*

Elias, Sherman, Joe Leigh Simpson, Alice O. Martin, Rudy Sabbagha, Allan Bombard, Barbara Rosinsky, and Lora D. Baum. 1986. Chorionic villus sampling in continuing pregnancies. I. Low fetal loss rates in initial 109 cases. *American Journal of Obstetrics and Gynecology* 154:1349–1352.

Eliot, Johan W., Robert E. Hall, J. Robert Willson, and Carolyn Houser. 1970. The obstetrician's view. In Robert E. Hall, ed., *Abortion in a Changing World,* 1:85–95.

Embrey, M. P. 1984. New prostaglandin delivery systems. In Elsayed S. E. Hafez, ed., *Voluntary Termination of Pregnancy,* pp. 67–74.

*Family Planning Perspectives.* 1983. Public support for legal abortion continues. 15:279–281.

Farr, A. D. 1980. The Marquis de Sade and induced abortion. *Journal of Medical Ethics* 6:7–10.

Finkbine, Sherri. 1967. The lesser of two evils. In Alan Guttmacher, ed., *The Case for Legalized Abortion Now,* Berkeley, Calif.: Diablo Press, pp. 15–25.

Finlay, Barbara Agresti. 1981. Sex differences in correlates of abortion attitudes among college students. *Journal of Marriage and the Family* 43:571–583.

Foster, Henry, Milton Smith, Charles McGruder, Floyd Richard, and Julian McIntyre. 1985. Post-conception menses induction using prostaglandin vaginal suppositories. *Obstetrics and Gynecology* 65:682–685.

Francke, Linda Bird. 1978. *The Ambivalence of Abortion*. New York: Random House.

Freeman, Ellen W. 1978. Abortion: Subjective attitudes and feelings. *Family Planning Perspectives* 10:150–155.

Freeman, Ellen. 1977. Influence of personality attributes on abortion experiences. *American Journal of Orthopsychiatry* 47:503–513.

Freedman, Mary Anne, David A. Jillson, Roberta R. Coffin, and Lloyd F. Novick. 1986. Comparison of complication rates in first trimester abortions performed by physician assistants and physicians. *American Journal of Public Health* 76:550–554.

Freud, Sigmund. 1963. *Sexuality and the Psychology of Love*. New York: MacMillan.

Gallup Opinion Index. April 1974 to June 1980. Princeton, N.J.: Gallup Poll.

Gallup Report. July 1981 to January–February, 1986. Princeton, N.J.: Gallup Poll.

Gaylor, Anne. 1979. The tortoise and the hare . . . and the power of language. *National Abortion Rights Action League Newsletter* January/February, vol. 11, no. 1. Washington, D.C.

George, B. James, Jr. 1972. The evolving law of abortion. *Western Reserve Law Review* 23:708–755.

George, B. James, Jr. 1967. Current abortion laws: Proposals and movements for reform. In David Smithe, ed., *Abortion and the Law*, pp. 1–36. Cleveland: Case Western Reserve Press.

Gerrard, Meg. 1977. Sex guilt in abortion patients. *Journal of Consulting Psychology* 45:708.

Gilligan, Carol. 1982. *In a Different Voice*. Cambridge: Harvard University Press.

Gold, Edwin M., Carl L. Erhart, Harold Jacobziner, and Frieda G. Nelson. 1965. Therapeutic abortions in New York City: A 20-year review. *American Journal of Public Health* 55:964–972.

Goodman, Ellen. 1985. *Keeping in Touch.* New York: Summit Books.

Gould, Ketayun. 1979. Family planning and abortion policy in the United States. *Social Service Review* 53:453–463.

Granberg, Donald. 1981. The abortion activists. *Family Planning Perspectives* 13:157–163.

Granberg, Donald and Beth Wellman Granberg. 1980. Abortion attitudes, 1965–1980: Trends and determinants. *Family Planning Perspectives* 12:250–261.

Greeley, Andrew M. 1985. *American Catholics Since the Council: An Unauthorized Report.* Chicago: Thomas More Press.

Grimes, David A. and Willard Cates, Jr. 1981. Dilatation and evacuation. In Gary Berger, William E. Brenner, and Louis G. Keith, eds., *Second Trimester Abortion,* pp. 119–133.

Grimes, David A., Willard Cates, Jr., and Richard Selik. 1981. Abortion facilities and the risk of death. *Family Planning Perspectives* 13:30–32.

Grimes, David A. and K. F. Schulz. 1985. The comparative safety of second trimester abortion methods. In Ciba Foundation Symposium 115, *Abortion: Medical Progress and Social Implications,* pp. 83–96.

*Griswold v. Connecticut,* 381 U.S. 479 (1965).

Guttmacher, Alan. F., ed. 1967. *The Case for Legalized Abortion Now.* Berkeley, Calif.: Diablo Press.

Hafez, Elsayed S. E., ed. 1984. *Voluntary Termination of Pregnancy.* Boston: MTP Press.

Hall, Robert. 1971. Abortion: Physician and hospital attitudes. *American Journal of Public Health* 61:517–519.

Hall, Robert, ed. 1970. *Abortion in a Changing World.* New York: Columbia University Press.

Hall, Robert. 1967a. Present abortion practices in New York state. *New York Medicine* 23:124–126.

Hall, Robert. 1967b. Abortion in American hospitals. *American Journal of Public Health* 57:1933–1936.

Hall, Robert. 1965. Therapeutic abortion, sterilization and conception. *Obstetrics and Gynecology* 91:518–532.

Hammond, Howard. 1964. Therapeutic abortion: Ten years' experience with hospital committee control. *American Journal of Obstetrics and Gynecology* 89:349–355.

Harper, Fowler. 1958. In Mary S. Calderone, ed., *Abortion in the United States,* pp. 187–195.

*Harris v. McRae,* 448 U.S. 297 (1980).

Harting, Donald and Helen J. Hunter. 1971. Abortion techniques and services: A review and critique. *American Journal of Public Health* 57:1937–1947.

*H. L. v. Matheson.* 450 U.S. 398 (1981).

Hawkinson, William P. 1976. Abortion: An anthropological overview. In Abdel R. Omran, ed., *Liberalization of Abortion Laws: Implications,* pp. 122–136.

Healy, David and Hamish Fraser. 1985. The antiprogesterones are coming: Menses induction, abortion, and labour? *British Medical Journal* 290:580–581.

Henshaw, Stanley K. 1986. Trends in abortion, 1982–1984. *Family Planning Perspectives* 18:34.

Henshaw, Stanley, Nancy J. Binkin, Ellen Blaine, and Jack C. Smith. 1985. A portrait of American women who obtain abortions. *Family Planning Perspectives* 17:90–96.

Henshaw, Stanley K. and Greg Martire. 1982. Abortion and the public opinion polls: Morality and legality. *Family Planning Perspectives* 14:53–60.

Henshaw, Stanley K. and Lynn S. Wallish. 1984. The medicaid cutoff and abortion services for the poor. *Family Planning Perspectives* 16:170–172, 177–180.

Hern, Warren H. 1984. *Abortion Practice.* Philadelphia: J. B. Lippincott.

Hodgson, Jane E., ed. 1981. *Abortion and Sterilization: Medical and Social Aspects.* New York: Academic Press.

Hogge, W. A., S. A. Schonberg, and M. S. Golbus. 1986. Chorionic villus sampling: Experience of the first 1000 cases. *American Journal of Obstetrics and Gynecology* 154:1249–1252.

Hogue, Carol J. R., Willard Cates, Jr., and Christopher Tietze. 1983. Impact of vacuum aspiration abortion on future childbearing: A review. *Family Planning Perspectives* 15:119–125.

Hogue, Carol J. R., Willard Cates, Jr., and Christopher Tietze.

1982. The effects of induced abortion on subsequent reproduction. *Epidemiology Review* 4:66–94.

Howe, Barbara, Roy Kaplan, and Constance English. 1979. Repeat abortions: Blaming the victims. *American Journal of Public Health* 69:1242–1246.

Hubbard, G. Wilkins. 1977. A review of the progress of psychiatric opinion regarding emotional complications of therapeutic abortion. *Southern Medical Journal* 70:588–590.

*In re Gault,* 387 U.S. 1 (1967).

Irwin, Theodore. 1970. The new abortion laws: How are they working? *Today's Health* 48:21.

Johnson, Jeanette H. 1984. Conception—the morning after. *Family Planning Perspectives* 16:266–270.

Jones, Elise F., Jacqueline Darroch Forrest, Noreen Goldman, Stanley K. Henshaw, Richard Lincoln, Jeannie I. Rosoff, Charles F. Westoff, and Deirdre Wulf. 1985. Teenage pregnancy in developed countries: Determinants and policy implications. *Family Planning Perspectives* 17:53–63.

Kerenyi, Thomas D. 1981. Intraamniotic techniques. In Jane E. Hodgson, ed., *Abortion and Sterilization: Medical and Social Aspects,* pp. 359–377.

Kinsey, Alfred. 1953. *Sexual Behavior in the Human Female.* Philadelphia: Saunders.

Kohl, Marvin, ed. 1978. *Infanticide and the Value of Life.* New York: Prometheus Books.

Kozol, Jonathan. 1973. A matter of life and death: The scandalous conditions at Boston City Hospital. *Ramparts,* pp. 21–25, 48–49.

Kummer, J. 1963. Post-abortion psychiatric illness-a myth? *American Journal of Psychiatry* 119:980–983.

Landers, Ann. 1985. Half-baked distortions used to make story sound true. *Greensboro News and Record,* July 15, 1985, p. A9.

Lauerson, Neils and Z. R. Graves. 1984. Menstrual induction and cervical priming prior to evacuation. In M. Toppozada, M. Bygdeman, and E. S. E. Hafez, eds., *Prostaglandins and Fertility Regulation,* pp. 91–106.

Lee, Nancy Howell. 1969. *The Search for an Abortionist*. Chicago: University of Chicago Press.

Levene, Howard I. and Francis J. Rigney. 1970. Law, preventive psychiatry, and therapeutic abortion. *Journal of Nervous and Mental Disease* 151:51–59.

Linn, Shai, Stephen C. Schoenbaum, Richard R. Monson, Bernard Rosner, Phillip G. Stubblefield, and Kenneth J. Ryan. 1983. The relationship between induced abortion and outcome of subsequent pregnancies. *American Journal of Obstetrics and Gynecology* 146:136–140.

Louisell, David W. and John T. Noonan, Jr. 1970. Constitutional balance. In John Noonan, ed., *The Morality of Abortion*, pp. 220–260.

Lucas, Roy. 1968. Federal constitutional limitations on the enforcement and administration of state abortion statutes. *North Carolina Law Review* 46:730–778.

Luker, Kristin. 1984. The war between the women. *Family Planning Perspectives* 16:105–110.

Luker, Kristin. 1984a. *Abortion and the Politics of Motherhood*. Berkeley: University of California Press.

Luker, Kristin. 1975. *Taking Chances: Abortion and the Decision Not to Contracept*. Berkeley: University of California Press.

Mabbutt, Fred R. 1972. What of private rights in a scientific age? *Current* (July/August), pp. 16–24.

Maguire, Marjorie Reiley. 1986. Pluralism on abortion in the theological community: The controversy continues. *Conscience: A Newsjournal of Prochoice Catholic Opinion* 7(1):1,3–10.

*Maher v. Roe* 432 U.S. 464 (1977).

Maine, Deborah. 1979. Does abortion affect later pregnancies? *Family Planning Perspectives* 9:98–101.

Marder, Leon. 1970. Psychiatric experience with a liberalized therapeutic abortion law. *American Journal of Psychiatry* 126:1230–1236.

Matejcek, Zdenek, Zdenek Dytrych, and Vratislav Schuller. 1985. Follow-up study of children born to women denied abortion. In Ciba Foundation Symposium 115, *Abortion: Medical Progress and Social Implications*, pp. 136–147.

Matejcek, Zdenek, Zdenek Dytrych, and Vratislav Schuller. 1978. Children born from unwanted pregnancies. *Acta Psychiatrica Scandinavica* 57:67–90.

McCain, Hugh. 1985. Abortion: A micro view. Presented at annual meeting of the Society for the Study of Social Problems. Washington, D.C., August 24, 1985.

McCormick, Richard A. 1981. *How Brave a New World: Dilemmas in Bioethics.* Garden City, N.Y.: Doubleday.

McGovern, Margaret M., James D. Goldberg, and Robert J. Desnick. 1986. Acceptability of chorionic villi sampling for prenatal diagnosis. *American Journal of Obstetrics and Gynecology* 155:25–29.

McLaren, Angus. 1981. Barrenness against nature: Recourse to abortion in preindustrial England. *The Journal of Sex Research* 17:224–237.

Means, Cyril C., Jr. 1971. The phoenix of abortion freedom: Is a penumbral or ninth amendment right about to arise from the nineteenth century legislative ashes of fourteenth century common law liberty? *New York Law Forum* 17:335–410.

Means, Cyril C., Jr. 1968. The law of New York concerning abortion and the status of the foetus, 1664–1968: A case of cessation of constitutionality. *New York Law Forum* 14:411–515.

Michel, Aaron E. 1982. Abortion and international law: The status and possible extension of women's right to privacy. *Journal of Family Law* 20:241–261.

Milbauer, Barbara. 1983. *The Law Giveth: Legal Aspects of the Abortion Controversy.* New York: Atheneum.

Milligan, J. E., A. T. Shennan, and E. M. Hoskins. 1984. Prenatal intensive care: Where and how to draw the line. *American Journal of Obstetrics and Gynecology* 148:499–503.

Minturn, Leigh and Jerry Stashak. 1982. Infanticide as a terminal abortion procedure. *Behavior Science Research* 17:70–90.

Mohr, James C. 1978. *Abortion in America: The Origins and Evolution of National Policy, 1800–1900.* New York: Oxford University Press.

Moore, K. L. 1982. *The Developing Human: Clinically Oriented Embryology.* 3d ed. Philadelphia: W. B. Saunders.

Mosher, Donald L. 1973. Sex differences, sex experiences, guilt, and explicitly sexual films. *Journal of Sex Issues* 29:95–112.

Munford, R. 1963. Interdisciplinary study of four women who had induced abortions. *American Journal of Obstetrics and Gynecology* 87:865–876.

Nathanson, Bernard N., with Richard C. Ostling. 1979. *Aborting America*. Garden City, N.Y.: Doubleday.

Nathanson, Constance A. and Marshall H. Becker. 1977. The influence of physicians' attitudes on abortion performance, patient management, and professional fees. *Family Planning Perspectives* 9:158–163.

NAS (National Academy of Sciences), 1975. *Legalized Abortion and the Public Health: Report of a Study by the Institute of Medicine*. Washington, D.C.

Nelson, George H. 1980. Prostaglandins and reproduction. *Obstetrics and Gynecology* 4:28–31.

Neubardt, Selig and Harold Schulman. 1977. *Techniques of Abortion*. 2d ed. Boston: Little, Brown.

Nolen, William A. 1978. *The Baby in the Bottle*. New York: Coward, McCann and Geoghegan.

Noonan, John T., Jr. 1979. *A Private Choice: Abortion in America in the Seventies*. New York: Free Press.

Noonan, John T., Jr. ed. 1979. *The Morality of Abortion*. Cambridge: Harvard University Press.

O'Donnell, Thomas J. 1970. A traditional Catholic's view. In Robert Hall, ed., *Abortion in a Changing World*, pp. 34–38.

Omran, Abdel R. 1982. Health and population dynamics: The vital connection. *Contraceptive Delivery Systems*, 3(314) Abstract 3.

Omran, Abdel R., ed., 1976. *Liberalization of Abortion Laws: Implications*. Chapel Hill: Carolina Population Center, University of North Carolina.

Packer, Herbert L. and Ralph J. Gampbell. 1959. Therapeutic abortion: A problem in law and medicine. *Stanford Law Review* 11:417–455.

Pakter, Jean and Frieda Nelson. 1971. Abortion in New York City: The first nine months. *Family Planning Perspectives* 3:5–12.

Pakter, Jean, David Harris, and Frieda Nelson. 1971. Surveillance of the abortion program in New York City: Preliminary report. *Modern Treatment* 8:169–201.

*People v. Belous* 71 Cal. 2d 954, 458, P. 2d 194 80 Cal. Reporter (1969).

Petchesky, Rosalind P. 1985. Abortion in the 1980s: Feminist morality and women's health. In Ellen Lewin and Virginia Olesen, eds., *Women, Health, and Healing*, pp. 139–173. New York: Tavistock.

Petchesky, Rosalind P. 1984. *Abortion and Woman's Choice*. New York: Longman.

Pfeiffer, Eric. 1970. Psychiatric indications or psychiatric justification of therapeutic abortion? *Archives of General Psychiatry* 23:402–407.

Phelan, Lana C. and Patricia T. Maginnis. 1969. *The Abortion Handbook for Responsible Women*. Canoga Park, Calif.: Weiss, Day, and Lord.

Philips, Susan V. 1980. Sex differences and language. *Annual Review of Anthropology* 9:523–544.

Pilpel, Harriet F. 1976. The collateral legal consequences of adopting a constitutional amendment on abortion. *Family Planning/ Population Reporter* 5(3):44–48.

Plagenz, Lorry. 1969. States legislate abortion reform, but hospitals are reluctant to comply. *Modern Hospital* 113:82–85.

*Planned Parenthood of Central Missouri v. Danforth*, 428 U.S. 52 (1976).

Plutzer, Eric and Barabara Ryan. 1985. When married women have abortions: The question of spousal notification. Presented at annual meeting of the Society for the Study of Social Problems. Washington, D.C.

*Population Reports*. 1985. Family planning programs. 13:J773– J812.

*Population Reports*. 1980. Pregnancy termination. Series F, No. 7. July. Population Information Program, Johns Hopkins University.

Potts, Malcolm. 1985. Medical progress and social implications of abortion: A summing up. In Ciba Foundation Symposium 115, *Abortion: Medical Progress and Social Implications*, pp. 263–269.

Presser, Harriet. 1977. Guessing and misinformation about pregnancy risk among urban mothers. *Family Planning Perspectives* 9:111–115.

Presser, Harriet. 1974. Early motherhood: Ignorance or bliss? *Family Planning Perspectives* 6:8.

Rains, Prudence M. 1971. *Becoming an Unwed Mother: A Sociological Account.* Chicago: Aldine, Atherton.

Ramsey, Paul. 1978. *Ethics at the Edge of Life: Medical and Legal Intersections.* New Haven: Yale University Press.

Ray, J. J. 1983. Attitude to abortion, attitude to life, and conservatism in Australia. *Sociology and Social Research* 68:236–243.

Reiss, Ira. 1980. *Family Systems in America.* 3d ed. New York: Holt, Rinehart, and Winston.

Robertson, John A. 1983. Medicolegal implications of a human life amendment. In Margery W. Shaw and A. Edward Doudera, eds., *Defining Human Life: Medical, Legal, and Ethical Implications,* pp. 161–173.

Rodman, Hyman. 1981. Future directions for abortion morality and policy. In Paul Sachdev, ed., *Abortion: Readings and Research,* pp. 229–237. Toronto: Butterworths.

Rodman, Hyman. 1971. *Lower-Class Families: The Culture of Poverty in Negro Trinidad.* New York: Oxford University Press.

Rodman, Hyman. 1968. Family and social pathology in the ghetto, *Science* 161:756–762.

Rodman Hyman. 1965. Middle-class misconceptions about lower-class families. In Hyman Rodman, ed., *Marriage, Family, and Society,* pp. 219–230. New York: Random House.

Rodman, Hyman, Susan H. Lewis, and Saralyn B. Griffith. 1984. *The Sexual Rights of Adolescents: Competence, Vulnerability, and Parental Control.* New York: Columbia University Press.

Rodman, Hyman and Jan Trost, eds. 1986. *The Adolescent Dilemma: International Perspectives on the Family Planning Rights of Minors.* New York: Praeger.

*Roe v. Wade,* 410 U.S. 113 (1973).

Roemer, Ruth. 1971. Abortion law reform and repeal: Legislative and judicial developments. *American Journal of Public Health* 61:500–509.

*Rosen v. Louisana State Board of Medical Examiners.* 318 F Supp. 1217 (E.D. La.1970).

Rosenberg, Leon. 1981. *Science* 242:907.

Rosoff, Jeanne and Asta M. Kenney. 1984. Title X and its critics. *Family Planning Perspectives* 16:111–118.

Rothstein, Arden A. 1977. *American Journal of Orthopsychiatry* 47:111–118.

Rothstein, Arden A. 1977a. Men's reactions to their partners' elective abortions. *American Journal of Obstetrics and Gynecology* 128:831.

Russell, Keith P. 1953. Changing indications for therapeutic abortion. *Journal of the American Medical Association* 151:108–111.

Safilios-Rothschild, Constantina. 1974. Why some women prefer abortion to contraception. *Contemporary Obstetrics and Gynecology* 4:125–128.

St. John-Stevas, Norman. 1964. *The Right to Life*. New York: Holt, Rinehart, and Winston.

Sarvis, Betty and Hyman Rodman. 1974. *The Abortion Controversy*. 2d ed. New York: Columbia University Press.

Saxen, Lauri and Juliani Rapola. 1969. *Congenital Defects*. New York: Holt, Rinehart and Winston.

Schardein, James L. 1976. *Drugs as Teratogens*. Cleveland: CRC Press.

Schell, Merrill S. 1977. Third party consent to abortions before and after Danforth: A theoretical analysis. *Journal of Family Law* 15:508–536.

Schneider, Carl E. and Maris A. Vinovskis. 1980. *The Law and Politics of Abortion*. Lexington, Mass.: Lexington Books.

Schoenbaum, Stephen C., Richard R. Monson, Phillip G. Stubblefield, Philip D. Darney, and Kenneth J. Ryan. 1980. Outcome of the delivery following an induced or spontaneous abortion. *American Journal of Obstetrics and Gynecology* 136:19–24.

Selik, Richard M., Willard Cates, Jr., and Carl W. Tyler. 1981. Behavioral factors contributing to abortion deaths: A new approach to mortality studies. *Obstetrics and Gynecology* 58:631–635.

Shaw, Margery W. and A. Edward Doudera., eds. 1983. *Defining Human Life: Medical, Legal, and Ethical Implications*. Ann Arbor, Mich.: AUPHA Press.

Shiota, K. and H. Nishimura. 1984. Epidemiology of induced abortion in Japan. In Elsayed S. E. Hafez, ed., *Voluntary Termination of Pregnancy*, pp. 3–10.

Shostak, Arthur B. and Gary McLouth. 1984. *Men and Abortion: Lessons, Losses, and Love.* New York: Praeger.

Shusterman, Lisa R. 1979. Predicting the psychological consequences of abortion. *Social Science and Medicine* 13A:683–689.

Silber, Tomas J. 1980. Values relating to abortion as expressed by the inner city adolescent girl—report of a physician's experience. *Adolescence* 15:183–189.

Simon, Nathan M. and Audrey G. Senturia. 1966. Psychiatric sequelae of abortion: Review of the literature, 1935–1964. *Archives of General Psychiatry* 15:378–389.

Simon, Nathan M., Audrey G. Senturia, and David Rothman. 1967. Psychiatric illness following therapeutic abortion. *American Journal of Psychiatry* 124:59–65.

Singnomklao, Tongplaew N. 1985. Abortion in Thailand and Sweden: Health services and short term consequences. In Ciba Foundation Symposium 115, *Abortion: Medical Progress and Social Implications,* pp. 54–67.

Smith, Harmon. 1970. *Ethics and the New Medicine.* Nashville: Abingdon Press.

Smith, Kenneth D. and Harris S. Wineberg. 1969–70. A survey of therapeutic abortion committees. *Criminal Law Quarterly* 12:279–306.

Smith, Roy G., Patricia G. Steinhoff, Milton Diamond, and Norma Brown. 1971. Abortion in Hawaii: The first 124 days. *American Journal of Public Health* 61:530–542.

Snell, Richard S. 1983. *Clinical Embryology for Medical Students.* 3d ed. Boston: Little, Brown.

Spitz, Alison M., Nancy C. Lee, David A. Grimes, Albert K. Schoenbucher, and Michael Lavoie. 1983. Third-trimester induced abortion in Georgia, 1979 and 1980. *American Journal of Public Health* 73:594–595.

Spitz, Irving M. and C. Wayne Bardin. 1985. Antiprogestins: Prospects for a once-a-month pill. *Family Planning Perspectives* 17:260–262.

Spivak, Manuel M. 1967. Therapeuic abortion: A 12-year review at the Toronto General Hospital, 1954–1965. *American Journal of Obstetrics and Gynecology* 97:316–323.

Stan, Adelle-Marie. 1986. Pat Hussey and Barbara Ferraro battle on. *Conscience: A Newsjournal of Prochoice Catholic Opinion* 7(3):1–4.

Steiner, Gilbert Y. 1981. *The Futility of Family Policy.* Washington, D.C.: Brookings Institution.

Stewart, Gary K. and Philip J. Goldstein. 1971. Therapeutic abortion in California: Effects on septic abortion and maternal mortality. *Obstetrics and Gynecology* 37:510–514.

Strong, Carson. 1983. The tiniest newborns: Aggressive treatment or conservative care? *Hastings Center Report,* February, pp. 14–19.

Stubblefield, Phillip G. 1985. Late abortion and technological advances in fetal viability: Some medical considerations. *Family Planning Perspectives* 17:161–162.

Stubblefield, Phillip G., A. M. Altman, and S. P. Goldstein. 1984. Laminaria treatment prior to late mid-trimester abortion by uterine evacuation. In Elsayed S. E. Hafez, ed., *Voluntary Termination of Pregnancy,* pp. 75–82.

Stubblefield, Phillip G., Richard R. Monson, Stephen C. Schoenbaum, C. E. Wolfson, D. J. Cookson, and Kenneth J. Ryan. 1984. Fertility after induced abortion: A prospective follow-up study. *Obstetrics and Gynecology* 62:186–193.

Such-Baer, M. 1974. Professional staff reaction to abortion work. *Social Casework* 55:435–441.

Szasz, Thomas. 1962. Bootlegging humanistic values through psychiatry. *Antioch Review* 22:341–349.

Tietze, Christopher. 1984. The public health effect of legal abortion in the U.S. *Family Planning Perspectives* 16:26–28.

Tietze, Christopher. 1983. *Induced Abortion: A World Review,* 5th ed. New York: The Population Council.

Tietze, Christopher. 1981. *Induced Abortion: A World Review,* 4th ed.

Tietze, Christopher. 1976. *Abortion 1974–75, Needs and Services in the U.S., Each State and Metropolitan Area: A Report.* New York: Alan Guttmacher Institute.

Tietze, Christopher. 1968. Therapeutic abortions in the U.S. *American Journal of Obstetrics and Gynecology* 101:784–787.

Tietze, Christopher and Sarah Lewit. 1981. Epidemiology of induced abortion. In Jane E. Hodgson, ed., *Abortion and Sterilization: Medical and Social Aspects,* pp. 39–56.

Tomlinson, Richard. 1984. Where population control cuts a different way. *Wall Street Journal,* June 20, 1984, p. 31.

Toppozada, M. 1984. Effects of prostaglandins on the human nonpregnant uterus and ovary. In M. Toppozada, M. Bygdeman, and E. S. E. Hafez, eds., *Prostaglandins and Fertility Regulation.,* pp. 27–58.

Toppozada, M., M. Bygdeman, and E. S. E. Hafez, eds. 1984. *Prostaglandins and Fertility Regulation.* Boston: MTP Press.

Tribe, Laurence H. 1985. *God Save This Honorable Court.* New York: Random House.

Tunkel, Victor. 1979. Abortion: How early, how late, and how legal? *British Medical Journal* 2:253–256.

U.S. Bureau of the Census. 1985. *Statistical Abstract of the United States: 1986.* 106th edition. Washington, D.C.

*U.S. v. Vuitch,* 305 F. Supp. 1032 (D.D.C.1969) and 91 S. Ct. 1294 (1971).

Van Nagell, J. R., Jr. and J. W. Roddick, Jr. 1971. Vaginal hysterectomy as a sterilization procedure. *American Journal of Obstetrics and Gynecology* 11:107–111.

Veatch, Robert M., ed. 1977. *Population Policy and Ethics: The American Experience.* New York: Irvington Publishers.

Walker, W. B. and J. F. Hulka. 1971. Attitudes and practices of North Carolina obstetricians: The impact of the North Carolina abortion act of 1967. *Southern Medical Journal* 64:441–445.

Walter, G. 1970. Psychological and emotional consequences of elective abortion: A review. *Obstetrics and Gynecology* 36:482–491.

Watters, Wendell W. 1976. *Compulsory Parenthood: The Truth About Abortion.* Toronto: McClelland and Stewart.

Wardle, Lynn D. and Mary Anne Q. Wood. 1982. *A Lawyer Looks at Abortion.* Provo, Utah: Brigham Young University Press.

Weisbord, Robert G. 1975. *Genocide? Birth Control and the Black American.* Westport, Conn.: Greenwood Press.

Weisman, Carol S., Constance A. Nathanson, Martha Ann Teitelbaum, Gary A. Chase, and Theodore M. King. 1986. Abortion attitudes and performance among male and female obstetrician-gynecologists. *Family Planning Perspectives* 18:67–73.

Westfall, David. 1982. Beyond abortion: The potential reach of a human life amendment. *American Journal of Law and Medicine* 8:97–135.

Westoff, Charles R. 1980. Women's reactions to pregnancy. *Family Planning Perspectives* 12:135–139.

Westoff, Charles R. 1973. *Toward the End of Growth: Population in America*. Englewood Cliffs, N.J.: Prentice-Hall.

Whittington, H. G. 1970. Evaluation of therapeutic abortion as an element of preventive psychiatry. *American Journal of Psychiatry* 126:1224–1229.

Williamson, Laila. 1978. Infanticide: An anthropological analysis. In Marvin Kohl, ed., *Infanticide and the Value of Life*, pp. 61–75. New York: Prometheus Books.

Winners and Sinners. 1982. *New York Times News Desk*, No. 411, July 6, 1982.

Winners and Sinners. 1981. *New York Times News Desk*, No. 406, August 21, 1981.

Wolfenden Report. 1957. *Report of the Committee on Homosexual Offences and Prostitution* (Sir John Wolfenden, chairman). London: HMSO.

Zimmerman, Mary K. 1977. *Passage Through Abortion: The Personal and Social Reality of Women's Experiences*. New York: Praeger.

# Index

Abortifacients, 3, 47, 57, 158; self-administered, 54, 55, 169–70

Abortion(s), 28, 75; adoption vs., 26, 87; availability of, 49, 83, 191; costs of, 101, 121–22; defined, 51; direct/indirect, 36; effect on subsequent pregnancies, 27–28, 68–70; in/and fertility control, 3, 13, 20; as issue, vii, 8 (*see also* Abortion controversy); numbers of, 1, 8, 45, 65; reasons for permitting, 136; relation with contraception and sterilization, 22–26; risks, complications in, 62–70; safety issue in, 49, 120; *see also* Early abortion; Late abortion; First trimester abortion; Illegal abortion; Repeat abortion

Abortion clinics, 82–83, 121, 170; *see also* Outpatient facilities

Abortion controversy, viii, 1–8; compromise possibilities in, viii, 42–43, 100, 157, 160–63, 165–70; future of, 133–34, 157–72; moral issues in, vii, 2, 31–35; *see also* Morality

Abortion decision(s), 39, 76, 102, 110, 123; emotional reaction to, 76, 86–87; and guilt, 78; locus of, 43, 71, 105, 118, 119, 182; male partner and, 81; for minors, 79, 110–14; morality of, 36–37

Abortion experience, 145, 152

Abortion facilities, 63, 64, 66; *see also* Hospitals; Outpatient facilities

Abortion laws, 3, 89, 94–95, 157; administration of, 175–79; constitutionality of, 94–101; history of, 173–91; as of Jan. 1973, 176–78*T*; liberalization of, 4, 14, 22, 89–90, 101–2, 150, 153, 159, 187; permissive, 90, 149; restrictive, 3, 7, 14, 149, 158–59; *see also* Reform laws; Repeal laws; State abortion laws

Abortion policy, 170–72; compromise in, 160–61; future of, 157–72; medical technology and, 163, 164–65

Abortion providers: emotional/psychological responses of, 76, 82–84, 87

Abortion rate, 22–24, 26; race and, 150, 153

Abortion ratio, 23–24, 153

Abortion services, 45–46, 66; access to, 18; effects of abortion on providers of, 76, 82–84; harassment of, 7; men's participation in, 82; *see also* Male partners

Abortion techniques, 49–62, 63; and future pregnancy outcomes, 68–69

Access to abortion, viii, 15, 17, 19, 83, 149; attempts to limit, 29, 119, 170–71; for blacks, 153; inequality in, 5, 47, 149–50, 151, 154, 190; laws and, 89–90; pre-legalization, 46

Administrative sanctions, 175

Adoption, 8, 75; vs. abortion, 26, 87

Akron, 125–26

Alabama, 173–74

Alaska, 102, 185, 187, 188

Ambivalence: in attitudes toward abortion, 41, 76, 143–46; toward fertility control, 16–19; about sexuality, 16–18

American Law Institute, 94, 161; Model Penal Code, 42, 43, 102, 184

American Medical Association, 47, 130

Amniocentesis, 57, 164, 168

Anesthesia, 49, 56, 65; local, 52, 56, 62, 76

Anti-abortion forces, 2, 7, 133–34, 173; and abortion law reform, 99, 101, 104–5, 107, 116, 119; language use by, 146–49; and repeal laws, 187; *see also* Pro-life forces

Anti-abortion laws, 126, 183; intent of, 90–94, 99, 100